HEALING THE SHAMED

Empowering Victims of Childhood Sexual Abuse

JOHN J. GLANVILLE

ISBN-13: 978-0992559700
ISBN-10: 0992559707

Edited by Susanne Lakin

Cover design and interior layout by Ellie Searl, Publishista®

John J. Glanville
Zilzie, Queensland, Australia

CONTENTS

ACKNOWLEDGMENTS

First, I am grateful for my existence, without which none of my experience could have happened. In turn, my gratitude toward the "being" that breathed life into me is beyond measure. Then of course my parents, who came from traumatic upbringings to embrace life and give me the opportunities to live, love, and learn. Two people who, no matter what, have been a sanctuary in my time of need and always believed in me, even when I didn't. One taught me to be bold, the other to see the good in people.

To my brothers, without whom I would not have been shaped into the man I am. One afforded me the understanding that succeeding outside of what seemed "normal" growing up was merely a limitation set by social conditioning. My other sibling inspired me to not only think outside of mainstream ideas but have the courage and conviction to state those beliefs.

To my two children, who gave me reason to keep pushing through unbearable pain. Who always bring me joy and give me purpose. Who I know gained and understood what I attempted to teach them from the outset—that integrity is paramount in all things. You continue to make me proud.

To my "adopted" children: while it's been a rough path to tread at times, it has been of extreme worth to me on many levels. Without you I would not have learned valuable lessons. You also offered me the gift of experiencing the love of your own children, something I treasure beyond your knowing.

To all my close friends—the ones I trust to bare my soul, the ones who see through the tough exterior. The ones who know my heart. Thanks for your belief and love.

To my psychology lecturers who told me my writing style was "too flowery": thanks, and screw you.

To all my clients who wholly entrusted me to experience and partake of their reality: much, much respect. I hope you all found a safe place.

To my partner, Mia, the lady who developed me into someone I like. The one person who saw the light within and never relented in her pursuit to make me believe in myself. The person who made me recognize I had something to offer the world. The person who loves me unconditionally and has never made a single demand for me to change, but through her love aided to model my soul toward betterment. For your efforts, patience, and love I am eternally grateful.

And finally, to Susanne Lakin, my editor, who helped with not only the final product in a highly professional manner but encouraged me all the way and made me a believer. To Paige Duke, whose meticulous proof reading revealed more mistakes than a George W. Bush presidential term, and Ellie Searl, for her patience and willingness to accommodate my every "brain explosion" in the quality production and design of the book's art and format.

John J. Glanville

"The moment you doubt whether you can fly,
you cease for ever to be able to do it."
~ *J. M. Barrie*

INTRODUCTION

I VIVIDLY RECALL THE DAY I decided to embark on a career in psychology. I was sitting in a dusty old lounge chair in a dingy little shop selling secondhand furniture. I was so broke I couldn't afford electricity and had so few customers I spent most days sleeping in an old cot at the rear of the premises. I'd curl up in a fetal position and escape my groggy mind. It wasn't laziness; I was chronically depressed.

Sometimes I would awake from my slumber to find items had been stolen—I wasn't the best storekeeper. On occasion I would be awake long enough to make a sale. Those were happy moments—not because I'd acquired any degree of success but because it meant I could afford petrol to visit my kids hundreds of miles away. Times were tough, very tough, and I was in a very dark place. No one knew it at the time, but I was seriously considering "checking out."

As I sat in my drab, dirty genoa lounge on this particular day—awake—I was reading a book that not only changed my life but probably saved it: M. Scott Peck's *The Road Less Traveled.* (If you haven't done so, do yourself a favor and indulge in some profound wisdom.)

As I read Peck's words, devouring them like Pac-Man eating dots, I began to relate so deeply to what he offered that I had a moment of clarity.

The depression lifted for a time, and a thought came to mind: *Is this seriously all I have to offer?*

I looked at my surrounds, and a certain shame enveloped me. Embarrassment that this was what I'd settled for. A meager existence forged on the back of poor choices and no self-belief. Some part of me knew I could do better. Somewhere deep within that seemingly empty shell, a light flickered ever so faintly that lit the way to a possibility—a hope that I could dig myself out of the hole I was in.

Faith is a beautiful thing. It is the nutrient from which all growth springs forth. I recognized in that moment that there had been no light at the end of the tunnel because the light had never been external to myself; it was in me.

That day, I telephoned an auctioneer. A week later I'd sold off every piece of furniture I had in store for a tenth of its price. I locked the door to the shop, threw the key down a drain (my apologies to the landlord— a most generous man who helped me in every way he could), and walked away vowing a determination to fulfill my true potential. I decided, thanks to M. Scott Peck, that I was going to be a psychologist. For the first time in my life, I had direction. I applied to attend a local university and, not long after, received a letter of acceptance.

Venturing into full-time study was a bold step in my case; I'd been a terrible student at high school. I failed most subjects and was considered "dumb" by at least one teacher, while many others often informed me I was "wasting their time." The latter part was true; the former, I would discover, wasn't. The reality of my high school failings was I had no idea why I was there. That might sound very odd, but I never understood the point of the curriculum. Furthermore, I was very unsure of myself as a kid; for numerous reasons, I had become accustomed to the belief that I was not allowed to succeed. Avoiding the spotlight kept me out of harm's way.

My first day as a university student was intimidating. I looked out over the hordes of faces in the lecture theatre and old wounds began to open. Doubt crept its disease through my entire being. *Screw that!* I gritted my teeth and looked out again over those two-hundred-plus faces. I made a decision there and then to overcome my fears. If these kids could do it, so could I!

I paid my way through stacking shelves in a grocery store. It was a humble existence with very little pleasures and comforts—just bare necessities. I kept late hours and was tired much of the time. I would ride a borrowed mountain bike (thanks, Dave) to lectures and use my neighbor's computer to write my assignments (thanks, Roy). I wasn't the greatest student for a number of reasons (thanks, Shane), but my main conflict was in my thinking, I didn't process information the way my teachers wanted me to. Their cut-and-dried applications of research findings meant very little in a philosophical sense to me. I wanted to think for myself and debate deep and meaningful topics, not be force-fed theories founded on statistical data. Regardless, I applied myself and ultimately became one of about twenty of those original two-hundred-plus students to graduate with honors.

However, by the time I graduated I'd become so disillusioned with the field of psychology I decided it wasn't for me. I felt I'd been taught nothing of worth, that I'd been shoveled a whole heap of bullshit in the form of academia that, in my opinion, was highly unlikely to be of any worth in the "real world." I felt duped. How a person could undertake such "study" and consider himself a worthy candidate to provide psychological intervention was beyond me. It felt fraudulent.

Subsequently, I reenrolled at the same university and began studying marketing. I was a few weeks into this new course when I received a phone call at home. I had applied for a job as an intern psychologist at a prison months prior and forgot all about it. I assumed I hadn't even gotten an interview because the space between my application and reenrolling in the university was many months apart. The call was a request to attend an interview at the prison. I agreed purely on the basis that I wanted to see the inside of a correctional facility; I'm a strange man.

I "suited up" on the day and performed well at the interview, probably because I was relaxed; I didn't need the job. Long story short: I got
offered the opportunity. And so I embarked on my new career as a prison
psychologist, all the while maintaining my marketing studies, "just in case."

A few weeks later, I quit those studies. I loved the work. I can honestly say it was the first job I'd had in my life—up to that point—for which
I sprang out of bed every day excited about being a wage slave. Each day
presented a whole new adventure. It was dangerous at times, extremely
confronting, and I found it strangely addictive.

I was required to run my first rehabilitation program, alone, within
the first month. This was an extremely anxiety-provoking situation, not
least because I was on my own in a room with ten offenders but due to
the fact that I was well aware I didn't know jack shit.

I pored over the content of the program manual in a way that I'd
never applied myself to my studies. I knew it back to front by the time
the course commenced. Unfortunately, things went south in the first five
minutes. During group introductions I mispronounced the name of a major prison "heavy." He was undertaking his first-ever program (and highly
reluctant to do so). He courteously responded to my error by pointing his
fingers at me in the shape of a pistol and pretending to blow my brains
out. It was an interesting introduction, to say the least.

However, one thing I took solace in was knowing that those ten prisoners had no idea that I was a greenhorn. I was able to bluff and wing my
way through a twelve-week course. The first thing I ditched was the manual prescribed to "teach" these men. Most of the time we spent talking
instead of me teaching. It was something foreign to my colleagues, and I
knew some of them didn't like my approach because it made their style
look bland and purposeless. As one prisoner said to me after I finished that
first course: "These rehab programs were totally shit until you got here." I
took that as a compliment.

In time I developed a reputation for being hard but fair. I always
ensure people know where they stand with me, and I have a very low
tolerance for bullshit. The inmates, like all people I come into contact

with, either love me or hate me. It is only after years of analysis on this point that I have come to recognize why some people detest me: my honesty scares them. Unfortunately, this was no different with my colleagues at the prison—many hated me. Not that I ever did anything wrong by them personally; that's one thing I know positively about myself—I do not intentionally go out of my way to hurt others.

Nevertheless, I often found myself the target of criticism for how I conducted business. I was labeled "too confrontational." This generally came from my peers—other psychologists. While I could tolerate their criticism, I could not tolerate them talking to prisoners about me, colluding with them regarding my reputation, manipulating them to make complaints about me, and at times, even informing them about my private life.

In due course, I relocated to the high-security area of the prison as a result of my relationship with my current partner, also a psychologist (another story for another day). My colleagues, yet again, took great delight in grinding my name, character, and reputation into the ground—something to this day I find incredibly strange, given they claim to be compassionate people who saw *me* as too confronting. I subsequently began working for a woman—another psychologist—I perceive as being one of the most manipulative and conniving people I've ever met. And I've met some masters. She made it her mission to ensure my character suffered complete assassination.

By this stage, I was growing tired of the environment. I wanted out, and it arrived in the form of an offer for promotion from head office. The new role was as a clinical assessor traveling to different prisons and interviewing sexual offenders for placement on relevant programs. My "snake in the grass" boss attempted with everything in her to block this success—not because she believed I was poor at my job but due to her personal issues with me and a strong desire to destroy my career. She wanted me trapped in her web where she could punish me as she pleased. I escaped.

I loved my new role. I had much independence in that I only answered to one person. The job was fascinating. I would spend all day talking to sexual offenders about their crimes, backgrounds, deviant thoughts, and modus operandi. I was required to collate the information, make an assessment, and then recommend a suitable program placement. I met some of the most evil people in that position—people with no regard for the welfare of others and no desire to change. People who enjoyed the idea of watching the world burn. Child killers, serial rapists—you name it, I interacted with them.

After about a year, I was again promoted. I was appointed as team leader to the sexual offender programs unit in my original prison location. However, this soon encompassed having to supervise an additional two teams in other prisons. The position essentially entailed supervising other clinicians and monitoring their facilitation of program delivery. This meant I could attend, engage in, and cofacilitate upward of four or five different sexual offender programs in a single week. Subsequently, I was privy to numerous discussions on the subject, and to this day am still amazed that I hear new material. In this field, you *never* know it all.

The work my teams produced was high quality. It was also incredibly intense, draining, yet highly fulfilling, and—for the most part—these teams comprised people I respected greatly for their abilities, support, loyalty, and virtues as human beings. To even set foot in this realm, you must be conscious of your own baggage. If you're not, you will sink, very quickly. However, most who do sink don't even know they have. Before too long they are convinced they are saving the world and connecting with offenders in a way that is implementing positive change; they aren't even aware they are being manipulated. Worse still, they don't realize they are simply someone who shouldn't be in this line of work. It most definitely isn't for everyone. I've witnessed many therapists collapse under the weight. The pressure is immense. Think about it: you're responsible for making a determination on whether a sexual offender is rehabilitated. You get that wrong and there are enormous consequences for some innocent person down the track.

During this period, I was slowly burning out. The content of the work had little impact on me. The politics of the environment was slowly decaying my spirit. Covering ass was always high on the agenda along with ticking boxes and producing appropriate statistics. These are the things politicians value. I don't. As such, I became embroiled in skirmishes with my superiors, usually because they wanted to compromise important aspects of rehabilitation for administrative bean-counting. Then came the point when I had a run-in with an international researcher who attempted to bully me into a point of contention I absolutely disagreed with. I stood my ground on a matter he proved he knew absolutely nothing about in terms of Australian Aboriginal culture and overstepped a mark due to his massive ego that had the potential to cause major rifts in the local community as well as in the program. From that point, at his recommendation, I was labeled recalcitrant.

Things got tougher for me from that point on. I no longer attended work with the passion I once had. I became so despondent I took stress leave. A couple of weeks into that leave, I received a voicemail message informing me my contract had been terminated and to "drop my laptop off at the front gate of the prison." I'd served my prison term. I didn't know it at the time, but I was free at last.

The way things had ended was kind of surreal. I spent some time lazing around the house thinking about my future. I determined I would enter private practice. I would no longer place myself at the mercy of the juggernaut that is politically driven. Instead, I would work for myself. I would conduct therapy how I wanted. I would undertake helping people—offenders and victims—without the imposed limitations of bureaucrats possessing no concern about human beings, only for budgets and elections. And so I ventured into a new vocational world.

The majority of my work these days encompasses working with sexual offenders on parole orders. I have people around me in "the system" to thank for that. People who have stuck by me and knowingly appreciate my efforts and ability to undertake this work for the right reasons. People with some spine and willingness to put the safety of the community above politics, personal agendas, and egos.

For all who love me, for all who despise me, and for all that I stand accused, I know this much about myself: I'm good at what I do.

CAVEAT

The following discussions between client and therapist have been altered for reasons pertinent to confidentiality. Names have been changed, characteristics swapped, stories intertwined, and details added and/or subtracted. This has been undertaken out of respect for privacy.

Some of the content may be "triggering." Please use appropriate judgment in determining whether to continue reading.

Until It Sleeps

Where do I take this pain of mine?
I run, but it stays right by my side.
So tear me open, pour me out;
There's things inside that scream and shout.
And the pain still hates me.
So hold me, until it sleeps.

~ James Hetfield (Metallica – *Load,* 1996)

CHAPTER ONE: SMILING JOEY

I RUMMAGED HASTILY THROUGH THE paperwork in front of me, conscious of the necessity to extract as much information as possible in the next five minutes. However, my efforts were proving futile. I was at every moment too readily distracted by the prison officers nearby; their presence made me uneasy. It was as if they possessed the capacity to make a person feel inferior without the utterance of a word. I hated that feeling. More to the point, I hated the control they had over me. It was a raw nerve from years gone by, anxieties from my youth of not being good enough and not fitting in. A weakness I wore openly in my teens that attracted the types who like to deride others to lift themselves up. Prison officers possessed the same bully mentality: the need to dominate, control, and degrade.

Through the surveillance window, I occasionally glanced up to see them "busily" making coffee. They appeared to be engaged in derisive-type banter. At least that was my impression, given I couldn't hear a word they were saying. The sudden synchronized darting of their eyes as I looked in their direction reinforced my belief that they were probably being derisive of me. It wasn't uncommon for "screws" to direct snide shots at the "care bears"—the name they liked to call psychologists.

I didn't care what they thought of me or my profession so long as they left me alone. I had worked in the system long enough to understand the power games and how to avoid attracting their unnecessary authority. I put aside my paranoia, refocused, and promptly went back to skimming my documents.

I knew this interview would be a difficult one. It had come about as a result of a request from my boss—an assessment of a particular sex offender for suitability for an upcoming rehabilitation program. In and of itself, the request was no big deal. I had interviewed hundreds of sex offenders. However, in this instance, it was the first time I was going in cold. I'd had no time to read up on the case because the directive to assess this prisoner had come only minutes prior.

In no time, the heavy steel handle rattled and turned, and the iron door swung open. In walked a young man of no more than eighteen. He wore a huge beaming smile. His beyond-pearly-white teeth and perfectly positioned dimples gave him an aura of being angelic. He was burly, fit; almost athletic. Though I'm not inclined that way, I could tell he was attractive. Moreover, I could tell he knew he was attractive. I stood up, and he politely offered his hand.

"Hey, I'm Joey," he said.

"John," I replied. Our hands came together and shook.

Joey broke eye contact. "Where do I sit?" he asked, looking at the three chairs surrounding the desk to our left.

I pointed to the seat closest to him. "You have to sit there. It's protocol."

He took his position and looked up at me. Still smiling, he asked, "Why's that?"

His ignorance surprised me. Joey had already served about two years of his sentence; such matters were common knowledge among inmates.

"Safety. Under the desk on my side is a duress button," I replied, making myself comfortable.

Joey was still smiling. It was like he had this perfect Cheshire Cat grin permanently imprinted on his face. "What's a duress button?"

I looked up from my documents. *Surely he can't be serious?*

Joey responded to my confused look with a rapid burst of laughter.

I rolled my eyes at his juvenile antics, but smiled. After all, he was barely an adult.

"Ha! Got ya there, didn't I, Boss?" Those teeth were now starting to piss me off.

"Yeah, I guess," I said, unfazed.

"No seriously, Boss, I did! You should have seen your face!" He banged his fist on the desk for emphasis as he delighted in his own wit.

I didn't think it was quite the victory Joey was making out, so I rained on his parade by getting down to business. "Do you know why you are here?"

Joey, still smirking, looked at the paperwork on the desk, then back at me. "Nope, no idea."

"Well, I'll tell you why I'm here," I commenced. "I'm here to interview you about your offense and assess whether you're suitable for placement on a sex-offender program."

Bam!

Suddenly Joey wasn't the jovial spirit he was a minute ago. The angelic Cheshire Cat morphed into a vicious wounded pit bull. Rage seemed to ooze from every pore. It was as if he had literally boiled in his own anger before my very eyes.

Joey regained composure, though the remnants of his fury still lingered between us across the desk. He slid down his cheap sunglasses from atop his head to conceal his eyes.

I broke the tension. "Is a program something you would be interested in, Joey?"

There was a long silence, the air still thick with his vitriol.

"It's not a matter of whether I'm interested at all, now, is it? You fucking idiots make us do these programs, and if we refuse—well then, we simply have no chance of getting out. It's total bullshit!"

Joey was right. If a sex offender refused to participate in a therapeutic program, he jeopardized his chance at freedom. The system viewed it as the sex offender declining an opportunity to gain insight into his antisocial behavior and therefore considered that the offender remained a risk to the general public. Basically, it was an offer presented under the illusion that the offender had a choice, but it was entrapment. It was simply a ruse that dangled a carrot. It was the government's means to make offenders jump through hoops, a political agenda to win votes.

"Is that a yes or a no, Joey?" I pushed.

He sat with pursed lips. I could hear him grinding those pearly white teeth, his jaw rigid in its side-to-side motion.

"What the fuck do I have to do, and how long's this shit gonna take?"

"Just answer some questions. Should be over in a couple of hours." I waited for it . . .

"A couple of hours! Are you fucking kidding me?"

"Nope," I said, pretending to be unperturbed as I prepared to lie. "Now, I've read your file inside and out. I've drawn some conclusions based on the police transcripts, but I'd prefer to hear from you about your offense, if that's okay?"

Joey took his crappy sunglasses off and began cleaning them with his prison-issue brown T-shirt. "Yeah, police transcripts—fucking bunch of lying assholes," he muttered, more to himself than to me.

Again Joey was correct. The police often did exaggerate their account of proceedings. Their justification, if there was any, was to trump up charges in the hope that something would stick. While that may seem applicable to those who were guilty, it didn't protect those who were innocent.

"If you recall, Joey," I said, "you did plead guilty to all the offenses in court. You didn't contest the police version."

I already knew what his next statement would be. I'd heard it a zillion times before.

"Only because my barrister told me to!" he countered.

I paused for a moment. I knew he wasn't going to like my next comment; however, I needed him to realize I was not going to get sidetracked by his smoke and mirrors.

"Yes, Joey, there's a good reason for that. It's because he knew you had absolutely no chance of getting off those charges. He went for an early plea to get you the shortest sentence possible."

Joey sat with his arms folded, sunglasses once again concealing his eyes. He knew he was trapped in more ways than one. I could sense he was summing up how much I knew about him, how much I knew about his crime, and whether he was going to be able to get away with lying by omission.

Although his shades hid his eyes, I could tell they were burning a hole in the files on the desk. Right at this moment, he would give anything to know their content. For Joey understood that whatever he was about to disclose would incriminate him in a future program. In other words, he would not be able to go back on what he was about to offer up.

"So," I began, "can you tell me what happened in as much detail as possible, please?"

Joey nervously ran his fingers through his hair, sighed, then turned his chair so he did not have to see me.

"I was only fifteen at the time," he said as his body slumped. He had submitted.

"I was at a party with some friends, and I met this chick. I can't remember her name, but she was interested in me. Well, I thought she was interested in me. Turns out she wasn't." He paused in a somewhat reminiscing fashion.

Pretty straightforward case, I thought, relieved—given I had not done my homework. "Go on," I requested.

"I was a bit drunk, not wasted, but I started smoking some weed. I shared a joint with this chick, and I put it on her."

"Asked her for sex?"

Joey looked at me with contempt. "Uh, yeah. Anyway, she was pretty hot, and I was pretty horny. So as I said, I put it on her, but she told me to fuck off."

"Then what happened?"

"What happened? I hit the bitch is what happened. Not hard or nothing, but I could tell it hurt her. Then she took off with her friend, and I felt really embarrassed. It was a bad scene, man—really bad, because people were watching this shit go down."

It seemed Joey had a conscience. "So you were embarrassed about everyone seeing you hit her?"

Joey looked confused by the question. "No," he said condescendingly as he shook his head, "I was embarrassed because the bitch had the hide to reject me in front of all those people."

I nodded and continued to take notes, wondering where this was leading. "So then what happened?"

"I left the party. I stole a couple of beers out of the fridge to drink on
my way home. By this stage I was feeling pretty fucked."

"As in drunk and stoned?" I clarified.

"Yeah, and I have to tell you things start to get a bit sketchy from here,
but I'll do my best to remember."

My "bullshit detector" went berserk.

"All I remember is walking along some street. It was pretty late at night,
and it was really hot; it was summer. Then I noticed this house with a door
open. There were lights on at the back but no light at the front, and the door
was open. I mean, seriously—can you believe these people leaving their
fucking front door open?"

I didn't respond. Joey continued.

"Anyway, I thought, 'Awesome—I can get in and see if there's anything
worth stealing.' So I snuck up to the front door and stuck my head in. I
listened, and I could hear voices and a television toward the back of the
house where the light was. I crept past the foyer and into a room. There was
nothing in there, so I went to an adjoining room. Now this is where it gets
a bit hazy," he said, looking at me to see if I was falling for his story of ill-
fated amnesia at the precise moment of his worst act. Again, I didn't respond.
His shifting in his chair alerted me to the likelihood he was agitated by my
non-acknowledgment of his attempted bluff.

"Go on," I half demanded.

Joey swallowed hard. "Like I said, I went into the adjoining room. I
could tell it was a kid's room, and I saw this cot." He paused, visually assessing my reaction from the safety of his shades.

"Then I saw this little girl asleep in there, and for some reason I got this
idea that I'd like to do bad stuff to her. I think it was because of the rejection
by that chick at the party." He looked at me, hoping I would approve of his
"wonderful insight." I kept writing. He quickly backtracked. "Or maybe it
was because I was so stoned and drunk?"

Again, I sat motionless.

"So I got in the cot and covered her mouth because she woke up. I told her to be quiet, then I did stuff to her and left."

He could not get that last sentence over and done with quick enough.

I kept my head down and continued to take pseudo-notes, all the while wishing I had read those damn files. Joey's eagerness to terminate his version of events at the point he did is typical of most sexual offenders. They like to omit the worst bits.

He wasn't getting off that easy.

"So let's go back to when you got in the cot. What happened from there?" I asked.

Joey became rattled. I watched as beads of sweat formed on his forehead. A long silence ensued while he gnawed away at a thumbnail, sitting back occasionally to assess the damage, viewing it from different angles. And then he began.

Approximately an hour later, the interview was over. I had forced myself to listen to Joey's story—and I do mean I literally had to force myself. I wanted to leave that interview room a number of times. Up to that point in my career, I had never been affected by a case. There are not many crimes that get to me emotionally, but this one did. Out of respect for the child and her family, and my concern over potential vicarious trauma to my readers, I have not provided the details.

However, I live with those details, and sometimes they creep up on me. They infiltrate my mind, and my body responds with an aversive shudder, dispelling them to a deep, dark place where they lie dormant until they pervade my conscience again, triggered by reminders of that innocent little girl's suffering. And yet, with regard to the ripple effect of "Smiling Joey's" despicable act, I am an outer ring, far removed from the violent splash that created the turmoil in what used to be the calm, clear waters of a child's innocence and her parents' faith in humanity. I cannot begin to imagine their pain.

Although I've never met her—I don't even know her name—I sometimes think about that little girl and all she endured. I wonder how her life panned out. I wonder about her struggles, her anguish, her torment, her fears, and whether the demons within ever sleep. I wonder about her family and their likely rage-based guilt at the injustice, the "why our daughter?" and the cruel "if only" mentality. I've long considered how I might help them.

It was during one of these contemplative states that I realized I could do something. I could help utilizing my experience working with sexual offenders and their victims. I recognized this knowledge could be put to broader use beyond the framework of my vocation as a criminal psychologist, to offer something more uplifting and powerful. It could be used as a very important means to aid victims in understanding the mind-set of their perpetrators, for I came to comprehend through interactions with victims that understanding the assailant can help them heal.

When one becomes enlightened to the mentality of a sexual predator, one unequivocally becomes aware that they, the victim, are not to blame, for blame is the evil legacy of the perpetrator that tortures the soul. It is a residue cancer composed of toxic emotive energies. Energies that slowly corrode one's spirit long after the physical invasion has taken place. These poisonous energies are at the core of the victim's self-directed blame and are an obstruction to healing. These energies are the emotions of guilt and shame.

Chapter Two: Guilt & Shame

*"You may think you can hide your shame by not talking about it,
but in reality, it's your shame that's hiding you."*
~ Adam Appleson

Jade

"I KNOW I'M NOT SUPPOSED to, but I just feel so guilty, so ashamed of what took place," she said, fiddling with the gold bangle on her wrist. It looked expensive, and her caressing of the band meant it had probably been given to her by someone she loved deeply.

"It's as if this 'thing' in me, a separate being, tells me it was my fault, that I did something wrong. There've been times when I felt I was on the cusp of letting go of the guilt, but then that 'thing' shows up again and whispers, 'yeah, but remember you did this' or 'you did that; you were a part of it,' and I'm back to square one," she said, tears streaming down her face.

Jade was a classy, attractive twenty-something-year-old woman. She attended therapy, worried her life had lost purpose. By her own account she had every reason to be happy—recently engaged, successful career, upcoming holiday to Europe—but none of this seemed to fill the void she felt inside. She put it this way: "My soul feels empty."

Over time I built an effective rapport with Jade, to the point she trusted me enough to disclose she had been sexually abused for a good portion of her childhood.

From the time she was four, Jade and her grandfather had formed a very special bond. Wherever Grandpa was, Jade could be found. Jade's grandparents lived on a large rural property. Her mother and father lived next door on similar acreage; thus, the family spent much time together.

Her grandfather, upon retirement, built a shed for his hobby of wood-turning. The shed was equipped with all the mod cons—practically another home—and was about a half-mile walk from the house. No one but Jade and her grandfather ventured up there much.

One day Jade's mother walked over to the shed. As she got close, she began to doubt if Jade or Grandpa were around; it seemed much too quiet. The wood lathe was not turning, nor could Jade or her grandfather be heard talking. Oddly, the shed was closed up. Jade's mother tried the door, but it was locked. She decided to head back to the house but thought to try the rear entry to the shed. When she opened the door, she saw her naked seven-year-old daughter being sexually abused by Grandpa.

"When you say you aren't supposed to feel ashamed and guilty, what do you mean, Jade?" I asked.

She stared at the clock on my office wall—the one that hadn't worked in three years. Its hands were permanently fixed at ten to four for no other reason than I couldn't be bothered to change the battery.

"Your clock's wrong," she said with a smile.

"No, it's just stopped," I replied. There was a silence. "Is the question too hard?"

"No. I want to answer it," she said, gently running her index finger along the rim of her bangle so that it spun slowly on her wrist. "It's just that I don't think I've ever verbalized what the true underpinnings of the emotions are. I mean, I've gone there before, but I stop short of admitting too much—if that makes sense?"

I nodded and waited. Silence is a therapist's most influential tool, yet many never discover it.

"When I think about it, the guilt and the shame are really two separate entities." Again she waited for my thoughts. I waited longer.

"One seems to be a symptom of the other," she concluded.

Impressed by her insight, I asked, "Which comes first, Jade?"

"Definitely the guilt," she said, as another tear made its way down her cheek. "Definitely the guilt," she repeated in a whisper.

"That's very much what I have come to understand," I said. "Other sexual abuse victims say exactly the same thing."

Jade looked up immediately. "Really? So it's normal?" She seemed genuinely surprised.

"Absolutely," I reassured her.

She relaxed. The weight she carried disappeared as she momentarily found sanctuary in the notion that maybe these emotions were not limited to her own experience, that these were normal feelings felt by others who had suffered in the same vein. Then the serenity was gone, and suddenly the tortured expression returned.

"It just happened, didn't it?" I ventured, needing to seize the moment.

"What's that?" Jade replied, my question jolting her back to the present.

"The little voice," I said. "The one that tells you you're no good."

Jade looked helpless. "Hmm," she acknowledged.

"What was it saying?"

She thought deeply. "That I was no good. Kind of like a fraud. That I was covering stuff up." She stared at my clock again.

"It's still ten to four, Jade," I teased.

She smiled.

I leaned forward and looked her in the eye. "What's 'the stuff,' Jade? What's 'the stuff' that this voice holds you ransom with?" I asked softly.

The tears began to well and slowly made their way down each side of her face. She didn't sob. She didn't move. She didn't make a sound. It seemed as though each teardrop held a story of its own, and she sat there remembering each of those stories as they ran down her cheeks. She was looking at me, but through me. I knew she was back in her grandfather's shed. Then the demon was exposed . . .

"I feel guilty because I feel partly responsible."

She paused. Then, with all her might, she exorcized the rest. "There were things I did that were wrong."

The words were broken up by her sobs.

I waited for her to compose herself. After a while, she sat waiting to continue.

"Let's start with one of those presumed 'wrongs' that are at the lesser end of the scale in terms of creating shame for you," I posited.

Jade looked pensive, then verbalized her thoughts. "You know, now that I'm thinking about it—now that I've let myself 'go there,' in front of someone, no less—there's really only a couple of memories that drive that horrible feeling in me."

"Did you want to talk about them?" I asked in hope.

. She nodded. "I remember this thing we would do at family dinner on Sundays. We all had our designated place at the table. I was always seated across from Grandpa, and sometimes our eyes would meet." She slowly shook her head.

"It's okay, Jade—no judgment, no guilt," I told her.

She courageously continued. "It was really weird, when I think about it. They were lustful looks. Not just on his behalf—on mine. It was as if I knew how to flirt at six years of age. He would wink at me, and I would feel butterflies in my stomach. He would rub my leg under the table with his foot, and I would feel sexually excited. I know that's disgusting, but I thought it was okay. Honestly, I did," Jade said, attempting to convince me of her naivety.

I didn't say anything. I didn't want her to finish at that point, with me reassuring her that she had committed no wrong. It was obvious she had done nothing wrong. She had been a child, but Jade had to come to that realization herself.

"Well, that's not entirely true," she said.

"What's that?" I asked.

"I knew we were doing something wrong. Grandpa emphasized that all the time. He would say things like, 'We will get into very big trouble if anyone finds out what we're doing' and 'This is just our secret.' I recall the one line that convinced me to keep my mouth shut was him telling me, 'If anyone finds out, they will stop us from coming up to the shed, and you won't be able to see me anymore.' That one scared me the most because, as much as I hate to say it, I adored my grandpa."

"I think that's perfectly rational, Jade."

She looked shocked. "You do?"

"Sure. I mean, like you said, you were just a kid. Your whole perspective on what was taking place was founded on what your grandpa told you. He was obviously someone you loved. I assume you trusted every word he said?"

She sat back in her chair and considered what I had just said. "Yes, I did, but I find I have incredibly conflicting feelings about him now. I am angry, but at the same time, even after all of this, I still love him. Is that wrong?"

I didn't answer straight away—not by choice; it was just a tough question. She sat waiting patiently for my response.

"I think it's like that clock," I said, pointing to my run-down piece of plastic crap that hadn't worked in three years.

Jade laughed. "How so?"

"The time is not wrong; it just 'is.' Even if it were 'right,' it wouldn't be 'right' in some other part of the world. So it's neither right nor wrong; it just *is*," I said, satisfied with my analogy because that piece of crap had actually served a purpose.

Jade sat looking at my clock, occasionally blinking away tears. "Yes, that's true."

We sat silent for a while, then Jade made a statement that was monumental in her coming to terms with her guilt. "I guess I have to differentiate between Grandpa's behavior and my own. Mine was the result of his influence. Like Newton said, 'Every action has a reaction,' so I guess my reaction wasn't right or wrong, it just *was*."

"Exactly!" I said with excitement. "Now, with that in mind, and going back to what you said earlier about shame being a different entity than guilt, and that the former is a symptom of the latter, can you see now why you feel so much shame?"

Suddenly she came back to life. "Oh my God! Yes!"

It was as if she had been hit with a defibrillator. "If I think I am guilty of things that I assume I did wrong, then it's a natural progression that I would then feel shame."

"So in reality, you are carrying shame that isn't even yours to carry," I offered. "It was 'given' to you as a legacy of someone else's behavior for which *they* should feel guilty."

"Oh my God!" Jade exclaimed again. "That is so true!"

I worked with Jade every week for many months. Every session, she got stronger. Throughout intervention she, bit by bit, cut the emotional cancer out. The last of which happened during the following discussion.

"I think I've come a long way," Jade declared.

"I agree," I said, smiling. I was very proud of Jade and the work we had done. I admired her bravery.

"I think I'm almost finished," she added assertively. "There's just one last thing to discuss. It's one I've been holding back. It's about the actual sexual abuse by Grandpa."

She waited for a response, but seemed to have become conditioned to my use of silence, so she continued.

"I can say this to you openly because I know I don't have to feel guilty and therefore ashamed. For too long I've beaten myself up over my memories of the abuse because I always remembered enjoying the sexual part when it took place."

She looked at me; this time I gave her a response.

"Jade, a *lot* of people do. It's a taboo subject because people don't want to believe it can happen that way, but it can, and sometimes does, happen that way. Certainly, it's not that way for everyone, but it is for plenty of others. The fact that it's off limits to discussion among the general populace means these victims often suffer in silence, forever trying to come to terms with something that simply eats away at them every day."

She nodded. "I know what Grandpa did was wrong. I feel I both love and despise him. However, the conflict about the abuse—my feelings about it and my feelings about him—have well and truly been resolved," she stated boldly.

"Go on?"

Jade sat up straight. I'd never seen her so strong.

"He was wrong. He abused me. I was a child who simply reacted to the actions of what I thought was love from my grandpa. I did nothing wrong. I thought nothing wrong. I felt nothing wrong. I have nothing to feel guilty about. Therefore, I refuse to carry the shame for someone else's wrongs."

With that, Jade took off her bangle and placed it in her handbag. I never saw her again.

ERROL

Errol sat nervously playing with his mobile phone while I completed the induction documentation for his consultation. I got the impression he was a bit of a diamond in the rough. He was approximately fifty, large, untidy, and wore a cowboy hat.

His hat was disgusting; it looked older than he was. Rings of sweat stained the brim, and there was a hole in the top that looked like the result of a cigarette burn. He seemed out of place in my office. He wasn't the type I encountered seeking psychological intervention.

"Do you have to do that for every appointment?" he asked, pointing at the paperwork.

"Yes, it's a pain in the ass," I said as I filled in the last section.

"Typical of today's world, all this bureaucratic bullshit—we have the same problem where I work. Not to mention all this occupational health and safety shit that just gets in the way and makes life harder," he stated, placing his phone in the pocket of his grubby denim jeans.

I couldn't help but agree. It was the very reason I had embarked on establishing my own practice.

"So what brings you here?" I asked.

"My wife." He laughed. Then Errol got serious. "Look," he said, "I really don't want to be here. I want to tell you that straight up. I'm here because my missus thinks I have something from my past to deal with."

"And do you?" I gently tested.

The question affronted him. "I told you—I don't want to be here," he said tersely.

"Errol," I said, ensuring our eyes met, "you seem like the type of guy that respects honesty, so I'll be up front with you."

He became attentive, his eyeballing demanding I continue.

I leaned back in my chair to demonstrate I was no threat. "You said you didn't want to be here, Errol. That's different from saying you don't need to be here. So forgetting your wife for a minute, do *you* think you need to be here?"

Errol unconsciously mirrored my behavior and relaxed into his seat. He seemed to be absorbing what I'd said. Gently he took off that repulsive cowboy hat and placed it on the floor. "Yeah, I need to be here," he said.

I respected his courage. "So where do we begin?" I prompted.

Errol gathered his scruffy, ZZ-Top-style beard in one hand and ran his closed fist all the way down to the bottom of his whiskers, repeating the motion over again as he sat thinking. "I have no idea, all I can tell you is I have a bad temper. I just lose it over stupid stuff."

"Seems like as good a place to start as any," I encouraged. "When did you last lose it?"

Errol half grinned. I sensed the smirk was a cover for profound sorrow. "Last night," he replied.

"Okay, so what happened?"

Errol let out a deep breath and resumed stroking his whiskers. "I had a few drinks. I was watching the football on TV and my team lost. I was so pissed off I threw a beer at the plasma screen," he said sheepishly.

After an in-depth discussion about the failings of our respective football teams, I asked, "What do you think throwing that beer was about?"

Errol answered straight away. He was quite black and white in his thinking style. "I don't know. I think I was just pissed off that my team lost. I'm a passionate supporter."

"Me too," I related. "I get pissed off as well. However, what I've come to understand about that gutted feeling after a loss is this: it seems to manifest as anger, but it's actually another thing entirely."

Errol looked puzzled that a deeper reason may have existed outside his rigid mind-set. "Like what?" he asked.

"It's a feeling of pain—not in the physical sense but in an emotional sense. It hurts," I offered.

He was nodding. "Yep, that's exactly how it feels."

I sat for a moment looking at the ceiling. As I did, I made the following comment: "You know, Errol, I just thought about it, and if I scratch a little deeper and get honest about it, that pain is there because I identify with my team *so* strongly that I take the loss personally."

He immediately identified. "I'm hearin' ya," he said emphatically.

We sat in silence for a little while before I asked, "You know what I've learned about that from personal experience and working with people in here?"

"What's that?"

Here was my opportunity. "What I've learned, Errol, is that taking the loss personally has to do with a sense of shame. Now, if I'm right about that, I'm wondering if your wife asked you to come see me because she thinks your issues from the past have to do with a sense of shame."

Errol sat like a deer caught in the headlights. "Yeah, big-time," he admitted solemnly.

I didn't say anything else. I just waited. I'm sure to Errol the silence seemed an eternity, but I didn't see the point of pushing him. I'd let him offer up his past in his own time. Finally he spoke.

"I feel like running out that door, but I know I can't. I know I need to be here. I'll just start by telling you the basics—that's all I feel comfortable with at the moment. Is that okay?"

"No problem," I said. "You set the pace."

Errol wriggled in his seat, tussled with his beard, and primed himself. Then the valve on Errol's internal pressure cooker slowly released for the first time in his life and allowed his pent-up rage to slowly escape.

"When I was a kid—about nine—I was sexually abused, and I don't think I've ever dealt with it. Not in a productive way, at least. I've used drugs and alcohol as escapism for many years. Although I don't do the hard drugs I once did, I still smoke weed like a chimney and drink too much. I know

I've been a real prick to my family over the years. I find I never live up to my own expectations as a husband and a father. I might do a hundred good things and then fuck it all up with one stupid act, like last night."

"Ah, we all fuck it up occasionally," I sympathized, knowing it to be true in my case. "So let's go back to the concept of shame and the abuse you suffered. Generally what I find is that shame is the back end of another emotion, that being guilt. So in respect to the abuse you suffered, what might you feel guilty about?"

Errol seemed like he was standing on the edge of a cliff, unsure whether to take a leap of faith or remain in the comfort of what he had always known. Luckily, he leapt.

"My abuser was my cousin; we were the same age," he said forlornly, head bowed.

"Same-age sexual abuse is a very common occurrence that often goes unreported," I said.

Errol's brow furrowed. "Common?" he asked.

"Yes, very."

He raised his eyebrows. "I've never heard of it before."

"There's a good reason for that." I nodded in agreement. "People are like you, Errol—they want to forget it, sweep it under the carpet and pretend it never happened because of the guilt and shame."

"Yeah, well that makes sense."

"Yes, it makes sense, but often what is logical is not productive. As you know all too well, if it's not dealt with, it can manifest in other destructive ways."

There was a long silence. I figured I'd let Errol assume the direction of where we would go from here. After grooming his whiskers for a time, he eventually spoke up. "I feel like it's always lurking there in the shadows—this secret that I'm terrified will come to the surface and others will find out."

I looked at his frightened face. "Errol," I said, "did you ever consider that every single person you meet in life has some skeleton of some description in their closet that they, too, hope never gets out?"

The robust man let out a chuckle. "That's probably very true."

"Whether you let people know or not is entirely up to you," I said. "Personally, I think it's not really about hiding the secret. It has more to do with understanding the need to *keep* it a secret."

Errol quickly responded to this supposition. "Well, that's pretty obvious, isn't it? I don't want to feel ashamed."

Errol, unwittingly, had provided me a foundation upon which I could address his needs. "You only feel shame because of your presumed guilt based on what you think you did was wrong."

He nodded with beard in hand.

"That being so," I added, "what was it you did that was wrong?"

He looked frustrated. "I already told you. I was abused by my cousin, who was the same age."

I shook my head. "No, Errol, you're not listening. Again, what did *you* do that was wrong?"

Errol's brain searched for a wrong. It was as if he needed to find something he could condemn himself with to justify his guilt and shame. "I willingly engaged in the act," he said. "In fact, at times I even sought him out," he openly confessed.

"And why did you do that?" I asked.

"Who knows?" he replied. The helplessness in his voice had returned.

"I can hazard a guess."

He looked surprised and eager to hear my hypothesis. "Yes?"

I braced myself. "Because you didn't know any better, and it felt good."

"It felt good?" He looked repulsed.

"I want you to really think about this next question, Errol. You aren't allowed to answer with 'I don't know.' You have to think about it. So here goes. For what other reason, if any, would you seek your cousin out for sexual activity?"

I sat back and waited, detached from Errol by continuing to look directly at the floor beneath my feet. I could sense he was twisting and pulling at that beard as the cogs in his brain slowly began to turn. Finally the beard tugging turned to stroking in alignment with the cogs becoming free and gaining momentum. He looked up. "You're right," he declared.

His body slumped into a heap. "I hate myself. I'm not that," he stated despairingly.

"You're not what?"

He looked distraught. "I'm not some sick homosexual, incestuous kid-fucker!"

"No, but you were a little kid with no understanding of sex until your cousin introduced you to it. Errol, look at me," I demanded. He complied. "The only reason you apply those labels is you have taught yourself over the years that the actions you partook of imply you fit in those categories. So let me ask you this: Have you, since the time with your cousin, sexually engaged with a male child or relative?"

"No," he replied.

I was vigilant to maintain his eye contact. "If we go back to our prior discussion about you feeling guilty for seeking out your cousin, take a look at that kid—you. In all seriousness, do you consider he was some sort of deviant?"

His body language changed immediately. "No way. That kid just didn't have a fucking clue. That kid was just doing what his cousin taught him to do, and continued to do it because it awakened his sexuality."

He'd finally gotten it.

"So, is there any person in this scenario who should feel guilty?" I asked.

Errol frowned. "My cousin, I guess." Within seconds he showed deeper analysis of this supposition. "But then, where did he learn it? If he was abused, then he was the same as me—just a dumb kid with no real idea what he was doing."

I genuinely thought long and hard about Errol's question. "I can't answer that, Errol. He may have been introduced through abuse or pornography—who knows? Whatever he feels about it now is his to deal with. Only he knows what went on for him, and if he suffers, then he probably needs to be more like you."

"How's that?" he asked.

I leaned forward. "Courageous in confronting his demons."

He sat back in his chair and soaked that up. I think it made him feel good. There was no beard tugging and no furrowed brow. He looked relaxed.

"I haven't spoken to him since we were kids," he said softly. "I avoid him at all costs. Last year I didn't attend our family reunion because I thought he might be there."

"And was he?"

"No," said Errol, resting his hands on his large belly like a bearded Buddha.

"I wonder why?" I asked, hoping he would take up the challenge.

"I know why," he retorted pronto. "Guilt and shame."

Errol continued to work through his past with me. At his last session, his wife also attended. It was an extremely emotional consultation, as she came to learn how her husband now understood his abuse, his misplaced guilt, his misplaced shame, and how he no longer hated himself. The removal of his long-held self-loathing meant he was no longer a slave to his anger. Errol came to realize he had nothing to be ashamed of. He also had no beard. The cowboy hat was gone, and he had started to go for evening walks to lose weight. It seemed his former self was being replaced with a new one—someone he took pride in, someone void of shame.

Errol's parting words to me were interesting.

"I've never told you this, but after that very first session I had a really vivid dream."

"About?" I asked curiously.

"I dreamt I saw myself as a little boy, and this heavenly figure appeared. I think it was Jesus. He sat down with the boy and put his shame into a little trinket box. Then they tied a ribbon around it and started walking toward a bright light. Jesus was carrying the box and holding the boy's hand. I watched until they disappeared into the light. It was the most serene experience of my life," he said as tears welled in his eyes.

"I think that dream says a lot, Errol."

"Yes, it was like that little boy had died and gone to heaven. He'd taken all his shame with him. He was no longer needed here," he said emotively.

"Why didn't you tell me about it?"

Errol paused for a minute. "I don't know," he said. "I'm not a religious man, and the whole Jesus thing sort of made me feel—"

"Ashamed?" I interrupted.

Errol smiled.

SARAH

"I have these recurring nightmares," Sarah said as she picked at the skin around her fingernails. The flesh looked raw, and her nails were chewed to the quick.

"I've had them for years," she added. "The content differs, but it's very much the same theme over and over again."

"What theme would that be?" I asked, assessing the stress machine seated before me.

Her eyes surveyed her fingers for the next point of attack. "I'm always being chased," she said, "but here's the weird bit—I'm being chased by me!"

"What do you mean?" I asked.

"In the dream I'm me chasing me, but it's me as a child. I look like that little guy Chucky in those horror movies, but I know it represents me," she said as she sat on her hands, a conscious maneuver to desist her anxiety-driven habit.

"How do the dreams end?" I asked, somewhat aware what this symbolism might represent.

"Um, they kind of don't," Sarah said as her hands reappeared. She grimaced in pain; the cuticle of her pinkie finger was bleeding. "I just wake up scared and upset. It's relentless. It seems to go all night."

"Do you believe there is a deeper, subconscious meaning at work?" I asked, wishing to test her openness to the value of the dreamscape.

"Oh, definitely!" she said excitedly.

"What's your interpretation?"

Sarah looked at me somewhat condescendingly. "It's telling me I'm running from something."

I nodded in agreement. "I also think it's something from your past you are running from, given you see yourself as a child. If I took it a step further, I might even suggest the Chucky doll is a part of your past that you see as evil or bad. And a step further would be that the dream never really ends because you have never really confronted little Chucky."

Sarah looked at me. I could tell by her face that she was about to erupt with emotion. And out it came—an ash cloud of long-repressed grief. I handed her a box of tissues. There weren't many left by the end of the session. Other than my brief analysis of her dream, we didn't talk about anything. I simply let her cry.

Intervention with Sarah was like pulling teeth. She was a master of the "one-word response" and adept at taking the conversation to places of no relevance whatsoever. After our tenth session, I'd had enough.

"Sarah, with all due respect, I don't know if you're ready to deal with your problems," I offered cautiously.

"What makes you say that?" she replied, beginning her finger-wounding ritual.

"In ten sessions, we haven't progressed. For example: remember those 'Chucky doll' nightmares you told me about when we first met?"

"Aha," she said, biting what remained of a nail.

"Remember how you had a massive emotional reaction to my interpretation of your dream?"

"Aha."

"Tell me what I know about your past," I said in challenge.

She looked up from her nail biting. "You know everything about my past: where I grew up, my school, my friends, my upbringing, my jobs. You even know about my sex life!"

"Is *any* of that relevant to your reaction in that first session?"

She looked angry. "Of course! It's all part of who I am, where I'm from!" She frowned at me like a cross school teacher.

"So then, tell me, Sarah, what *is* your problem?"

"That's your job," she snapped.

I contemplated what she was saying, and what followed was a mini awakening. "You're doing it right now." I laughed.

"Doing what?" she demanded.

"Avoiding the question. More to the point, you're making it my responsibility to justify your attendance here. That's not my job, Sarah; it's yours," I said, returning the ball to her court.

Sarah didn't respond. She simply ate her fingers some more. I was just about to accept defeat when she spoke. "I just can't go there."

I attempted to make it safe, but keep it real. "You don't have to. You don't have to be here. You don't have to do this, but what's obvious to me is that you most definitely need it."

She sat with her eyes closed. "It's just too hard," she conceded. "It will open up the floodgates, and I don't know if I can stop it once it starts."

That was true. I had seen her emotional reaction before, and it was like floodgates opening, and there didn't seem to be any dam wall that could withstand the torrent. I thought for a while about how to approach the matter, then it dawned on me. "Sarah, do you keep a journal?"

"Yes, I've kept one ever since I was a little girl. I love to write."

"Is there a journal you have that outlines the problem?" I asked.

"Yes," she said. Her prompt response took me by surprise. It was as if the issue being in written format was entirely separate from the one she was being asked to verbalize.

"Would you be willing to photocopy the relevant pages and post them to me?" I almost begged.

"Sure," she said nonchalantly.

A fortnight later, Sarah attended her appointment. By that time I had received her letter. She sat down and instantly began the finger sabotage. She looked at me wide-eyed and nervous.

"I understand why it's been so difficult for you now," I began.

She shifted in her chair. The finger picking became more intense. I grabbed her hands and she froze.

"Stop picking away at yourself," I said softly.

She went limp and began to weep. Not inconsolably, but in a way I had seen many times before: tears well, then fall. No sound, just tears.

"It's my fault," she whispered.

The tears continued to descend. Her mascara left black streaks down her cheeks, but she seemed oblivious. Her suffering had been intense and lengthy: many, many years of heartache.

"What happened is not your doing, Sarah. I know that what I'm saying only seems like words, but if you allow me, and I hope you do, I will help you see how none of this is your fault—none of it." I did my best to assure her.

"I should have done something that night," she said in a voice littered with regret.

That night . . .

Sarah was thirteen years old. She lived with her mother; her dad had long since left the scene. On occasion, Sarah would stay in her mother's room. She would drag her mattress in and fall asleep watching television. Not because she was a fearful child but because she just liked being close to her mother.

On this particular night, a man broke in. Sarah awoke to her mother being raped. Fearing for her life, she slid under the bed, where she stayed until the vile act had been completed. Luckily the offender did not detect her presence.

"I could have called the police. I could have snuck out into the kitchen," she insisted.

"And he would have seen you," I stated firmly.

She paid no attention to my observation. "I just should have done something."

It's sometimes difficult to know what to say in these moments. However, I find if I wait long enough, something outside myself sends me clarity, gifts of astuteness.

"Sarah, do you have children?" I asked. The seemingly out-of-context question stunned her back to the now.

"Yes," she said, wiping her nose with one hand while chewing the other. "I have a boy and a girl."

"How old is your daughter?"

"Ten," she said quite proudly.

I stared at her intensely, "Sarah, if a similar situation occurred at your home—by that I mean if the same thing happened to *you* as had happened to your mother—what would you hope your daughter would do?"

"Hide, protect herself." Her response was immediate and full of valor. It was obvious she loved this child with all her heart, which would make my point even more emotive and easier for her to comprehend.

"Would you in any way whatsoever expect her to protect you?"

She looked amazed. "God, no! I would be willing to die before that!"

I smiled. "Just like your mother did, Sarah."

I left her to ponder that for a while. It seemed to resonate with her. I paid close attention to her demeanor, and, as expected, the sadness returned.

"How do I get over this?" she entreated. The bleakness in her voice was a reflection of the helplessness she felt.

For the first time, I really felt Sarah wanted my help. That she was reaching out to me and not the other way around. I think it was the first time she actually knew she needed it. I looked her in the eyes. "By understanding that you have nothing to feel guilty about. Nothing."

"Easier said than done," she lamented.

I waved her response away. "Wrong. You did it two minutes ago when you engaged in the logic of what I said."

She suddenly sat up and paid more attention.

"Your emotions took a backseat," I continued. "Those emotions you feel are your conditioned response because you have always thought about the entire event from a perspective of you not having done enough. You think about it from the point of view that you were wrong in some way. When you think like that, you *will* feel guilt. When you feel guilt, you invariably feel shame. So by that reasoning it's perfectly logical that you have long felt the way you do and that you have struggled in life. But, Sarah, what if you didn't think about it that way?"

For the first time, I saw her hang on my every word. "I get what you're saying. I really do, but I just can't force myself to see it any other way," she stated with frustration.

"What's to force?" I asked. "Let it come, Sarah. Let it present itself to you. Your dreams have been guiding you toward that for a long time—deal with your past. That time has come. Reframe the event. Present it to me another way."

Sarah thought for an eternity, but there were no tears. Something had shifted. Then, like an oyster opening, a pearl was presented. "My mother saved me," she said with a quiver in her voice. "She loved me so much she sacrificed herself."

I felt a lump in my throat.

"Holy shit!"

Her use of the *S* word startled me; I'd never heard Sarah swear.

"What is it?" I asked.

"Something just occurred to me." She was almost joyous. "Not once did my mother yell for help during that whole ordeal. She knew I was in the room, but she didn't yell out to me. She knew if she did, he would have known I was there."

"Your mother is very brave," I said sincerely.

"Wow! She is! She really is!"

We both sat for a while. I broke the silence.

"Let's do one more hypothetical to cement this point. I want you to detach from the whole offense but maintain everything you know about it. I want you to be an external observer seeing it all unfold from each perspective: yours, your mother's, and the intruder's."

"Okay," Sarah replied.

"Imagine you are on a jury in a courtroom, and the person on trial isn't the intruder—it's the thirteen-year-old girl. Would you find her guilty of anything?"

Barely had I got the sentence out before Sarah vehemently replied, "Not in a million years!"

I continued. "As a juror, being entirely objective, who is to blame?"

"The intruder," she replied confidently.

"Who is guilty?"

"The intruder," she said even more resolutely than the first time.

"Who should feel guilty?"

"The intruder," she said again.

"Who should feel ashamed?"

"The intruder." She smiled.

Needless to say, Sarah changed after therapy. I once bumped into her socially. She showed me her long manicured fingernails. "I stopped picking myself to bits," she said with pride.

CONCLUSION

The many differing scenarios involved in the suffering of people at the hands of offenders are endless. My inclusion of the three case studies—Jade, Errol, and Sarah—in no way encapsulates the full gamut of people's experiences. They are simply three people I remember and admire due to their courage to let go of what they came to realize was destructive, who rose above adversity to become an inspiration—if not to anyone else but themselves.

I truly hope they have helped you see that guilt and shame are caustic to the soul, how these emotions are cancerous and eat away the spirit of the sufferer. Moreover, I hope if you are a sufferer, you will find the courage to reclaim your true identity. To reclaim the peace that is rightfully yours.

I want you to know, with everything in you, that guilt and shame are completely misplaced emotions in victims. They are not the victim's to own or preserve—period. They belong to perpetrators—those individuals who committed wrong.

Chapter Three: 70%

"You are all things. Denying, rejecting, judging or hiding from any aspect of your total being creates pain and results in a lack of wholeness."
~ Joy Page

MANY YEARS AGO I ATTENDED a seminar presented by a researcher who specialized in the area of sexual offenders. I distinctly recall a statement he made during his lecture. He was discussing various studies and made the comment that only 30% of sexual offenses are ever reported. Many people in the audience were shocked by this. Their surprise exponentially increased the more he talked.

The researcher went on to say that of this 30%, only half resulted in authorities pressing charges. Of those charges, approximately half made it to court. Of those that made it to court, only half result in convictions. So roughly, 3.5% of all sexual offenses result in an actual conviction against the offender. Personally, I find this astounding because I think it speaks volumes about our legal system (but that's a whole other book). However, for the purpose of this chapter, I wish to focus on the proposed reporting percentage—the estimate of 30%.

I have researched this projection via reputable websites on the Internet and, essentially, the quoted number is always identical. The first point I wish to make is that the presumed number can only ever be a guess. It can never be a "scientific fact" because there is no valid means to accurately assess such data. How can we measure all "non-reports" of sex offenses when we don't even know they exist?

I expect you are by now assuming I am suggesting the 30% guesstimate is exaggerated; however, from my experience, I would say it's likely too conservative.

Working in private practice, I have seen thousands of adult clients. A portion of these people were victims of childhood sexual abuse. Oddly, they rarely attend therapy for that reason. Typically they presented with some other surface-level problem that was the result of the childhood trauma. However, my main point is this: I can honestly say that of all these victims, only a handful reported the offense to authorities. Thus, in my opinion the much-posited estimate of 30%—based on what I've seen and heard in my consulting room—is possibly far lower. Perhaps even to the extreme of being a single-digit percentage!

Regardless of which is correct, and for the sake of saving argument, let us presume the 30% estimate is accurate. When people hear this, they are immediately taken aback. Why?

It would seem to me they automatically jump to emotive notions about fairness. People detest the idea that there may be numerous sex offenders "out there" going undetected and not being brought to justice. In my view, this is an unproductive mind-set. It implores a witch-hunt mentality that shifts all the focus to "catching" the offender and overlooks the blatantly obvious: the victim.

If greater emphasis were placed on the needs of the victim and coming to understand why a massive 70% (at least) do not report being sexually assaulted, two things would be achieved. One: we would apprehend more offenders because more victims would be forthcoming, and two: the needs of the victim would be better met (than they currently are), given their preparedness to disclose.

So why are victims of childhood sexual abuse reluctant to come forward?

First, we need to differentiate between non-reporting as a child and non-reporting as an adult. The latter differs greatly from the former, namely because as adults, victims are able to see through the manipulative tactics of the perpetrator. Since I will cover the deceptive ploys of offenders in later chapters (and, therefore, how they operate to gain access and escape detection), the current section is dedicated toward understanding adult survivors and their reluctance to report even after the veil of trickery has long been removed.

There are many reasons why victims do not pursue justice. As far as I can tell, almost every one of these reasons has its root in the toxicity of guilt and shame, which if you recall is the "property" of the offender. If that cancer is not eradicated from the victim as early as possible, it grows. Over time, it continues to feed on the guilt and shame absorbed from the broader dynamic of the victim's life.

RUBY

Ruby sat before me, staring out the window. "I saw Uncle Ray on Sunday," she said casually.

"Oh," I replied. Her disclosure caught me off guard. "How did you find that?"

She persisted in staring out the window. "Same as I always do."

I waited for her to collect her thoughts as she watched a little boy run playfully from his mother in the car park. "You know what I hate most?"

"What's that?" I asked.

"I hate that he thinks he can talk to me like normal. As if nothing ever happened," she said, while simultaneously smiling at the little boy still evading his mother.

"I'd love to say to him, 'Look, you asshole—don't talk to me,' but I can't," she said coolly.

I joined in her voyeurism. "What stops you?"

Suddenly Ruby was back in the room. She looked at me sternly. "Others," she said dejectedly. "I'm constrained by the feelings of others."

"Others?" I asked.

She turned her attention back to the proceedings outside, scanning for the little boy, who had since departed. "All of them," she said. "But mainly my aunt and cousins."

We remained sitting in silence. We both sat fixated on two pigeons perched on the handrail. "Don't you ever feel like just blurting it out?" I eventually asked.

Ruby kept staring. "It's kind of weird. Sometimes I want to shout it from the rooftops. Other times I just want them all to go away and stay away and never come near me, never talk to me, never contact me—just leave me out of it."

"Do you feel the same when you're alone with your aunt and cousins and he's not there?"

Ruby considered the question for a time. "No," she said finally. "It's different. I'm more at peace then—unless of course they mention the asshole. Especially if they mention him in a positive light. Then I feel the anger in the pit of my stomach, and I just want to get the hell out of there in case someone notices."

I could understand her perspective. It certainly was a situation that would likely get the better of me, which led to my next question. "Why do your aunt and cousins have such an influence over your silence?"

She turned sharply, looking at me as if I had no heart. "I don't want to ruin their lives!" she said in amazement. "It would tear their family apart!"

"So you sacrifice yourself for their happiness?" I countered.

Ruby went back to her window observations while mulling my question. "In a way, I guess I do," she conceded. "But it's not that I want to be a martyr. I just think blurting it out would simply add to the destruction he's already caused."

"Isn't that his to deal with, Ruby?"

"You're assuming they would all believe me. It's been over twenty years. How would I prove it? It's my word against his," she said. "Besides, when the shit hits the fan, of course they would believe him. So not only would I have been subjected to his perverted ways as a kid, I would also lose my relationships with my aunt and cousins and who knows who else?"

She had a point. There was a lot to lose and a lot at stake. I decided to push a bit further. "So even after twenty years, he still has control." I leaned back in my chair and asked aloud, "How can you get it back?"

She turned from the window. "What?"

"The power—how can you get it back?" I asked again.

She looked engrossed. This time she didn't turn to the window. "I've never really thought about it," she admitted. "I've just always accepted that the way it is is the way it is."

I shook my head. "If you had accepted it in a positive way, wouldn't you have closure?" I queried.

"So what are you saying? I haven't accepted it?"

"I think we both know the answer to that, Ruby." I repeated the question. "How can you get the power back?"

Ruby sat upright. "I'd like to confront him alone so I wouldn't have to worry about my aunt," she said staunchly. "I'd like to let that slimy bastard know I still remember."

"What would be the benefit of that?" I asked.

She didn't have to think long. "He would be the one uncomfortable around me—not the other way around. He would live in worry that I might speak up. I could dump all my baggage back onto him where it belongs!"

I never saw Ruby again after that session. I consider that one of two things happened: either she confronted her Uncle Ray or she didn't. I prefer to think it was the former.

JACK

Jack was a thirty-year-old mechanic. He operated his own business and always attended our sessions dressed in overalls. I found him to be quite articulate and a deep thinker.

"Why does society make it so difficult?" Jack asked.

"What do you mean?" I responded as I watched him clean his black fingernails with his car keys.

He looked up, suddenly realizing he was tending to his oil-soaked nails in public. He seemed embarrassed and stopped immediately. "It's just so hard to deal with because of the way society dictates to you that you're a victim of a disgusting act. Society says sex offenders are the lowest scum in the bucket, especially child sex offenders, so if that's the case, what does that say about me?"

I didn't respond. After a short pause he continued. "To me, it tells me there's something wrong with me. I'm so weak and vulnerable that I'm seen by these scum as easy prey. And while society sees him as a monster, I'm seen as the little bitch of that monster."

I contemplated his words. As I let them sink in, Jack spoke again. "That's why I've never said a word about what happened to me as a kid— not even to my wife. Why would I want the person I love to know that about me, let alone the rest of the world?" he said angrily.

"How do you think I see you, Jack?"

"Well that's pretty obvious" he said dryly. "I'm sitting in a shrink's office, aren't I? Obviously you think there's something wrong with me."

I laughed. "You came to see me, remember?"

He seemed to find my comment somewhat amusing.

"Why did you come to see me, Jack?" I pressed.

Jack was looking at his feet. His steel-capped boots had seen better days. He put his head in his hands. "I just needed to spill my guts," he said helplessly. "I'd stored this stuff for so long that I just couldn't do it anymore. It was killing me. I couldn't tell anyone—not even the police."

"Why not?" I semi-protested.

He looked up. "What are they gonna do?" he asked sarcastically. "Question me over and over again. Make me relive the whole thing in explicit detail. Do you know what that would be like?"

I remained quiet.

"It would be like watching my wife die a slow, painful death and then being forced to think about every single detail of her suffering over and over again." He grimaced.

I waited again.

"Then you know what comes next? I have to go to court, and the same thing happens again. So what if the son-of-a-bitch gets convicted? Big deal! He'd probably get a five-year sentence with parole after two or three. Then

I'd feel utterly pissed off! That's all my childhood innocence is worth? Five years of his fucking life?"

I sat silent.

"And then you know what happens?"

I shook my head.

"The asshole gets released and I relive it all again. It just never ends," he said.

Jack sat back in his chair with his arms folded, letting me know he was done.

I gathered my thoughts. "Has it ended by you *not* going to the police?"

He looked surprised, as if that was the last question he expected me to ask. "I suppose not, but this has got to be less traumatic."

"Not from where I'm sitting," I joked. Luckily he laughed. "Maybe you have society's perception of your position a little skewed?"

"No, I don't," he said confidently. "I'll tell you something. If my sexual abuse was exactly the same in every detail but instead of a man, the abuser was a woman, I wouldn't be sitting here. I wouldn't feel the need."

I looked at him quizzically.

"There wouldn't be a need because I wouldn't feel any shame. Society wouldn't see it as such a terrible act. It would have been a twelve-year-old boy's conquest. And you know what? I'd probably look back on it with fond memories."

I began to think deeper about Jack's theory. The longer I sat in thought, the more difficult it got to answer him. On one hand, the moral conditioning in me said "you have to say it's wrong" while on the other, my personal reality was saying "state the truth." I decided to run with the truth.

"You know, if I'm honest, I think I would too."

Immediately Jack relaxed. "Thank fuck someone can be honest with themselves!" he said with great relief.

My admission seemed to give Jack permission to open up further. "You see, I've given this much thought. The *type* of sex offense is very important in society's view as to whether the victim supposedly suffers. Man with boy is a big no-no. So too man with girl, as is woman with girl. But woman with boy—that's different. That's no big deal, apparently."

I nodded. "Why do you think that is?"

Jack had an answer at the ready. "You may think this is stupid, but I think it comes down to the act of penetration."

He waited for my response. Before I could answer, he began talking again. "Let me ask you this: How many male patients have you had over the years that came here because they couldn't deal with being abused by a woman?"

"None," I admitted.

"That's because they don't see it as abuse. Even if a kid was younger than twelve—say eight—they would still be conditioned to believe it was something positive. Men like the idea of sexually aggressive women. It's why the porn industry is so big. Think about this. If a few guys went camping and were sitting around a fire bragging about their first time and one of them said, 'When I was eight my hot, blonde, twenty-five-year-old schoolteacher seduced me,' the rest would be like, 'You lucky bastard!' But what if it were a girl sitting around that campfire telling the exact same story except the teacher's a male? Big problem!" he said, emphasizing his point by widening his eyes.

"So what you are basically saying, Jack, is a double standard exists?"

"Yes!" he said emphatically. "It pisses me off no end. Why do I have to feel like shit because society says my abuse was more wrong?"

I waited to see if he was going to answer his own question. This time he didn't have a preconceived thought.

"But if what you're saying is true, isn't the double standard created by males?" I speculated.

"I guess so," he said.

"So if the double standard is created by men, and you are a man, aren't you part of the society that perpetuates the double standard?"

Jack seriously considered my question. "I hate to admit it, but the answer is yes."

I continued. "With that in mind, are you saying all sex with children should be okay?"

"Of course not," he replied harshly. "What I'm saying is there shouldn't be any difference across the board. Sex with children no matter what the gender should be seen as wrong."

I nodded. "So if I extrapolate on that, it might be fair to suggest that what you are really saying is you envy others who don't have to feel the way you do about yourself? Basically it's not fair?"

"Pretty much," he agreed.

We sat in silence for a moment. Jack went back to cleaning his fingernails.

"Do you think life is fair, Jack?"

He scoffed aloud. "Hardly."

"Then why are you fighting so tenaciously against reality?"

Jack looked puzzled. "What do you mean?"

"If you believe life isn't fair, and that's reality, why do you fight against it?"

"Because it should be fair," he said with a twinge of frustration.

I leaned forward in my chair. As he looked me in the eye, I whispered, "But it isn't."

Jack became agitated. "So we should all just stop fighting against wrongs? That's stupid," he said derisively.

It was time for some tough love. "You aren't fighting against wrongs," I said. "You're bitter because the world doesn't see you how you want to be seen. Maybe the world is wrong about that. But it seems to me you want the world to accept you without having to put your ass on the line."

Jack sat staring at me. "Go on," he said. I liked the fact he was so principled with his honesty. It made him open, and open clients are the easiest to work with.

"If you want society to truly 'get' what you are saying, you need to be bold. If you were bold, you wouldn't suffer in silence. You would be openly stating the matters you have spoken about today. And yes, that means you may get hurt, but that's the reality of life, Jack. If you make yourself vulnerable, you can get hurt, but you also open yourself to receive intimacy."

He sat nodding.

"You make great points, Jack," I continued. "And people would benefit from understanding those points, but here is my question to you: How can people gain an appreciation of those points when you—the best teacher possible, the person who lives it every day—is hiding away too scared to educate them?"

I only heard from Jack once more. He sent me a letter. Inside the envelope was a business card from his mechanic shop. On the back written in pen was one word: "Thanks."

RONALD

"I remember the first time it happened," said Ronald. He was a slightly built man, balding, with thin round-rimmed old-style glasses. He looked like an accountant, but he was actually a chef.

"Mom and Dad had gone out and asked our uncle to babysit." He sighed. "When it was time for bed, he made us have a shower. I was too little to realize it was a bit odd for him to be in the shower with me and my older sister. He became *the* babysitter after that. As in 'the one Mom and Dad always asked for.'"

Ronald paused as he squinted through his spectacles in a manner that suggested he was discomforted by his recollections. "From there it turned into other things. He focused more on my sister than me. She was a bit older and a girl, so I guess he liked that better. After a few times, he gave instructions for me to touch my sister, and vice versa."

"Does your sister remember?" I asked.

Ronald pushed his glasses back up his nose with his index finger. "I'm sure she would. We never talk about it."

"Did you ever tell your parents? Was it reported?" I asked.

Ronald shook his head. "By the time I realized what he was doing, it was too late. In the end, I couldn't tell anybody."

"Too scared?"

"As a child, yes. I thought I'd get in big trouble," he said immediately. However, the remainder of his reply took some time. "As an adult, no. I feel like a hypocrite."

His response interested me. "How so?" I asked, probably a little too eager than required.

He took his glasses off and breathed on the lenses before giving them a quick polish with a handkerchief he produced from his trouser pocket. "This is the hard part," he said. He finished cleaning his spectacles, placed the hankie back in his pocket, and wriggled a bit to get himself comfortable in preparation for what he was about to say.

"After he introduced me to sexual stuff, I introduced another kid to it," Ronald said ruefully. "He was my best friend. It only happened twice."

"Why did it stop?" I asked.

"I somehow came to the conclusion that it was wrong."

"Do you still see your uncle?"

"No," Ronald said as he shook his head. "He died in a work accident a few years back." There was not a trace of emotion in his voice.

"Even though he's gone, you still keep the secret?"

He looked at me strangely. "Yeah, well, it's one thing to go to your parents and say, 'Hey guys, remember good ol' Uncle Steve? Well, he used to touch me and Claire.' You're in a whole other ballpark when you have to add, 'Oh, and by the way, Mom and Dad, I became a pedo myself.'" With that Ronald broke down.

The wretched sobbing was relentless. It was the release of a festering poison, years of guilt and shame coming to a head, ejected by an inner goodness that had long been suffocated in the bottom of his soul. His childhood innocence was now making a bid for freedom. I did not interrupt or even attempt to console him. To do so would have been contrary to his needs. He had too long been forced to hide the rawness of his true suffering.

Finally Ronald stopped crying, his glasses in one hand and his handkerchief in the other.

"You okay?" I asked.

He moved his head slightly, motioning a single nod as he closed his bloodshot eyes.

I waited a while. "Ronald," I began, "your actions after your own abuse were the result of what you learned."

He opened his eyes. He looked different without his glasses, less fragile. "I've thought about that," he said. "But if that's true, then isn't it the same for my uncle? I mean, he probably was acting on what he had learned too, right?"

"We all have a history, Ronald," I said. "And just as we have that history, we have responsibility. The difference between you and your uncle is that you were a child; he was an adult."

I let Ronald take that comment in before continuing. "His responsibility, by and large, far, far exceeded yours, Ronald. You stopped when you deduced for yourself, even as a child, that it was wrong. Your uncle, on the other hand, as an adult didn't."

Ronald sat silently, head in hands, staring at his feet. The ensuing silence made him uncomfortable enough to sit up and put his glasses back on. He looked at me in anticipation.

"I want to ask you a question," I said. "The question is based on what I've just said, and I want you to answer it from the part of you that has just rid yourself of all that emotional poison. I want you to answer it from the part of you that just pushed all that poison up and out of you."

He nodded. "Okay."

"Who's responsible?"

Ronald sat nodding. "He is."

For the remainder of the session we didn't speak. Ronald simply sat with his eyes closed, smiling. It wasn't a broad smile; it was serene and subtle. He was at peace.

I am uncertain whether any of the people in these scenarios reported their childhood abuse post-intervention. Maybe they didn't need to. Maybe simply offloading the burden through talking was enough. What has become obvious to me, though, is this: if a victim is able to openly explore their experience, they are better able to rid themselves of the emotional pus that has festered within for years. They can begin to slowly squeeze it out, lance the emotional boil, and begin tending to other significant matters in their lives, such as relationships.

CHAPTER FOUR: TRUST & INTIMACY

"Intimacy is being seen and known as the person you truly are."
~ Amy Bloom

WHEN I WAS ELEVEN, I was in a bank holdup. I was waiting in line to withdraw five dollars from my account, excited at the prospect of buying some football trading cards. Just as the teller called me forward, a voice boomed, "Get back against the fucking wall!"

I remember turning to my right, and there, almost pressed against my cheek, was a man in a balaclava with a shotgun in my face. I took flight and ran as fast as I could. I found a small alcove between some people's legs and hid there as I watched the proceedings. In less than a few minutes, the bandit had a bag full of cash and was gone. I didn't really feel overwhelmed after he had fled. In fact, I remember trudging back up to the teller and asking if I could still withdraw my five dollars.

My inclusion of this story is to point out that such a traumatic event in my young life has, to my knowledge, not affected me greatly in adulthood. However, I also recall a trip to the dentist at around the same age, whereby this "butcher" extracted two of my teeth. That event scared the hell out of me—so much so that I only returned to a dentist about six months ago at the age of forty-one. Obviously that childhood trauma had a pronounced effect on me.

I'm sure there are others out there who would be more traumatized by the armed holdup situation than the dentist experience. That's the thing with trauma—there is no right or wrong. Events are construed in the minds of people and interpreted in ways that make sense to them. In other words, what constitutes trauma is relative to the individual.

Responses to trauma are similarly just as unique. For those of you who have suffered childhood sexual abuse and are traumatized, your symptoms are not wrong. They are perfectly logical. They are typically defense mechanisms put in place from times long ago with a view to protecting yourself. The problem is, when you continue to utilize strategies you implemented as a child, you are relying on outdated techniques to get your current needs met.

These problems (or defense mechanisms) manifest in such a way that they produce the totally opposite outcome of what the person desires. And what I have come to understand through conducting therapy is that victims of childhood sexual abuse desire acceptance, validation, security, and unconditional love.

These qualities are the cornerstones to the foundation of any loving relationship. And the foundation of all loving relationships is intimacy—a closeness afforded by trust. In adulthood, many victims lack the trust required to establish intimacy in their relationships. This is because they have had it completely annihilated. Sadly, they can also lack the mistrust required to offer self-protection. Thus, for victims, the concept of intimacy can be daunting, even terrifying.

ANNA

"I don't want to get too close to him," Anna said. She sat fiddling with the hem of her dress. It looked outdated. It was floral and something reminiscent of the seventies.

"But didn't you say you've been married for fourteen years?" I enquired with some disbelief.

Anna looked up, clearly nervous. My question had made her defensive. "Yes," she replied with caution.

I paused for a time to allow her to settle then addressed her in a gentler tone. "How long has it been this way?" Her eyes remained fixated on her hem. It seemed she was wondering why she continued to wear that dress when it would probably be best used as a rag in someone's workshop. "Since we've been together—seventeen years."

Working with Anna was like getting a wild bird to eat from my hand. I approached the next question with discretion. "Do you trust your husband?"

Her maintaining focus on her hem was evidence she was not spooked. "Yes, well, no. I don't know," she stammered. "I do, but I don't mean in a conventional sense."

I nodded. "You mean, as in you trust that he won't cheat on you, but you don't trust him emotionally?" I clarified.

"Yes, that's it, exactly!" Anna said, straightening out her dress so that it sat flat on her knees.

"Why don't you trust him emotionally?" I was sure the question didn't come out as an accusation.

"I don't know."

I smiled at her. "Anna, you didn't think long enough to give a response of 'I don't know.'" She gave a nervous laugh. I repeated the question.

"I'm scared of being affectionate and making myself vulnerable," she announced.

The promptness of her exclamation surprised me. It was as if it was just sitting there waiting to be prompted into a verbalization. "Vulnerable to what?" I asked.

"I don't kn—" She stopped midsentence, perhaps conscious of the likelihood I wouldn't settle for her answer. She grinned at me, then looked thoughtful. "Him, I guess. I don't want to be vulnerable to my husband."

"Do you love him?" I said in a soft tone to allow her to be honest in her reply should it be perceived as negative.

Anna looked soulful. "With all my heart," she said sincerely. "But that's the problem. I want to give myself to him, but I just become . . . I'm not sure what the feeling is."

"Anxious?"

"Yes. It's so uncomfortable, I go into a spin."

"Do you feel that way if he's affectionate toward you?"

"Worse," she said fervidly. "I have this overriding need to escape, like I'm trapped and going to die. So I do the very thing I hate."

"What's that?"

"I reject him," she said as the tears formed in her eyes. "I hurt him over and over again. He thinks it's him. He thinks I don't love him, and I can see why. My words don't match my actions, but if only he knew what my heart holds. If only he knew."

I left her to her thoughts for a while. "I want you to think about the last time he tried to show you affection," I began.

"Uh-huh," she replied between sniffs.

"When he attempted to show you affection, what were you feeling in that moment?"

Anna's response was instantaneous. "Panic!"

"Okay, now I want you to really think about this next question: What were you thinking in that moment?"

She gave the request due consideration. "I have to get him away from me. I have to reject him so we don't get too close. I have to stop him from wanting sex."

I respected her honesty but did not respond. To do so would have cut Anna off from tapping in to her honorable disclosure. I wanted her to make the next link.

"How can I let him touch me? When he does, I just get flooded with memories. It makes my skin crawl. I panic. I don't enjoy it, and I ruin sex for him."

"Is your husband aware of your childhood abuse?"

"Kind of," she said. I could tell by her voice that it was a half-truth.

"So you have told him your father sexually abused you?" I asked, as least threateningly as possible.

"No," she half-smiled.

"Then what does 'kind of' mean?" I asked in jest.

"He knows there is probably something that happened because of my issues with sex."

Her response was my "in." "But your issues aren't with sex," I immediately countered.

Anna looked up in surprise. "They aren't?"

"No." I cut my answer off, hoping she would think for herself. Hoping she would explore beyond what she had verbalized thus far.

Suddenly she looked as if she had gained insight that afforded clarity. "My issue is with intimacy, not sex."

I smiled and nodded in confirmation. "To say your issues are with sex," I said, "is like putting the cart before the horse. The sexual problem is a symptom of the intimacy problem."

The wild bird was now eating freely from my palm. "So how can I fix that?" she requested eagerly.

"Yes, how can you fix that?"

Her eagerness turned to thoughtfulness. "I suppose I have to trust him."

"That being the case, what is the first thing you could trust him with?"

"My past," she said. "But that makes me nervous. What if he doesn't want me after I tell him what happened to me?"

"Isn't that the point of trust?"

"I don't get you."

"Anna, there are no guarantees," I said gently. "He might not want you."

She looked stunned. I held my hand up as indication for her to allow me to finish. "I think it's highly unlikely he would toss you out like garbage, but it seems to be a valid fear for you, so I'll ask you this. Let's say you told him everything that your father did. Then after entrusting him with that information, this man you have loved for seventeen years up and left. Would you really want to be with someone like that, someone so unfeeling and so overtly cruel?"

"No," she said boldly. "But he isn't unfeeling and cruel."

I smiled. "Then I guess you don't have a reason not to tell him."

Anna grinned.

I continued. "So he's a good man, and you trust him?"

She nodded ardently.

"Okay, so let's venture into the future for a minute. Let's just for this moment pretend you told him everything, and he responded like the caring man you know him to be. What would your life be like?"

Anna began to swell with emotion. The prospect of a closer tie to her husband filled her with joy. "Better, much better. I'd feel like I could be myself."

"What is it you fear most about telling him?"

"That he won't want me," she replied as the anxiety-provoking thoughts infiltrated her rationale.

"That he will reject *you*," I said sternly, hoping she would pick up on my emphasis.

Abruptly the anxiety was gone. "Oh wow!" she said excitedly. "That's what I do to him! The thing I fear is what I project onto him!"

At our last session, after Anna had taken the intrepid step of informing her husband about her past, she asked me the following question: "What would you have said to me in that previous session if I had said I didn't trust my husband, that he *was* cruel and unfeeling and I couldn't tell him?"

I thought for a moment. "What is it you have learned is the basic foundation of relationships?" I returned her serve.

"Intimacy," she said.

"And what is the key ingredient to obtaining intimacy?"

"Vulnerability."

"And when you make yourself vulnerable, what do you place in the person you make yourself vulnerable to?"

"Your heart, your trust."

"And if a relationship doesn't have trust, what has it got?"

"Nothing."

"So if someone said to you their relationship had nothing to offer, that they could not fulfil their development as a person, that they had to limit their growth and hide away and never reveal who they truly are for fear of cruel rejection, what advice would you give them?"

"Leave."

"There's your answer."

JOSEPHINE

Josephine sat eating her large bag of potato crisps while occasionally washing them down with a swig from her big bottle of Diet Coke.

"Why do you bring those here?" I asked, motioning at the food items.

She looked shocked. "Oh, sorry. Does it bother you?"

"I didn't say it bothered me. I asked you why you bring them."

"I don't know—habit, I guess," she said, ashamed.

Josephine was an extremely large woman—so large she took up most of the space on my two-seater couch. She would sit with her legs spread so her large stomach would fall between her knees. From this position, she could more readily access her foodstuffs.

I shook my head. "That's a cop-out answer. What's the real reason?"

Josephine rolled her bag of crisps up and placed them on the floor. "You mean the story behind the habit?" The regret in her voice was beyond sad.

"If you like," I said sensitively.

She went to reach for her Diet Coke and thought better of it. "It makes me feel more comfortable."

"Does it help you deal with the anxiety generated by coming to see me?"

"Yes. It's just another example of how I use food to feel secure."

"Are you consciously aware you bring that stuff?" I gestured at the food.

"Yes," she admitted shyly. "I stop at the supermarket and load up before I get here. I know I'm doing it, but I feel like I need it. No different than any other addict in times of stress."

"In the moment you are purchasing that stuff, do you consider your weight and health problems?"

Josephine contemplated the probe. "Yes, I have to say I do. But the need is too strong. It's like I justify it in my head by saying things like 'It's okay—you're allowed this one. You deserve it for going to therapy in the first place.'"

"Then you consciously override logic? Your desire to comfort yourself due to expected anxiety overrides the need to develop a healthier approach to life?"

"I guess so," she acknowledged timidly.

"When was the first time you ate like that?" I pressed.

"What do you mean? As in when was the first time I hate consciously?"

I noted her Freudian slip. "What did you just say?"

Josephine looked confused. "When was the first time I ate consciously?" she repeated.

"No. You said 'hate' consciously, not 'ate.'"

"Did I?" she said, bewildered.

I looked at her with intent. "I think that's really the crux of the matter here."

She remained silent. "Hate consciously?" she then whispered.

Josephine placed her food in her bag. I assumed she was intending to leave. To my relief, she put the bag to the side of the couch. "When I was thirteen, I never looked like this," she specified boldly.

I never entered the indignity of requesting she clarify what she meant by "looking like this." It would have been an insult and founded on fraud. I would rather her think I was rude than dishonest.

"I was slim," she continued. "I wasn't your average teenage girl. I actually loved my body shape."

I ventured into the abyss. "Was it about that time the eating began?"

Josephine looked repentant. "Yes," she said ruefully. "I couldn't shovel it in quick enough. I had been powerless for too long. So I made a decision to take control; eating was the one thing I had control over."

"Powerless against whom? What?" I asked.

She seemed tentative but simultaneously appreciative of the candid discussion. "My stepfather," she eventually confided. "He sexually abused me for years."

I remained quiet in the hope she would offer up any additional information of significance to her.

"My mother even knew about it."

I waited some more; nothing was forthcoming. "You informed her?" I asked.

"Yes. I fell pregnant at twelve. I had to tell her. I told her it was his."

"His, meaning it was your stepfather's?"

"Yes," she confirmed. "Mom made me get an abortion. Not a word was ever spoken about it again."

"What? She stayed with your stepfather?" I said in disbelief.

"Yes." She nodded. "To my knowledge, Mom didn't even question him about it. She just went on in life like nothing ever happened."

I was amazed at her mother's cruel insensitivity. "And you?" I asked compassionately.

"I was twelve. I couldn't make heads or tails of it. I assumed I must have done something wrong. So I just shut my mouth."

"And the abuse—did it continue?" I asked, in hope of a negative reply.

"Yes, it went on until I was about fourteen."

"What happened?" I asked, in hope of some positive outcome.

"I got fat," Josephine said. The entire time of our discussion, she showed no sign of breaking down. However, stating the obvious released a solitary tear. "I ate and ate and ate until I was so fat he wouldn't want me," she added in anger.

There was a long pause. I was attempting to digest how a mother could put her own selfish needs before the protection of her daughter. "Why do you still eat that way?" I finally asked.

"Protection."

"From?"

"Being hurt. I don't trust anyone. If you can't trust your own mother to protect you from a predatory animal, who can you trust?" she avowed.

I nodded in agreement. "Do you trust yourself?"

Josephine shed another tear. "No," she said. "I have no discipline."

"I disagree entirely."

She stared at me perplexed. "What?"

I returned her stare, but mine had a decided purpose. "I want you to listen to what I'm about to say. Listen from a new perspective and with objectivity. Don't listen to the old ways. Listen to what I'm saying. Can you do that?"

"Yes."

"The problem is you have too much discipline." I let that sink in. "In fact, Josephine, you are so highly disciplined that even though you know it's not normal, kosher, or protocol to bring food to therapy for an emotional eating problem, you do."

I could see I had sparked her interest. "You are so disciplined that you continue to eat and eat and eat in light of the fact that you are morbidly obese and posing serious risks to your health. Now, if you were doing that because you had no logical reason, no prior conditioning, no need to protect yourself, I'd say *that* was a lack of discipline. You are entirely dedicated to an unproductive and much outdated 'security system.' It's time for an upgrade."

I sat back in my chair and left her to ponder my comments.

Josephine shook her head. "God, I've never thought of it like that."

That day, Josephine hired a personal trainer. She went home and discarded every single bit of junk food in her fridge and pantry. She completely redirected her discipline. One year later, Josephine has shed kilos. As disciplined as she was, she has *never* missed a training session.

TINA

"Do you think a person can ever get over being sexually abused as a child?"

"Depends what you mean by 'get over,'" I offered.

I liked Tina. She was bubbly and charismatic. She also possessed an innocent type of honesty that I imagine many people would appreciate, and sadly, a few would exploit. She was pretty without being stunning, and seemed carefree.

"I don't know—like, get over it. Get to a point where it doesn't affect them anymore," she said in her quirky happy-but-discerning way.

I considered her query. "The answer is yes and no. I think the memory always remains. What the person does with those memories is what determines whether it affects her in positive or negative ways."

Tina looked surprised. "Positive ways?"

"Yes, using it as a means to propel herself forward."

"Oh, I see what you mean." Tina thought for a moment, then proposed a question designed to "pump up her tires." "Do you think I do that?"

"No," I stated bluntly.

She looked dejected. "Why? I don't let it get to me. I'm not depressed. I have a good life," she argued.

"You're sitting in my office for a reason."

"But that's different."

"Is it?"

She sat up straighter. "Yes, as a matter of fact it is, Mr. Psychologist."

Tina waited for a reply; she didn't get one. My silence frustrated her; subsequently, she felt the need to talk. "My not wanting a partner in life has absolutely nothing to do with my being sexually abused as a kid."

I looked at her cynically. "If that were true, Tina, why would you begin this conversation by asking me if a person can ever get over being sexually abused?"

"I don't know. I was just thinking about it."

"So what exactly were you thinking about?"

She giggled. "No, it's embarrassing."

I coaxed her. "Believe me, I've heard it all."

She took a breath. "Well," she started, "I was just wondering why I have absolutely no sex drive. None. It's like I'm asexual."

I raised my eyebrows. "You asked the initial sexual abuse question after thinking about that, and you believe they are not connected?"

Tina laughed. "Well, now that I'm consciously making the links, I can see where you are coming from."

"So you have no attraction to males?"

She almost fell out of her chair. "Yes!" she said aghast. "I'm not a lesbian!"

Her reaction was less than subtle for someone claiming to be asexual. "I didn't imply you were. I merely asked if you're attracted to males because you said you might be asexual."

"Well, yeah, I'm attracted to males, okay. Very much so. I just don't do anything about it."

"Have you ever had a relationship?"

Tina folded her arms. "Once," she said defensively.

"How long ago?"

She looked depressed. It was the first time I had ever seen her bubbly persona disappear and give way to the hidden, deep-rooted emotions she had come to conceal. "Do we have to talk about this?"

"No," I said faintly. "We can talk about whatever you like."

I broke eye contact with her. I wanted Tina to feel at ease, that she was under no obligation to discuss something she wanted hidden. Of course this was not what I hoped for. It was my intention to crack her open like a walnut, but I had to be disciplined in allowing her to reveal herself, not have me use a hammer to shatter her shell and quite likely damage the soft goodness within.

"I broke it off after about three months," she divulged brusquely.

I remained silent.

"I couldn't please him in the bedroom. Oh my God! I don't even know you, and I'm telling you this stuff!"

I looked at her in a way that showed I understood how vulnerable she was making herself.

"Yeah, well, anyway. I broke it off after three months and swore I would never have a male in my life again. The end."

"When you said you couldn't please him in the bedroom, what did you mean?"

Tina looked at me as if she absolutely knew I was going to pose that particular question. "This is really embarrassing." She was blushing.

"It's okay," I said. "No judgment here, if you want to tell, you can."

Her red face gave over to a depressed expression once again. "It just wouldn't fit in," she revealed. "We tried many times, but it was impossible."

I could almost feel her despair. At this point, she was highly fragile but also highly open to ingesting new information. "I would like to ask you a very personal question."

"Oh God," she laughed nervously. "Okay, what is it?"

"When you were attempting sex, did your vagina go into spasm?"

Tina looked quizzical. She eyed me as if I was some kind of seer with a crystal ball. "Yeeeeesss," she said in a drawn-out manner.

I nodded. "Tina, it's a condition called vaginismus."

She almost jumped from her chair. "What! It has a name?"

I couldn't tell if she was excited or traumatized. "Yes. It's actually not that uncommon," I said as she sat on the edge of her chair enthralled by my every word. "Basically, the vagina spasms whenever penetration is attempted. It's like the blinking of your eye. If it feels endangered of being damaged, it blinks. Vaginismus is not too dissimilar to that blink reflex. The spasm is designed to protect you from what you anticipate will be painful penetration."

Tina looked gobsmacked. "So other people have this problem?"

"Yes, particularly women who have been raped."

She literally fell back into her chair and let out a huge sigh of relief. Just as spontaneously she was back up in my face. "So I'm not a freak?" she demanded.

"Not at all."

Again Tina fell back in her chair. She was in her own head. I decided to let her stay there until need be. Her frown slowly disappeared. "So this is the result of being sexually abused as a child?"

I was cautious with the tone of my reply. "I believe all the evidence points to as much."

She looked at me with total helplessness. "I've craved intimacy for so long, but I just couldn't let myself go there because of this. I was just too embarrassed."

It was the first time I had seen Tina cry.

"Many women feel the same way," I consoled her.

She took some time to soak in what I was saying. Gradually she returned to her normal self.

"It's amazing really, isn't it?' she posited.

"What's that?"

"This reflex action I have to protect myself. I think it's totally amazing!"

"The mind is a very powerful thing."

Bam! There she was right back in my face. "Can it be fixed?" she pled.

"What's to fix? Given what you went through as a child, it makes perfect sense you would respond in such a way. Fixing it implies it's broken. It's definitely not broken. It's doing a great job. However, it's a response fixated on the past. You are in a different place in life, and therefore what was once a great means of protection has now become a hindrance to your development. But, yes, it can be altered."

I referred Tina to someone with more expertise in the area than myself. I don't know if she "fixed" her problem. Her case was one of many that evidenced to me how childhood sexual abuse destroys a victim's capacity to partake of intimacy, albeit in an "amazing" way.

ARNOLD

Arnold was a professional athlete. He was extremely fit, confident, and self-assured. I respected him for the simple fact that he never treated others like they were beneath him. He appeared to have a genuine desire to connect with people and gave of his time freely and generously. However, as with most victims of childhood sexual abuse, Arnold had demons he hid from others.

"After sex, I just feel the need to get the hell out of there."

"Run?" I asked.

"Yeah, I get flustered, really anxious."

I found it difficult to envisage Arnold being flustered about anything, given that I had watched him in his chosen sport.

"As if something bad will happen?" I suggested.

"Kind of," he said. "It's more that I feel trapped and just want to escape."

"Escape from what?"

He thought for a moment. "The situation."

"Which is?"

Arnold looked reluctant to "go there." "The deed's done. I feel like just cleaning up and taking off."

I considered what he was saying. "Do you feel guilty?"

He became alert. "Yes! Very!"

"Why?"

His alertness sank back into shame. "I feel like I've used my partner for my own needs, and there's all this mess, and I just want it cleaned up so I can move on."

"Do you ever hold her after sex?"

He shook his head vigorously. "No, I'm outta there."

"Does she notice?"

"Yep, she always asks me to just stay and cuddle, but I tell her I'm not comfortable lying in my own mess. And, yes, I'm very aware that relates to what we have talked about in regard to being raped as a boy. I would feel so used, dirty, and ashamed, I would literally run to clean myself up."

I was impressed with his insight. "I'm still getting paid for this session, right?" I joked.

He laughed. "We'll see."

The feel in the room went back to solemnness. "Is that the only reason you run?" I asked.

"It just feels wrong to me."

"Wrong or uncomfortable?"

"That's more accurate—uncomfortable." I let Arnold rest on that point. Before too long he produced more information as a result of me saying nothing. "Within me, I know the right thing to do is stay and hold her, but it feels so uncomfortable."

His use of a value judgment for such a situation alerted me. "Why do you see it as the 'right' thing to do?"

His glance suggested he found my question odd. "I should want to, shouldn't I?"

"Should you?" I retorted immediately.

"Yeah, women like that," he said calmly.

"Do you?"

Calmness gave way to angst. "No."

Arnold's rapid and emotive response sent alarm bells ringing. Not only for me, but he too appeared to understand something about his delivery was important.

"So forget about what you assume your partner wants for a minute," I said. "Would you like to stay and be intimate with her after sex?"

His reply was immediate. "Absolutely."

"Why?"

Arnold deliberated. "I want her to know I love her."

"No," I stated firmly. My response caught him off guard. "I said forget about what *she* wants for a minute. Would *you* like to stay and be intimate after sex?"

His demeanor changed as if to say he now understood where I was coming from. "Yes," he replied.

I could sense Arnold was on the verge of tapping into some long-repressed emotions. "Why?" I continued.

"To feel loved," he said as the tears streamed down his face.

I offered him some tissues. "And you leave because . . . ?"

"I don't feel worthy of it," he said, accepting my offer.

I knew I had to keep whittling away. The time was ripe; he was open to it. "You don't feel worthy because . . . ?"

Arnold's highly emotive state also meant he was extremely honest. "I feel like I've used her for my own pleasure, and if I'm intimate with her afterward, it's just a lie."

"As in fake?"

He nodded.

"So you desire that emotional connection with her, but resist because you feel like you used her during sex, and to show her such affection afterward would be false?"

"Exactly!" Arnold said, as if for the first time in his life he was truly understood.

I decided to test his insight. "What do you think the problem is here, Arnold?"

"I'm scared of intimacy?" he asked.

I shook my head. "I believe that is the back end of the problem. The issue for you begins before the after-sex intimacy."

With that, I sat back and pretended to be disengaged. I wanted Arnold to think deeply about what I had just said. Suddenly he spoke up. "Yes, you're right."

I probed further. "When does the problem begin?"

"During sex. No, before sex," he corrected himself. "The problem begins before sex because I don't see sex as an intimate connection. I see it as sex."

I smiled. "And how do you view sex?"

"As an act designed to fulfil selfish needs."

Arnold briefly went silent, then made a comment that opened him up. "No wonder I feel guilty and want to escape; I feel like my abuser."

I motioned with my hands for him to continue. This was his "lightbulb" moment.

"If I see sex as just this deed I perform for my own selfish gratification, and think I use my partner to obtain that end, it naturally follows that I would feel like a fraud if I snuggled up to her afterward."

He relaxed into his chair.

I pressed some more. "What needs to happen?"

He became attentive again. "I need to change how I view sex."

"How do you want to see it?"

"As something I *share* with my partner."

I let that sink in for him before progressing to my next question. "To obtain what ends, besides the obvious?"

"Connection," he said serenely.

Again, I let him rest with that notion to cement it for future use.

"Do you think your partner uses you for sexual pleasure?"

The inquiry jolted Arnold from his peaceful state. He looked intrigued. "I'm not sure," he said. "I've never really thought about it. I guess she has to. If I'm not involved, then she has no one to use. I suppose it depends on the definition of the term 'use.'"

"That's a very good point. Do you think she uses you but not with a sole intent to entirely satisfy herself? By that I mean, do you think she wants you to use her to please yourself?"

Arnold was coming back to life. "Yeah, I would say so."

"Why would she want that?"

"To please me, to feel wanted, to feel connected."

The penny had dropped.

ANGELA

"Do you think it's wrong that I'm a prostitute?"

I found the question affronting and quite odd. "Why do you ask?"

Angela smiled flirtatiously. "I'm just interested to know."

"That's not the reason," I said, void of emotion. "Why do you ask?" I repeated.

She recoiled from her "little girl" act. "I suppose I want your approval."

"Why?"

"I want everyone's approval," she said with a dour look.

"Why?"

"It makes me feel better about myself." If anything, Angela was honest.

"Why don't you feel good about yourself?"

"Because I'm a prostitute," she said, her tone intimating that I was a fool.

"So when you ask me if it's wrong that you're a prostitute, what are you hoping I say?"

Angela directed her striking blue eyes to her stockings. She pinched the material between her fingers and let go, allowing it to twang against her skin. "That it's okay," she said sadly.

"And my approval will make it all good?"

She looked at me despairingly. "Probably not."

I altered my posture as a prelude to illustrate the importance of my next question. "Do you think it's okay to be a prostitute?"

She didn't have to think about her answer. It was obviously a topic she considered a lot. "Yes and no," she said. "Yes, because it makes me feel wanted. No, because it makes me feel ashamed."

The massive conflict made sense. "How does it make you feel wanted?"

"Men are willing to pay to have sex with me," she said as she continued her stocking twanging. "I used to go out on the town most nights of the week. I took a new guy home nearly every night. I figured, if I'm going to be promiscuous, I may as well get paid for it. So I placed an ad in the paper and here I am."

I nodded. "How does it make you feel ashamed?"

"There's no honor in it; any idiot can do it."

Angela sat waiting for a query. She obviously felt silence was an uncomfortable tenet. "There is another aspect to it," she said. "It's clichéd, but I also like the control and power I have. I know that's the result of being sexually abused by my father and my uncles and being raped when I was at university. That's pretty much when I became promiscuous."

One would never have suspected for a minute Angela's past was littered with such trauma. She presented as cool and calm. She was classy and articulate. I refocused. "Those events are quite traumatic. You don't express much emotion when you discuss them."

"I've cried too many tears," she replied stoically.

"Which one affected you the most?"

"The rape," she said without hesitation. "He was my boyfriend. He was abusive, extremely violent. One night he assaulted me so badly I thought I was going to die. I finally got the courage to report him to the police. I made a decision that night that nobody was hurting me anymore. The next night, he broke into my apartment and beat and raped me. I never saw him again."

"Did you report it?"

"Nope." Her response was so matter-of-fact it had to be a ruse designed to repress the real pain.

"Why?"

Angela shrugged. "I felt it was my lot in life. I felt like I attracted men like that because it's what I deserved."

I really felt for her. "Do you feel you are deserving of better now?"

"I feel I'm worth nothing to anyone, least of all myself."

"So the prostitution serves the purpose of power and control over men, and at the same time a sense of being wanted?" I posed.

Angela slowly nodded. I noted she was doing her absolute best to refrain from crying. Her lipstick-caked bottom lip quivered.

"You okay?" I asked. She waved me away with a courteous grunt as she fetched tissues from her handbag.

I waited until she regained her composure. "So when you say it gives you a sense of being wanted, do you mean sexually or just wanted?"

Angela delicately and deliberately ran the tissue over her eyes so as not to disturb her makeup. "Wanted in general," she replied. "I like the lonely guys the best, the ones who like to talk. I like that they just want to spend time with me, talking. It sounds stupid, but it makes me feel special."

"I don't think it's stupid. It makes perfect sense, given your history. Let me ask you something: Do you trust men?"

She was now sitting upright. She reminded me of a schoolgirl wanting to impress by having the best posture in the class. "That's hard to answer," she said. "I do, but I don't. I seem to trust the wrong ones."

"Why do you think that is?"

She pursed her lips and squinted as she took a moment to think. "I make myself too available. I'll do anything to win their approval."

"What are you like in relationships?"

"Submissive," she answered with ironic assertiveness. "I'm totally controllable because I fear abandonment."

I considered her comment. "Besides the control element, how do you think that relates to your work as a prostitute?"

"My clients need me more than I need them. I can't be abandoned because there's always someone else willing to pay."

"Those lonely guys you spoke of—why do you think they pay to have a conversation?"

She smiled. The very thought of these men, regardless of the fact that they were lonely and desperate, made her feel good. "They lack love, and they crave intimacy."

I primed myself for the big question. "What is it you crave?" I asked sharply.

Her blue eyes looked sad. "Love. Intimacy."

"Do you think those lonely guys get their needs met via you?"

Angela reverted to her thinking pose: pursed lips and squinting eyes. "I suppose they do," she said. "They keep coming back."

"Doesn't that suggest they don't?"

"I don't understand." She looked puzzled.

"If their intimacy needs were being met, surely they wouldn't need you."

Angela didn't respond, so I continued. "Surely they would be making changes in their lives outside of your services to create intimacy? It seems to me they use your services because they are too scared to seek intimacy. Your services make it easy for them; there is no risk involved."

She nodded. "True, very true."

"What about you?" I asked. "If you crave love and intimacy, Angela, and you keep going back, what does that say about you?"

"Exactly the same thing," she acknowledged as the tears began to flow.

I didn't interrupt her pain. I let her be. Angela cried a river. After every shred of that negative emotion had been exhausted, she sat up and stared. It was as if she was in a trance. She simply sat staring into space. Suddenly I saw her eyes change. "Something just occurred to me," she declared.

"What's that?" I asked gently.

"All this time I thought I was in control of the sex with my clients, but really, what is actually taking place is I'm just abusing myself. I'm trying to control my abuse, not stop it. I'm abusing myself so no one else can."

It was truly one of the most remarkable insights I had ever witnessed from a client. I don't know what happened to Angela. I never saw her again.

CONCLUSION

The message of this chapter has been to offer insight on how victims of child sexual abuse are often forced into an emotional conflict. That is, by virtue of their abuser's selfishness, their intimacy boundaries shrink. They become so contracted so as to form a prison cell. Subsequently, the very walls that protect them confine them. It is difficult to reach out to others when you are living in a crypt—an emotional coffin.

That is not to say victims do not desire intimacy. I believe you can discern that from the cases presented. Victims yearn to be intimate. They yearn to allow themselves to trust. They yearn to love. However, because every innocent part of their humanity has been "used," they revert to protective strategies that, while keep them "safe," are entirely unproductive in the adult world.

When you cannot connect with others, or do so in self-destructive ways, inevitably you become bitter.

CHAPTER FIVE: HATE

"In time we hate that which we often fear."
~ William Shakespeare

MICHELLE

"HATE IS SUCH A STRONG word," she said.

I shrugged. "Isn't that why you chose it?"

Michelle unstrapped her red high heels and sat-crossed legged on her chair. She examined my response to having placed her feet on my furniture; it was an act of defiance. She flicked her long blond hair from her face.

"Is it wrong to hate your own mother?" she asked, her hair, strand by strand, made its way back to its previous resting place. Her face became partially obscured as she sat waiting for my reply. My nonresponse unsettled her; she soothed herself with her own voice. "Most people would say it's wrong," she offered.

"Why's that?" I probed.

She looked up, seemingly relieved I had broken my silence. "It's just not supposed to be that way."

"Maybe, but in your situation—as a child—you went to her and told her you were being molested. Not only did she call you a liar, she also took your stepfather's side."

I let Michelle absorb my words before making eye contact. "Is *that* wrong?" I asked.

"Yes," she said determinedly.

"Then I guess your hate is justified, given that you see what she did as being wrong."

She seemed bewildered by my statement. "Don't you see it as wrong?"

I shook my head. "It doesn't matter what I think. It only matters what you think."

Michelle still looked confused. "So you don't agree?"

"No, I didn't say that." My tone was soft. I didn't want to scare her off. I delayed my next comment so as to give it greater emphasis. "My opinion of your mother's actions is irrelevant in the context of *your* hate. It's *your* emotion due to *your* experience. The meaning *you* have assigned to the event entitles *you* to feel hate."

She began caressing her temple with deliberate tension, her spindly fingers working overtime to massage an answer from her brain. "But hate is such an awful emotion. I *hate* that I hate."

Michelle kept kneading her head with her eyes closed. She was in cognitive torture; she wanted to rid herself of this destructive emotion, yet at the same time felt the need to safeguard it.

"Then why hang on to it?" I asked.

Michelle ceased massaging. "Because I really do *hate* her," she said bitterly. Her words dripped in acid.

"Didn't we already cover this bit?" I joked. It was an attempt to break away from the power of her emotive state. She smiled unconvincingly, stopped massaging her temple, and began rubbing her shoulder blades. I waited for her to settle.

"Why do you keep the hate?" I repeated.

Michelle flicked her hair from her face. "Wouldn't you hate her if she were your mother?" Her question was genuine and begged for validation. As much as I wanted to say yes, I knew I couldn't.

"It's not about my views," I offered. "Why do you keep the hate going?"

My persistence in the same line of questioning began to take its toll. Michelle asked for a break.

I watched her out the window furiously puffing on cigarettes—sucking in smoke with the ferocity of a high-powered vacuum cleaner. Occasionally she would stop and stare at something in the distance, then shake her head. I wondered what she was thinking. Finally she stubbed out yet another cigarette, tilted her head, blew the smoke in the air, and trudged back into the building.

The room filled with the scent of stale tobacco. Michelle took up her seat and swept her hair from her face. "I don't know any other way to process this," she said irritably. "My mother knows I hate her, and to be honest, I like it that way."

"Why's that?"

"Well," she began as she placed her pack of cigarettes in her handbag and retrieved a hair band, "it keeps me at a safe distance; it allows me to keep clear of her. But the best part about that is she doesn't like that I keep the hate going. She wants me to forgive her, and because that's what she wants, I don't. You see, keeping the hate going is a constant reminder to my mom that she's an incredibly shitty parent."

I fiddled with my pen by taking it apart and piecing it back together. Doing so enables me to get the client to focus on my actions at times when I believe my forthcoming question may be too threatening.

"So you do it to punish her?" I asked.

Her gaze darted from my pen to my eyes. "I guess," she said as she began to rub the nicotine stains on her fingers.

I approached with caution. "You intentionally seek to hurt her?"

"Only because of what she did!" Michelle shot back. "I think it's a fairly natural reaction."

"I didn't disagree with you," I said calmly. "I was simply asking if you intentionally do it to hurt her."

Michelle looked guilty. "Yes then!" she said aggressively, "I do it to hurt the bitch!"

I let her simmer. After a few minutes, she was a little less emotive.

"Why do you want to hurt her, Michelle?"

She looked up, her eyes a combination of sadness and rage. "It gives me power," she stated fearlessly.

"Over?"

"The situation."

"Didn't you tell me earlier you hate that you hate?"

"I do," she acknowledged, "but the power the hate brings is too strong to give up."

I considered her response. "So you would rather have power over your mother than feel good within yourself?"

Michelle's defenses reignited. "I'm not going to be all chummy with the bitch and pretend it didn't happen!"

I remained composed. "Who's asking you to?"

"You are!"

"Actually, I'm not," I said staunchly. "However, it's interesting that you assume as much."

"Why?" she demanded as she flicked her hair.

"Because the very concept seems to make you incredibly nervous."

She didn't respond immediately. She dabbed a finger on her tongue and moistened the outer edge of the middle finger on her opposite hand and proceeded to rub at the yellowish stain vigorously.

"It does make me nervous. It scares the shit out of me."

I could sense this was a moment of opportunity simply based on the fact she'd taken time to consider what I'd said and formulated a response. "You said earlier your hate keeps your mother away; I think that speaks volumes."

"I'm scared of her. Well, not her exactly. I'm scared of the situation. She caused me so much pain—I'll never put myself in that predicament again. So if I hate the fat, ugly bitch, I don't have to deal with her. I can keep her at arm's length." Her defensive edge remained.

I faked thinking. I wanted Michelle to perceive I didn't have an answer at the ready. Rapid fire in questioning can be perceived as aggressive, thus the occasional pause works wonders when planning to ask difficult questions. I began taking my pen apart.

"Can't you do that without hating her?" I asked as she watched me remove the inner spring.

"Huh?" she half-grunted.

"I'm just looking at what you said from another angle. You said you hate to hate, so I'm assuming that particular emotion makes you feel bad. More to the point, it makes you feel bad about you?"

"Yes," she replied placidly. "Hate is an awful emotion. Not only is it awful, it's false too."

I looked up from my pen mechanics and gazed at her curiously, in turn, inciting Michelle to clarify her comment.

"It's false in the sense that it gives a feeling of strength, but at the same time, it makes you feel like an evil person—sadistic, even." She swept her hair from her face.

"I don't like that feeling," she continued. "I think there's something in everyone that just knows that feeling isn't right. It doesn't sit right. It's weird because you kind of get addicted to it."

My facial expression insisted she clarify.

"It feels satisfying in a sadistic way, but at the same time it feels wrong in your soul."

I smiled in agreement. Her analysis, I thought, was brilliant.

"So why continue using hate as a means to keep your mother away?"

"I don't really need to, but I think it comes back to the control and power it gives me. It comes back to that feeling I just described—that feeling of power—but at the same time knowing it's wrong and doing you no good."

"Can't you keep her at a distance but without the use of hate?"

"How?" she asked. Her query reeked of impossibility.

I leaned forward. "Let's imagine for a minute you were completely detached from this."

She suspended her nicotine-stain sanitizing and looked up with interest.

"Let's say this whole sexual abuse matter and everything that goes with it was a story you read in the newspaper. Would you feel hate toward the mother in the article?"

Michelle contemplated the question earnestly. "No, I'd feel pity toward her; she's a weak and selfish human being."

"Would you want to punish her? Would you want to control her?"

"No," she stated frankly, "my pity toward her would be out of utter contempt. I'd feel absolutely nothing toward her. I'd feel more toward the child. I'd want to help the child. I'd want to make sure that child is okay."

I smiled. "So all your energy would go into helping the child heal?"

Michelle looked up as she looped her hair through the eye of her elastic band.

"Ah, now I see."

BILL

Bill was a fifty-year-old trucker. He was tall, slender, and stiff in all bodily mechanics to the point that he looked as if he needed thawing out. He was warm but distant: a wall built to keep people away and maintain his isolation. However, if one were able to get inside Bill's wall, one soon came to realize he possessed a heart of gold. The problem was, Bill's gilt heart was being corroded by hate.

"I got arrested last year because of him," he said provokingly.

"I thought you said he died ten years ago?"

"He did," Bill laughed. "He got prostate cancer—poetic justice in my opinion—serves the bastard right."

Bill was discussing Father Brown, a deceased Catholic priest. This "man of the cloth" had a despicable history of raping young boys, including Bill. It is unknown how many offenses the good Father was responsible for; however, it was estimated his victims numbered in the thousands. The "holy man" died in prison at the age of eighty-two.

"So how did you get arrested?" I asked.

Bill looked delighted I had returned to the original topic. "I got really drunk on Christmas Day. That day always has mixed emotions for me. It's the day I'm with the people I love, but it's also the day I was first raped by that evil son of a bitch."

Bill took a moment to compose himself. His jovial state became sullen, then all of a sudden he was excited again. "I drove my car up to the cemetery and found where that asshole was buried. I sat straddling his tombstone while drinking a bottle of Jack Daniels. Just as I was about to head home, I took a piss on his grave. It was really bad timing."

I sat confused. Bill smiled mischievously. "Just as I started pissing on the old bastard's grave, his whole family rolled up with bunches of flowers and shit."

He sat awaiting my response. He initially chuckled a little. Then his chuckle turned to a nervous smile as he perceived I must have disapproved. The truth was, I didn't know how to respond. Part of me found his story hilarious, part of me found it disrespectful, part of me felt sorry for the family members simply wanting to pay their respects on Christmas Day, but most of me felt incredibly sad for Bill. Sad because I could not even begin to fathom the intensity of hatred a person must feel to justify desecrating a burial site.

"You think I did the wrong thing?" he asked accusingly.

"It's not that, Bill. I just feel really sorry that you have suffered so much that pissing on his grave gave you some semblance of retribution."

Bill looked disappointed. It was as if the story he felt proud of telling—the one he thought would be readily embraced and acknowledged as an appropriate form of vengeance—spontaneously combusted between his delivery and my receiving.

"I want you to understand something," I said. "It's not that I disapprove of what you did. I understand why you did it. I just don't see how it helps you."

"It helped me at the time." He grinned. It was a smile designed to coax me into altering my stance.

"What about his family, witnessing that?" I pressed gently.

"Fuck 'em!" he let loose. "They shouldn't be mourning the loss of that sack of shit! The world's better off!"

"Not to them," I said firmly.

His eyes popped. "Fuck 'em!" he yelled again.

I waited for his rage to subside. "What do you feel toward them right now, right in this instant?"

"I hate the assholes!" he shouted, void of thought.

I remained with the same posture and composure. I wanted Bill to believe his anger and hatred had no effect on me. "Why do you hate them?"

He looked surprised. "Because he's a fucking pedophile!"

His anger scared me, although I didn't let him know it. I determined we had come this far; we had passed the point of no return. Pulling out now would be pointless and likely damaging.

"He was obviously more than just a pedophile to his family," I suggested politely.

"Fuck 'em!" he half yelled, half whimpered, as he burst into tears.

Bill sat sobbing, his gasps expelling years of anguish and frustration. I let him be.

I wasn't sure if Bill would attend his next appointment. I wasn't sure if I'd taken him to a place previously that he acknowledged as being of worth to his healing. To my relief, I opened my office door to see him sitting patiently in the waiting room.

He greeted me with the same warmth he always did and immediately launched into discussion from the previous session.

"When I got home from last week's appointment, I was a mess! I swore I wouldn't come back here." His tone confused me. I expected anger, but he seemed excited.

"Why did you?"

"My wife, Erin," he said emotively. "After she settled me down, she asked about the session and what happened. I told her how it went, and she consoled me. I had to go on a road trip the next day, and when I got up she was already awake. She said she was coming with me."

I half-smiled. The gesture was enough for him to continue.

"We began talking, like, *really* talking. She asked again about the session and then asked me to pull the truck off the highway. I was a bit worried she was going to tell me she was leaving or something, but she held my hands and told me she loved me with all her heart. She told me I was a good man. She told me I was a good father. Then she told me pissing on Brown's grave was wrong."

I perceived that contributing anything at this point was futile. Nothing I could verbalize would add to the current discussion, so I remained silent. Not because it was a tactical move; I simply had no idea where he was heading.

"I didn't say anything at first," he continued. "I just listened. I told her I loved her too. Erin fell asleep next to me after I hit the highway, and I started thinking about what she said. I began to wonder why she wanted me to know pissing on Brown's grave was wrong. I felt different. I was thinking about the whole thing clearer than ever, without the anger. If she had done it any other way, I think I would have just got pissed off."

"Like you did with me?" I tested.

"Yeah, exactly." He chuckled. "I started asking myself what it was that Erin was seeing that I wasn't. Then I thought about you and how much I fucking hate you." He looked up to check my reaction.

"Go on." I smiled.

"And then it started to fall into place. I started to think about why I hated you, and all I could come up with was that you actually had the balls to tell me the truth. You didn't pretend to laugh along with my story and humor me. You told me *your* truth; that made me respect you. Then I started thinking about it from that filthy old pedo's family's point of view, and I recognized what you were trying to get me to see: them being there paying their tributes to him on Christmas Day is their truth. It's how they see him. Just because they see him that way doesn't mean they accept him only as a boy-raper. They remember him how they want to remember him."

I was in awe. Bill's wife's input and the gentle manner in which she intervened had obviously impacted the trucker massively. It had made him stop and take toll of her perspective in a way that he felt no threat.

"Then there's my viewpoint," he continued. "Which is completely valid. In my view he's a fucking monster and an animal—always will be in my eyes. But then I got to thinking some more about his family being there on Christmas Day. Even though they know he's a pedophile, they still made the effort to show him that unconditional love."

"Go on," I encouraged him. His insights were impressive, to say the least, but not as inspiring as what was to come.

"Yeah, well, as I was saying, they made the effort on Christmas Day, the day dedicated to family. They were there for him, and here I was, drunk and pissing on the grave of a dead man. I should have been at home. At home embracing the love of my own family and being grateful for what I've got." The tears welled in his eyes.

"When Erin woke up, I pulled the rig over. I said, 'Erin, I don't hate him anymore.' She looked shocked. She became emotional; she could see the change in me. I could tell by her eyes she could tell she had the *real* me for the first time in our marriage. I said, 'Erin, I don't hate him anymore because he isn't going to take me away from you, our children, and our grandchildren ever again.'"

SOPHIA

Sophia's father was an abusive alcoholic. He would beat her mother into submission and, in due course, considered Sophia his sexual property. From Sophia's recollections, she had been raped almost every day from the age of nine, sometimes in front of her siblings. She eventually fled "home" at the age of twelve and spent her teenage years on the streets of Sydney. There she partook of any and every behavior that aided her survival. Her life eventually took a turn for the better when she met a church pastor.

Sophia was now twenty-nine, married, a mother of two, a devout Christian, and worked part-time as a receptionist.

"So you found all of them?" I asked.

Sophia nodded soberly. I could feel the vibe of her energy. Finding her lost family members had not ended well.

"All but my father. I have no desire to connect with him. I have no inclination to find him. As a Christian, I would have to forgive him. I don't want to be in that position," she said sternly.

"What about the others?"

"My mom's in yet another abusive relationship," she said as she rolled her eyes. "I found her through a private detective. I wanted to find out where she was at in her life before I allowed her back into mine. Seems she never learned a thing. She's right back where she started."

Sophia sank into her chair, then rose up stoutly. "I don't want her around my kids," she avowed. "I've worked too hard to let her destroy what I have. My kids deserve better." She took a sip of water from her bottle and swished it around in her mouth before swallowing.

"And your brother and sister?" I enquired hopefully.

"Trent's in prison. Apparently he lost the plot and has a substantial criminal history. He's doing twelve years for shooting a guy over some bad drug deal. The private detective told me in no uncertain terms not to go anywhere near Trent. He said he was a bad person."

"Your sister?"

Sophia's face changed; through her eyes, I could see her heart sink. "Abbey committed suicide when she was thirteen."

It was obvious they'd been close.

"She took an overdose of Mom's sleeping pills," she added. "That's all I know."

At this precise moment, Sophia was an open wound. My mind was saying, *Back off*, but my gut was saying, *Do it.* I always follow my gut.

"The anger is missing from your voice when you discuss Abbey," I pressed.

With that, Sophia broke down. Her head collapsed into her hands as she wept in agony. She didn't sob; she wailed like a mother grieving the loss of a child.

"How embarrassing," she said bashfully after some time. "I've never cried like that before. It was kind of weird."

I waved her comment away. "Happens in here all the time."

Sophia smiled in acknowledgement of the likely truth of my admission.

"I want to ask you something about your reaction, if that's okay?" I hoped she would be brave enough to discuss the depth of her suffering.

She nodded, somewhat apprehensively.

"In my experience, overt sadness—like you displayed earlier—is usually a masking emotion. Often what lies underneath is anger."

She thought for a moment. "Yes, I suppose that's true. I'm incredibly angry at my father *and* my mother."

I went on. "Typically, what then lies under the anger is the root emotion. I find in most cases when sadness is the surface emotion the root emotion is often guilt."

Sophia's face turned remorseful as the last word left my mouth. She closed her eyes and sat breathing heavily, too heavily for a person in a static state.

"I hate myself," she whispered faintly. "I'm a terrible, terrible sister."

I didn't need to ask why.

She wiped her tear-drenched face with a tissue. "I should never have left. I bailed on Abbey. She probably became his sex toy. She probably committed suicide because of that."

Sophia became emotional again. I didn't say a word even though I knew she wanted me to intervene. I waited to see if there was anything else she needed to get out. I didn't wait long.

"If I hadn't left," Sophia continued, "she wouldn't have had to go through what I did. I should have stayed and protected her. It's my fault. Her blood is on my hands!"

"I can see what you mean," I said without a trace of compassion.

Sophia's face lost its sullen expression. Instead, she looked astonished. Her crying ceased instantly.

I took it a step further. "You're right. If you had stayed, then Abbey would still be alive."

Sophia sat looking at me dumbfounded. This was my opportunity.

"Tell me your absolute honest thoughts about me right now, Sophia, without worrying about my feelings," I said with every ounce of integrity I could muster.

She looked tentative. She needed to give herself permission to be honest. In hindsight her hesitance was probably due to her religious views more than a desire to comply with social etiquette. Luckily she went with her gut.

"I think you're a fucking moron," she said brusquely.

I smiled. "There's no need to hate yourself, Sophia."

CONCLUSION

Those of you who are victims of childhood sexual abuse must understand, there is no right or wrong way to feel about your past. The means by which you make sense of your experience is rightfully yours. I can only offer what I know by virtue of working with people in therapy.

What I have come to understand is that those who dispose of hate as a means to deal with whatever it is that haunts them inevitably become stronger. In that regard, it is my opinion that the emotion of hate, while offering a sense of power, actually weakens people. It is an emotion that can be abused, like substances, to cover true suffering. As such, people can just as easily become addicted to hate as they can to alcohol, drugs, gambling, and other vices. It keeps the victim in a victim mentality. It enslaves.

Chapter Six: Knowledge Is Power

"Real knowledge is to know the extent of one's ignorance."
~ *Confucius*

I WRAPPED MY HANDS IN the warmth of the Styrofoam cup and took a long sip. The aroma of coffee wafting past my nose prepared me for the richness of the taste to come. I savored the flavor as I watched some children playing boisterously in the park opposite me, their vigilant mothers positioned immediately to my left. Being bored, I eavesdropped on their conversation. They were discussing child sex offenders.

"I'm so glad they have the 'Stranger Danger' program at school," stated one woman.

The others wholeheartedly agreed with her.

"Yes," said another. "It makes me breathe a little easier knowing Jacob understands what to do."

"I always pay close attention when I pick Chloe up after school, just to make sure no one suspicious is hanging around," another chimed in.

I rolled my eyes.

"What's the point?" I muttered under my breath, but the words had come out louder than intended. The group stood staring at me.

"Pardon?" asked a lady holding a baby.

"Sorry, I shouldn't have been listening," I backpedalled.

She laughed. "Well now, this would be the first time a man wanted to hear what a bunch of women were talking about."

Her friends seemed a little less inclined to embrace me. I smiled and swigged my coffee and hoped to God she wouldn't press me for an answer. I wasn't that lucky.

"Did I hear you correctly—you don't see the point?"

I put my hands up in a gesture of surrender. "I don't want to fight."

She smiled. The others were still a bit wary.

"Why would you say that?" she challenged.

I've been surrounded by ten offenders during program facilitation and have never been as scared about being honest as I was with that group of women at that moment. "Um, I just think it gets a little too much airplay," I said timidly.

"You obviously don't have children," one woman said, going on the attack.

I sipped my coffee.

"I have children," I replied calmly.

"And you think teaching them about 'Stranger Danger' is a waste of time?" she asked in a tone that failed to hide her scorn.

"Not completely. I just prefer to focus on what's important. I taught them about reality."

The lady holding the baby reinvolved herself. "And that is?" she asked politely.

"That if they *were* to be sexually abused, the person to most likely do it would be someone they knew, not a complete stranger."

None of the women said a word. I felt braver.

"How many kids were abducted from the school your child attends in the last year?" I asked Baby Lady.

"None," she said sheepishly. "But that might be because of the 'Stranger Danger' message," she hurriedly threw in.

"Maybe; I didn't say it was a complete waste of time."

I took another hit of caffeine. "How many kids have been abducted in the school's history?"

"I'm not sure. I'm guessing none," she conceded.

"How many kids currently attending that school do you reckon have been, or are currently being, sexually abused?"

The group looked horrified (I never have been one for social graces).

"I'd like to think very few," Baby Lady replied. The others agreed.

"If you can believe the statistics, one in five kids will suffer sexual abuse of some kind, so 'very few' is probably an extremely conservative guess," I argued.

They looked shocked.

"One in five!" declared one lady.

"I highly doubt that," said another in an attempt to wipe away her friend's fears.

I shrugged. "It's what the research says."

They seemed too unsettled to go back to their banter. Some looked at each other, and some looked at me.

"Let's say you're right," I said to Baby Lady. "Let's say it is only a few. How many do you think know their abuser?"

"Hmm, logic tells me all of them," she admitted.

I stood up from the park bench and threw my empty coffee cup in the adjacent rubbish bin.

"Thanks for the conversation."

I walked away feeling pleased with myself. Not because I was a smartass, but because I knew I had at least made those women think outside the typical rigid conceptualization regarding sexual offenders. Hopefully, they were disturbed enough to research the facts for themselves.

To be informed you must sift the chaff from the wheat with respect to the truth about sexual offenders. For example, researchers—based on recidivism rates—continue to espouse the view that sexual offenders are the least likely to reoffend. Of course the "Average Joe" is taken aback by this "fact." "Average Joe" assumes all sex offenders are psychopaths who will reoffend at every opportunity, as shown on television. The reality is, sex offenders *are* the least likely group to reoffend—*as a whole*.

It's true that a massive majority of sexual offenders will only ever commit a one-off offense and never do so again in their entire life. Yet there are others—such as the 453 pedophiles in a study by Abel (1994) that admitted to 67,000+ sex crimes against children—that do perpetually and predatorily recidivate. Thus, researchers are telling a half-truth when they say sexual offenders are the least likely to reoffend. And it's a very precarious half-truth because such generalized assumptions detract from the dangerousness of offenders that *are* predators. Dumping all sex offenders into one pile and implying they are the least likely to reoffend is like saying all domestic canines are safe. The truth is most are, but some aren't.

Whether the tactic is deceit, fear, or both, most predatory-type child sex offenders have spent many years mastering their craft. Remember that statistic from Chapter Two, regarding only 3.5% of offenders gaining a conviction? This suggests 96.5% of offenders do not suffer punishment. Think about that from their perspective: it's worth the gamble. The odds imply extremely limited risk.

This is how the serial types become virtuosos. They offend and learn, offend and learn, over and over again. And, in so doing, better formulate their modus operandi. The offenders we know about are only the tip of the iceberg; most of the "experts" don't get caught.

In order to understand what a child sex offender is, you must first understand what they are not.

PEDOPHILIA—A BRIEF MODERN HISTORY

In the time of Sigmund Freud, pedophilia was considered so uncommon that the legendary psychiatrist deemed exclusive sexual interest in children as a "sporadic aberration." In fact, homosexuality was considered the affliction of the sexual deviant, so much so it was thought an illness.

When the American Psychiatric Association (APA) released the first edition of the Diagnostic and Statistical Manual of Mental Disorders (DSM-I) in 1952, homosexuality was included and defined as a sexual abnormality. In due course, the gay lobbyists began to make waves about the wrongfulness of "diagnosing" someone as homosexual. At this time, gay rights activists were united with pedophile lobbyists in an effort to have their sexuality accepted by mainstream society (yes, you read that correctly).

Over time, the homosexual activists broke away from the pedophiliacs and began demonstrating of their own accord. This came to the fore in 1970 during the APA's annual convention in San Francisco. Activists interrupted proceedings relentlessly and ridiculed any psychiatrist who had posited a belief that homosexuality was a mental disorder.

Around this time—and throughout the '60s—a major antipsychiatry movement was afoot. The gay rights activists attached themselves to the movement and subsequently, due to much protestation, when the DSM-II (7th printing) was released in 1974, homosexuality had been removed as an illness.

The exclusion of homosexuality as a mental disorder makes for interesting debate, namely because one must question the motive for its removal. Was it eradicated due to social pressure, or was it removed because it was no longer considered a disorder?

Dr. Jon Meyer, writing in *Comprehensive Textbook of Psychiatry, 4th edition*, states:

> This change reflected the point of view that homosexuality was to be considered a mental disorder only if it was subjectively disturbing to the individual. The decision of the APA Board . . . took place in the context of new sociological data, biological inferences, and de-emphasis of psychoanalytic observations.

If Dr. Meyer is correct, homosexuality was no longer considered an illness based on science. My main point of focus here is the reference to biological factors. If these are at play for people who are homosexual (i.e., they do not choose their sexuality), what must we make of pedophiles?

Almost every pedophile I've ever met told me they were born that way. Perhaps that's an uncomplicated "out"; they don't have to accept responsibility for their behavior. I might adhere to that cynical train of thought if the individuals I'm speaking about had reason to lie. However, some were serial offenders who openly acknowledged their attractions. They had no qualms in stating a belief that sex with children was completely acceptable. Hence, they had no reason to misconstrue or conceal their genuine attitudes.

Unlike homosexuality, the majority of modern-day society does not believe pedophilia is a sexual predisposition. In other words, there is no genetic or biological cause. Society prefers to believe pedophilia is a choice—because if it were any other way, it would evoke a major dilemma in exactly the same fashion that homosexuality did a few decades back.

I don't know about you—I can only speak for myself—but in terms of my sexuality I'm attracted to women. How do I know this? I feel it in every part of me. It just "is." When did I start to feel this way? As far back as I can remember. Can I change it? No. It is who I am.

Consider this in the context of pedophilia. If this is who they are, can they change it?

In my experience, the answer is a resounding no.

What am I proposing? That we legalize pedophilia, as was done with homosexuality?

No, never.[1] What I *am* saying is we need to improve our knowledge of the problem.

DSM-IV CLASSIFICATION OF PEDOPHILIA

If I were to ask you to define pedophilia, I wonder what your answer would be.

Most people have no idea. They assume it refers to some sick, twisted, debauched deviate with a tenuous grip on their sexual impulses who hangs out in public toilets awaiting their next child victim.

Wrong.

According to the DSM-IV, pedophilia is classed as a paraphilia:

---

[1] Of course this now leaves me open for attack from the politically correct brigade who can accuse me of suggesting homosexuality should be illegal. Get this message: I do not care one iota what consenting adults do between the sheets. I do care about children being exploited. Big difference!

> The Paraphilias are characterized by recurrent, in-
> tense, sexual urges, fantasies, or behaviors that involve un-
> usual objects, activities, or situations and cause clinically
> significant distress or impairment in social, occupational,
> or other important areas of functioning. (pp. 571–2)

In specific reference to the paraphilia of pedophilia, an individual can be diagnosed a pedophile if they meet the following DSM-IV criteria:

> Over a period of at least six months, recurrent, in-
> tense sexually arousing fantasies, sexual urges, or behaviors
> involving sexual activity with a prepubescent child or chil-
> dren (generally age 13 years or younger).
>
> [And:] The person has acted on these sexual urges, or
> the sexual urges or fantasies caused marked distress or in-
> terpersonal difficulty.
>
> [And:] The person is at least age 16 years and at least
> 5 years older than the child or children in Criterion A.
>
> Note: Do not include an individual in late adoles-
> cence involved in an ongoing sexual relationship with a 12-
> or 13-year-old.

Every time I read this criterion, it does my head in. I hope I can explain this precisely and laconically so you, too, can see why my brain feels like it's going to explode.

First, the criterion states that a diagnosis of pedophilia can only be applied if "the sexual urges or fantasies caused marked distress or interpersonal difficulties." In other words, if a person sexually abused numerous prepubescent children over a twenty-year period and felt no remorse, they cannot be diagnosed a pedophile.

In all my years, every single serial offending pedophile I've met showed not a scrap of remorse—not one smidgen. The reason is obvious. They believe what they are doing is acceptable. In my experience, these types represent the highest risk, yet they are not, according to DSM-IV criteria, pedophiles.

My next beef has to do with the notion that the sexual urges, fantasies, etc., are specified as having to last six months or longer. The reason I have issue with this is important in the context of this book—you must understand there is a decided difference between a pedophile and a child sex offender.

A person can be a pedophile and never have a physical sexual encounter with a child.

What?

Yes, read that again.

Many people, including therapists and researchers, make the erroneous assumption that anyone suffering a pedophilic condition wants to harm children. This is not the case. While most will fantasize about prepubescent children, the majority will likely never offend. They may struggle to understand their sexuality for the entirety of their lives. However, most pedophiles recognize their inclinations are morally wrong. As such, they refrain from exploiting children based on their own value set. This is exactly why the research pertaining to pedophiles is skewed—false, even—because it primarily focuses on individuals that have crossed the moral line (i.e., child sexual offenders).

Back to my original gripe. A time frame of six months for continued attraction/arousal/urges makes no sense to me. This is because a person can offend against a child and not be a pedophile.

Huh?

Yes, read that again too.

For example, a man may not be a pedophile, for he may not be attracted to prepubescent girls, yet he may lust for and eventually offend against his physically developed twelve-year-old daughter. If this desire had been building up over seven months, according to the DSM-IV, he is a pedophile. This invariably means a man with a one-off offense with no attraction to prepubescent body types is a DSM-IV classified pedophile, yet a self-proclaimed serial child sex offender, according to DSM-IV criteria, is not.

This brings me to the point of an age criteria. I completely fail to see the science in designating thirteen years of age as a means to determine someone's pedophilic interests. What if a child thirteen years or under does not have a prepubescent body shape? What if she/he looks like an adult?

Imagine this: you are walking down the street and pass a very attractive person. You think to yourself, "Wow!" and turn for a second glance. You feel all the excitement of the sexual attraction between you and that stranger. The next day you are walking down the same street and pass the same individual. This time they are wearing a school uniform. Does your sexual attraction from the previous day suddenly make you a pedophile? No, it makes you a normal human being. If you had sex with that person, and they were under the age of sixteen (in my country), that would make you a child sex offender, not a pedophile.

Recently I was having dinner with a colleague. I noticed him look at the waitress in a sexual way. I asked, "How old do you think she is?"

He blushed but was at least honest. "I'm hoping eighteen." He laughed.

Turns out she was thirteen.

If my friend lived in Colombia or Panama, he could legally have sex with that waitress. In those countries, a female is of legal consenting age at twelve (males fourteen). If he lived in Japan, Spain, or Syria, he could legally have sex with the waitress—the consenting age is thirteen (female and males). In Albania, Bosnia, Croatia, Estonia, Georgia, Germany, Hungary, Iceland, Italy, Liechtenstein, and Puerto Rico, he would have to wait another year (the consenting age for both sexes being fourteen). However, if he lived in Cameroon, he should probably best look elsewhere because in that country you must be twenty-one. How does the DSM-IV account for these cultural differences?

My observation of the problem within society is that anything and everything perceived to be sexually inappropriate or dysfunctional makes someone a "pedo." The word has been taken way out of context to the point it has no meaning other than a derogatory label. For example, I was watching a clip on MTV and said aloud, "Gee, she is one sexy woman." My stepdaughter sitting nearby contorted her face in disgust as she promptly informed me the girl on TV was "only sixteen." She got further repulsed when I said, "And? Sixteen is the legal age of consent in this country."

"Pedo," she replied.

What was I supposed to do? Suddenly say, "Oh, I didn't mean it. She's not sexy at all. In fact, I find her physically grotesque, and there isn't a sensuous bone in her body. She has no sex appeal whatsoever, and now we can all go back to being comfortable in my presence because by denying my attractions, I'm safe for human interaction, as I've obviously proven myself not to be a 'pedo.'"

I find it alarming when talking to teleiophiles (this is the label coined for people who have a "normal" sexual preference for adults of the opposite sex . . . I can feel my brain getting sore again) that they feel the need to ensure you understand they are not attracted to anyone under eighteen years of age for fear of being labelled a pervert.

Recently in a bar, I was discussing this very topic with a fifty-year-old man. He emphatically stated that even if he were single and approached by a beautiful eighteen-year-old woman, he would not have sex with her. His reasoning? "She's just a kid."

I argued he was confusing the issue, as I was stating the scenario based on attraction alone. To my surprise, he took it a step further. "I don't think I'd even be attracted," he said.

What was interesting about this little experience was that within a minute of that conversation ending, four beautiful young girls walked into the bar. None of them looked much older than eighteen or nineteen. Guess who was drooling in his beer glass as they walked by?

He gazed from the time the young ladies entered until the time it took them to exit through the far door, all the while staring at their "best parts."

I laughed as he noticed I had spotted his lusting stares. I shook my head and suggested he had just made a liar of himself. His reply was baffling, to say the least, "C'mon, it's a bar. They're at least eighteen."

In his mind, a matter of days, weeks, or months can determine what he is attracted to. What if they were seventeen years and 364 days old? Would they still be unattractive? Quite frankly, I find it exceedingly bizarre that a fifty-year-old man can be so out of touch with his sexuality.

The reason he and others have become conscious of repressing these attractions is that culturally we are being conditioned to believe such attractions are wrong. We fear that by stepping outside the politically correct framework we will be seen as sexually abnormal. As a result of this perceived "wrongness," there is currently an alarming movement taking place in the field of psychology/psychiatry. Certain researchers are advocating for the inclusion of two new disorders in the upcoming DSM-V (these are the same people responsible for inventing the term *teleiophile*). The "disorders" proposed are hebephilia and ephebophilia.

Hebephilia is defined as a primary or exclusive interest in pubescent individuals age eleven through fourteen. Ephebophilia is founded on the same premise except the attraction is to later adolescents age fifteen through nineteen. It is important to understand we are talking about attraction here, not offending. Merely attraction.

I do not consider this good science. It demonstrates the degree to which the psych establishment forgoes rigorous empirical testing to define a boundary for diagnosing mental illness. It is the result of the pressure being applied via sociocultural and legal norms to conform to a moral basis; no disorder should be founded on morality. Would you be comfortable being tagged with a mental illness if you found sixteen-year-olds attractive? I mean, seriously—has the world gone mad?

The biological reason for puberty is to reproduce. Biologically speaking, you are *supposed* to find pubescent individuals attractive. In fact, the only people who don't find pubescent individuals attractive are pedophiles. However, as human beings we have moral reasoning. We deduce the proper and right thing to do. Subsequently, it's illegal to have unconsenting sexual interaction with anyone we simply find attractive. It's also illegal to have sexual engagement with an individual under sixteen (in the country I reside in). Personally, I find lots of females sexually appealing. I also have cutoffs at either end of the spectrum (i.e., I don't find prepubescent girls or elderly women sexually appealing at all). Does that make me a teleiophilic, hebephilic, ephebophilic sex monster?

We also have the issue of a cutoff point of sixteen years of age being the chronological requirement to be diagnosed a pedophile. There is no science in this designated cutoff. It is simply a number plucked from thin air to coincide with the typical age of consent in the Western world. It makes no sense. There are simply too many variables at play, which is the problem when you attempt to create a "scientific" method to understand a dynamic concept such as human sexuality. It's impossible to have a "one size fits all" approach.

Human sexuality is highly complex. However, we (society) have been conditioned to believe sexual offending is very straightforward, black and white, cut-and-dried. This is simply untrue. Offenders are all unique. They are all different, and their reasons for offending are never simple. We, as a society, are way off the mark in understanding these people because regardless of what the academics preach, the information is limited.

This brings me to the next topic. There is no area with a greater chasm of noninformation than the area of female sexual offenders. It's as if female sex offenders simply do not exist, or, at the very least, are exceptionally rare. Subsequently, society deems females nonthreatening with regard to committing sex crimes. Evidence of this can be found in an article I recently read that told of a particularly odd occurrence that took place on a long-distance flight.

A child traveling alone had been seated next to a male passenger. The stewardess informed the man he would have to change seats and proceeded to ask a female sitting nearby if she would mind changing seats with the man because it was against company policy for the male to sit next to the child. The passengers exchanged seats, and the female was thanked for her consideration but not the man.

What the . . . ?

At least we can sleep at night knowing that no child is allowed to sit next to a male on an airplane. Under the same absurd premise, I should not be allowed to sit next to females travelling alone on planes because I might sexually assault them.

What took place on that flight is absolutely ridiculous for many reasons. However, for the sake of this chapter I would like to focus on the faulty assumption that a child in the presence of a woman is less vulnerable. Let's get this straight from the outset: there are *many* female child sexual offenders "out there." To believe otherwise is, quite frankly, naïve.

Occasionally we read about the female schoolteacher who ventures into a sexual relationship with a student, but not often. Yet I know from my high school years this definitely occurs, and it occurs frequently. I recall boys under sixteen having sex with at least three female teachers. Those boys will never press charges for all the reasons discussed by "Jack" in Chapter Three.

During my years working in prisons, I was regularly required to interview and assess offenders. Particularly when interviewing a sex offender, the topic of their introduction to sex was a standard part of the discussion. It was during these conversations I came to realize just how prevalent female child sex offenders are.

The following narrative is similar to many others I have heard.

BENNY AND ANDREW

I scoped the circle of participants in the room, wondering who among them was presenting next. They were a group of ten men. All had been assessed as medium-risk sexual offenders. I noted most were intently listening to the inmate currently speaking, except Benny.

Benny was obsessed with the scraps of paper in his hands. He furiously pored over his notes while nervously moving his leg up and down at high speed. I caught his eye and slowly mouthed the word *relax*. He smiled, then instantly resumed his leg shaking and note perusal.

Eventually it was Benny's turn. He was presenting his "autobiography" to the group, his story about his journey in life and how it related to his offending. He started by telling the others how he never knew his real parents and was placed into foster care as a baby.

"I liked living with those people," he said. "They were nice people. They were good to me. But they got divorced, and I was moved around all over the place after that. Then I got placed with this other family when I was about thirteen, but by then I was off the rails. I was always in trouble with the cops."

I was impressed. Benny was cruising through his presentation. He showed no signs of nerves whatsoever.

"Because we lived in a faraway spot in the bush, the welfare department would send a social worker out to see me. She was really nice. I liked her a lot. She would talk to me about my problems and shit; I liked that she took an interest in me."

Benny confidently placed the top sheet of paper underneath the others in his hands and continued. "She lived at the beach hundreds of miles from where we lived. She asked if I'd like to come and stay with her. I'd never seen the ocean . . ."

Bit of a boundary issue, I thought.

Benny continued. "We flew on an aeroplane. I was really scared, but so excited. I stayed with her for two weeks. My holidays continued right up until I was sixteen, and that was also my introduction to sex."

"What?" I asked, aghast.

Benny looked up from his notes. "Huh?"

The room kind of stopped. The rest of the group were looking at me.

"Sorry," I said, "I thought you said going to the social worker's house for a holiday was your introduction to sex."

Benny looked confused. "It was," he replied.

"Oh, okay. Did she have kids or something?" I reasoned.

"No," said Benny defensively, "I had sex with *her*."

"Who?" I sought clarification.

"My social worker."

I shook my head, not in disbelief but to try to recapture some lucidity. "Hang on; back up a bit. How old were you?"

"When I had sex with her?"

"Yeah."

"We had sex on my first visit; I was thirteen. We pretty much had sex every day for the two weeks I was there," he boasted.

"What the fuck!" piped up Levi.

Levi was a huge Polynesian man. His legs were covered in intricate tribal tattoos, and his muscles flexed and defined themselves whenever he made the slightest movement. Levi had been incarcerated for carnal knowledge. He had entered a sexual relationship with a fourteen-year-old girl who had told him she was twenty. On account of his lengthy criminal history, Levi was shown no mercy by the court and was sentenced to five years imprisonment. The entire group respected him out of pure fear. He had a reputation for being a hothead, and even though he spoke "funny," no one dared poke fun at him.

"How old dis bitch?" Levi demanded.

"I don't know—about thirty-five, I suppose," replied Benny, wondering what all the fuss was about.

"Did you report it?" I asked.

"Report what?"

Levi eased his hulking frame forward. "You stupid, Benny." Levi pointed at me. "John tryin' tell you dat bitch sexed abuse you."

"She sexually abused me!?" Benny retorted. The tone of his voice reflected his belief that the supposition was simply preposterous.

The group sat waiting for me to intervene. "Benny," I said, "last week Colin talked to us about his offense. Do you remember what it was about?"

"Yeah, he abused his stepdaughter."

"How old was she?"

"Fourteen, I think."

Colin nodded in confirmation.

"How old were you when your social worker had sex with you?"

"So I was sexually abused?" Benny laughed.

"Yes, you idiot, Benny," chastised Levi.

"But I liked her. I've never heard something so dumb. That's so stupid. I wasn't scared of her or anything. I liked it when she took me on holidays."

A few inmates giggled among themselves.

Levi looked at me. "I fink she a bitch, John."

"Why?" interjected Benny in defense of his teenage memoirs.

"She sexed abuse you, bro. If dat us do dat to girl, we in big, big troubles."

Benny looked at Levi incredulously. "Oh, maybe I do feel a little bit bad about it," he said sarcastically to the rest of the group. "Maybe I can claim me some victim compensation or some shit."

They roared laughing, except Levi.

"Benny, you a dickhead. She pro'bly still do dat shit to chil'ren."

The group immediately ceased laughing. I was worried the giant man might kill Benny, so I pulled him into line.

"Levi, remember to be respectful. You don't have to agree, but you don't have to call Benny a dickhead." It was an inward tongue-in-cheek reprimand that probably came out a little too truthful.

"Anyway, what do I give a fuck?" said Benny, his courage in challenging Levi the result of my interjection as opposed to genuine bravery.

"Kid still get sexed abuse by her," argued Levi. "I bet dat bitch tell you to shut you mouth?"

Benny nodded. "Yeah, she said if I told my foster family, I wouldn't be able to go on holidays with her anymore—so what?"

Levi was calmer. "Why you fink she say dat for you, stupid?"

Benny looked indignant. "To keep fucking me," he replied sarcastically.

The group broke into fits of laughter.

"And you think that's perfectly fine?" I asked.

"Let me spell it out for you," said Benny, "I. Don't. Give. A. Shit."

Suddenly a voice from the edge of the circle spoke up. "I just want to say something about my upcoming presentation," said Andrew.

Andrew was a very quiet and reserved group member. He was doing three years for sexually assaulting a disabled woman.

"I started my autobiography section the other night," he began. "When I got to the part about my introduction to sex, I wasn't going to write it, but I will now."

"What do you mean?" I enquired.

"My cousin used to get me to, you know, like, go down on her and shit. She was fifteen, and I was about five or six."

The group was still silent, waiting to see Andrew's reaction before committing to make light of his circumstance. There was no thought of respect.

It was merely a pause to gain confirmation to engage in their pseudo-bond-ing.

"How did that affect you?" I asked.

"To be honest, I never really thought about it much until the other night. Then when Benny started saying that stuff, it began to come back to me in more detail. I thought she was just a bit of a weirdo. When she got older, it stopped because I didn't see her as much."

"Why were you not going to include it in your presentation?"

"It wasn't that important."

"So you see nothing wrong with a girl that age making you—at five or six—perform oral sex on her?"

"Not really. It didn't damage me or nothin'."

I sat and waited. I knew I wouldn't have to address this issue; a strong personality in a rehab program is always a therapist's best friend.

"All you fuckin' idiots," Levi said. "If dat a man, we go prison. Lady don't get nuffin."

The entire group refused to make eye contact with the giant.

"So you think she's a sex offender?" Andrew directed his question to-ward me.

Levi couldn't help but involve himself. "Of course she sexed offender, you idiot, An'rew!"

I looked at Levi in a gesture to keep his cool. He simmered.

"How old were you when it ended?" I asked.

"I dunno—about eight," said Andrew.

"So your cousin was about eighteen?"

"Yeah," he confirmed.

"Is it illegal to have sex with eight-year-olds if you're eighteen?"

"Yeah, of course it is."

I shrugged. "It is what it is."

The conclusion was left to Levi.

"You a dickhead, An'rew."

———◆———

It wasn't something they as a group were ever going to get, simply because what was taking place was merely a reflection of societal attitudes about female child sexual offenders. It is difficult to envisage this communal position changing, given the main culprits of the fallacy are the men abused as children who do not see it as abuse. However, I digress. The real issue is this: yes, female child sexual offenders exist. They are more common than perceived.

CONCLUSION

There are many myths surrounding child sex offenders that dilute the more important information. Obviously I could have selected a multitude of other topics of an erroneous nature to write about. However, I chose to stick with two of the most salient issues so as to provide a backdrop for the chapters to come. Specifically, I wanted to illustrate some of the main fallacies surrounding these people as perpetuated by the mass media, the general population, and (sadly) researchers.

False, misleading, or hyped-up information is not helpful in understanding the mind-set of sexual offenders of any type. It merely serves to pigeonhole and profile them in a way that makes them even more obscure and therefore less detectable. In other words, the myths actually work in the favor of the virtuoso-type offenders because it cloaks them. While the ill informed are looking for the freak in the trench coat, the benevolent helper is working his/her "magic."

More pertinently to this book is that misconceptions propounded by society do not aid victims in understanding the mentality, attitudes, and psyches of their perpetrators. As I stated earlier, sexual offending is not cut-and-dried. I hope the following chapters help you fathom the inner cognitive workings of perpetrators. I hope these insights enable you to realize that in every way the abuse you suffered was not your fault. I hope they help you heal.

In stating the above, I need to provide a forewarning of the material to come. The content is raw, and as such may be triggering to those readers

who have suffered sexual abuse. It is impossible for me to highlight the cognitive distortions of offenders without presenting the details. The subject
matter is disturbing, not just for the obvious reasons (i.e., physical acts) but,
as you will see, due to the extent of the planning, grooming, and tactical
deceit—which is nothing short of unnerving. With this in mind, I suggest
you proceed with caution. Read with the intent of focusing on the acts of
the offenders that demonstrate their wiliness. If you can do this, you will,
without doubt, begin to see no victim is *ever* to blame.

CHAPTER SEVEN: THE CYBER PREDATOR

"We don't protect our young,
and we tolerate predators of the same species."
~ Andrew Vachss

ETHAN

THERE WAS NO OTHER WAY to describe Ethan: slovenly. Pure and simple, he was a slob. His hair was unkempt, his clothes unironed, his stomach protruded from his T-shirt, and his body odor was nothing short of vile. He attended therapy looking as if he had just that minute raised his head from his pillow. He was forever late yet always managed to squeeze out an excuse that contained just enough validity to presume him innocent.

I assessed the sorry sight of a man before me. He was a social outcast. Other than his appearance, there was a certain something about Ethan that was off-putting. He was simply uncomfortable to be around. He was gauche, and this characteristic stuck to you like walking into a spider's web; it freaked you out. It also initiated a chain reaction of social rejection cues that he either chose to ignore or was completely unaware of. The more cues, the more his "web" fused to your personal space.

Ethan's dress sense further implied he had never understood the basics of social presentation. In this instance, he wore an old faded "Fat Albert" T-shirt, loud board shorts, white ankle-length socks, and a pair of black leather shoes. For all his shortcomings, however, Ethan was highly intelligent. It was his life conditioning that had created a black hole in terms of social and emotional smarts. It was this void that intimated how he had come to be in my office.

"Where did you want to begin?" Ethan asked as he made himself comfortable.

The question surprised me. It was one I thought I should be asking. His confidence was odd—misplaced, even. Namely because he had nothing to be confident about, yet he presented as if he was the most special person on the planet. I immediately assumed he was the by-product of an environment in which his parents not only overprotected him but quite likely overindulged him in notions about his prized worth.

"The start is always a good place," I said dryly.

"Do you mean the start of my offending, the start of my life—what do you mean?" he asked pompously.

The question struck me as absurd. He knew full well why he was attending therapy. I sat waiting for him to continue to see if the uncomfortable silence had any effect on him. It didn't.

"Your offending," I said.

"Oh, okay," he replied with a puzzled twinge. His tone annoyed me; it felt false. "I thought you'd be all over that, to be honest. I thought you'd have read the court documents before I got here. Were you given the court documents?"

He was grating on my nerves already.

"I have the documents; I've *even* read them," I said patronizingly. He didn't catch on. He was too busy tending to his socks. He finished evening out the lengths and measured them against each other to ensure they were pulled up squarely.

"I had illegal porn on my computer," he said in an apathetic manner. He then sat back in the chair as if it was his favorite recliner and began picking the peeling transfer off his T-shirt.

"Go on," I requested.

Ethan looked at me oddly, showed me the palms of his hands, and simultaneously shrugged his shoulders. He didn't say a word, but the combination of signals was designed to sarcastically ask, "What else?"

I'd had enough.

"You honestly think you can come here and offer up that bullshit as a means to begin our discussions?" I stated matter-of-factly.

Again his three-combination body gesture came to the fore. This time it was even more pronounced.

I shook my head angrily. "Okay, fine, we do it the hard way."

He was still unfazed.

"I'll just assume everything the police said was true."

"It's not all true," he said confidently as he picked another piece of "Fat Albert's" head from his T-shirt, rolled it in his fingers, and threw it on the floor.

I waited and waited. And waited some more. Finally, once "Fat Albert" had all but disappeared, Ethan spoke up. "The number of images the cops say I had on my computer is a lie."

I acted composed even though I was relieved; I had won the battle of the wills.

"How many did you have?" I asked.

"Lots," he said.

I looked at him sternly, "Don't play me for a fool."

"I don't know," he replied with attitude. "Probably around a hundred."

I shook my head again. "You just don't get it, do you?"

He remained unruffled.

"How many times have you done this?" I asked heatedly, motioning with my hand at the space between him and myself.

"Seen a shrink? Never," he scoffed. He was above such folly.

"Well, I've talked to guys in your position at least a thousand times, so I've got a pretty good understanding of what rings true and what doesn't, and what you just said is complete bullshit."

He acted indignant; feigned emotions are always a surefire sign of a liar.

"Well, you tell me how many I had then. You seem to know it all," he barked.

"The police say it was in excess of ten thousand."

Ethan didn't respond. Instead he maintained his pseudo indignation and went back to picking his T-shirt.

"You do realize this isn't like 'normal' therapy?" I asked.

He kept harvesting what remained of "Fat Albert."

"It differs from normal therapy because you *will* keep coming here until you have satisfactorily engaged."

He looked up. "You can't do that!" he said defiantly.

I leaned into him to permeate his personal space. "I can't, but your parole officer will."

Ethan remained difficult to engage for a number of sessions. Many professionals reading this will attribute his resistance to my confronting style. I make no apologies for my approach. I prefer offenders of Ethan's ilk to know I'm not willing to adhere to *their* rules of engagement. Ethan was a master manipulator. He needed to understand I wasn't going to let him squeeze past me like he'd done with everything else in life to date. In time, he gave over.

"All right," Ethan declared forthrightly, "I'll be honest with you."

"I'm ready when you are," I said doubtingly.

He took a deep breath. "The cops are wrong about how many images and movies I downloaded."

I looked at him with a touch of contempt. I found it difficult not to roll my eyes. Then he stunned me.

"There were heaps more," he confessed. "There were thousands more they never found. I had them on DVDs, USB sticks, and hard drives. I hid them around the house and in the shed. They also never got the online conversations I had."

Of course the issue now was whether Ethan was genuine in his disclosure or simply telling me what I wanted to hear to hasten his therapy. I knew in due course I'd know the answer.

"Let's go back to the start," I said. "When did you first discover pornography?"

"When I discovered the Internet," he replied coolly.

"Which was?"

"About ten years ago, I was twelve. Mom and Dad got me a computer for my birthday. I convinced them to let me set it up in my room. It wasn't long before I started finding porn."

"What kind of porn?" He didn't realize it, but my question was loaded. I wanted to see if he was feeding me lies. I knew if he exaggerated his answer by telling me he went straight for the extreme pornographic genres (e.g.: bestiality, rape), he would be lying.

"Just normal stuff: naked women, sex, lesbian stuff."

His answer suggested he was honest. However, he was a slippery customer, and I wanted to be sure. I loaded another bullet.

"How did you find it?" If he concocted an extreme answer, the content was likely dubious.

"It was pretty innocent at first. I used to play games online, and I just started clicking links. After a while—as with everything on the Internet—those links led to porn."

I was convinced.

"So your parents had no idea?'

"Nope, none whatsoever. They thought I was doing my homework." He almost seemed proud. "I'd spend every minute in my room looking at porn. I'd look at it first thing in the morning, first thing when I got home from school, and last thing before I went to bed."

I waited for Ethan to continue. He seemed to want to tell it all. I could see by his lack of emotion these disclosures were by no means to clear his conscience; they were merely offerings to control and speed up the pace of intervention.

"I even started printing out pictures to take to school," he recalled.

"To show other kids?"

I thought he may have done this to gain acceptance in some way. I was way off. He didn't have that depth.

"No. I was a loner."

There was no self-pity in his reply. He didn't care he was a social leper.

"I used to take the pictures to school so I'd have something to jerk off to at lunchtime."

I tried to contain my surprise. "How many times a day were you masturbating?"

"As many as was physically possible—sometimes up to ten times."

"And now?"

"Not as much, probably about half that." His laid-back manner suggested he thought his libido was nothing out of the ordinary.

Note to self: don't shake his hand when he leaves.

"Okay, so take me back to the time just after you discovered pornography?"

"I got deeper and deeper into it," he said. There was still no emotion in his voice. "The normal stuff just wasn't doing it for me anymore. So I ventured into other things like bestiality and sadistic stuff."

"How old were you at that point?"

"I was still about twelve." Ethan balked for the first time. "I didn't know it was wrong. I mean, I saw these adults fucking animals, and I thought it was normal."

I nodded. "Did you try it?"

"No!" He relaxed once he realized I believed him.

"What was the attraction with it?"

"I don't know." He paused. "I think it was just another level of extreme. I think what would have turned me on was getting a girl to do it with an animal."

His candidness was not anywhere near as surprising as his indifference to discussing the topics being raised. It was as if there was no capacity for him to feel shame. Each deviant disclosure was literally like a bead of water sliding off a duck's back.

"Why would you want a girl to have sex with an animal?" I ventured.

"The control, I suppose. Making her think I was getting off because of her doing it but secretly getting off because I manipulated the stupid bitch to be a filthy whore."

"Did you get into trouble for anything inappropriate around that time?"

He looked surprised that I linked the question to the current theme. "Yeah," he said. "I got expelled from school for being inappropriate to girls."

"What did you do?"

"I'd follow them into the toilets and watch them. But that's not what I got expelled for. I got kicked out for touching one."

"What happened?"

Ethan's pupils became dilated. I could tell he was aroused thinking about the forthcoming story.

"It was at high school. We were made to do some stupid stage production. I didn't want to be in it, so I volunteered to look after the sets and the props and shit. I found a spot at the back of the stage where I could watch the girls getting changed. I'd sit there and jerk off."

Again he seemed to be reminiscing. I interrupted his thoughts.

"I thought you said you touched a girl?"

"I did," he replied as he awoke from his memories. "I'd sit within a few feet of where they would get changed. I was behind two drapes, and if I held them tight together and made a little hole I could see everything. One of them got too close and bent over in front of me. As she was changing her costume, I reached out and touched her pussy."

I didn't appreciate his use of that particular vernacular to describe the female genitalia. Not because I'm prudish; I simply believe it's inappropriate when an offender is discussing sex crimes. I believe it's disrespectful to the victim. At this stage I was willing to let it go. I knew Ethan was going to be in therapy for a long, long time. It was my intention from that point to let him speak freely so I could obtain as much information as possible. From this point, it wasn't about therapy; it was about assessing his risk—which, as far as I could tell, was the highest of highs.

"Were your parents informed?" I asked.

"Yeah," he said in typical blasé fashion. "They weren't too bothered I don't think."

"You don't *think?*"

He shrugged. "I wouldn't know. They didn't discuss it with me. They just told me I was changing schools and sent me to this Christian boys' college. I hated that fucking shithole, fucking God this and Jesus that."

I wondered how much of his hatred for the school was the result of having his sexual behavior challenged with regard to the Christian moral stance on pornography, sex, and masturbation. Or perhaps it was simply there were no girls?

Ethan observed me thinking. It was as if he was waiting for me to catch up. Once he saw me regain focus, he continued. "After they sent me there, I became more of a recluse. I just spent all my time looking at porn. I used to love saving it in files on my computer. It was like my big porn scrapbook. I had those files super-organized."

Ethan paused and frowned. "Weird thing though—I would never go back and look at my collection. I'd just keep them stored and love the fact I had them."

It made sense. The thought of new material being accessible 24/7 meant he was likely never satisfied with what he had, always being on the lookout for something better. I decided to take the conversation to a darker place.

"When did you start looking at child pornography?"

He didn't flinch. "When I was about fourteen. I wanted to see kids my own age fucking."

"What about children younger than you?"

He shrugged. "I looked at anything. But the younger girls didn't do it for me. I liked ones my age. I still like them at that age. That's when they're in the prime of their physical beauty."

"So they were all developed physically?"

"Yeah," he said as if insulted. "Why would I want to look at kids with no tits or hair on their pussy?"

His lack of awareness was disturbing and his answer vulgar. I sat thinking for a while. I didn't look at him. I didn't say anything, and I didn't move.

I was contemplating Ethan's lack of pedophilic interests. He wasn't perturbed by the silence and casually picked up a magazine from the table. He started flicking through the pages.

"The illegal material you were busted for," I started, "what was it?"

He looked up from the periodical. "Same stuff: girls around thirteen, fourteen, fifteen having sex."

He went back to skimming his magazine. The way he pressed his finger to his tongue to obtain moisture for separating the pages sickened me. I leant over and gently took the publication from his hands and returned it to the table. Oddly, his body language responded as if *I* were the rude one.

"So you never left that phase?" I asked.

"Nope, but even that wasn't enough," he said, disinterested.

"What do you mean?"

"I discovered Facebook."

I knew where this was headed.

"I could pretend to be people I wasn't. I'd make up all these bullshit stories and suck girls in. I could be cool on Facebook."

It was odd; his over-inflated ego suggested he already thought he was "cool." Yet his behavior online told the true story: somewhere deep down, Ethan knew he was nothing more than a pathetic, lonely loser.

"So you used Facebook?" I asked in the hope he would continue.

"Yeah, Facebook was the best; it was the easiest. I would go through heaps of profiles and find teenage girls—pretty ones. I'd set up a bogus account and find some random picture on the Internet of a good-looking young guy and post it as my profile pic. Then I'd slowly add random people as friends so it looked legitimate. When I had about fifty friends, I'd send a girl I was targeting a friend request. They would either add me or reject me. Most would add me."

His animation increased with every sentence. It was obvious this was the penultimate of his current erotic desires.

"Then what?" I asked.

"I'd bide my time. I wouldn't interact with her at all. I'd just study her. I'd go through her account with a fine-tooth comb and get to know everything about her: who her family were, who her friends were, what movies she liked, what music she was into, what her dog's name was. By the end, I pretty much knew everything about her."

At this point he was near drooling.

"Sounds time-consuming," I proposed.

"It wasn't about the time." His tone implied I didn't appreciate the hard work and patience involved. "I'd go through her photos online, the ones in her Facebook albums. I'd jerk off to the ones where she was in a bikini or something skimpy. After a while it wasn't enough though. That's when I'd want to start interacting with her to see if I could get her to have cybersex."

"How would you initiate that?"

"I'd wait until she posted a status update on her Facebook account that was sad or showed she might be upset about some bullshit."

His blatant disregard for another person's feelings to satisfy his own lust was appalling.

"I'd make sure she wasn't posting the update from her phone though," he added in haste.

"Why?" I asked in genuine curiosity.

"You can't really have a proper online chat if it's from a phone. It's too slow because it's too hard for them to type."

"How would you know it was from a phone?"

"Most kids have iPhones or BlackBerrys these days. When you post from those types of phones, it says so in their status update on Facebook."

He waited for my reaction. He was showing me how shrewd he was and needed some ego stroking.

"That's pretty clever."

Ethan smiled. My "praise" took it to a whole new level. I was about to find out just how "good" this guy was.

"So anyway, I'd make sure she wasn't updating her status from her phone. I'd make sure she was at home at her keyboard in her room."

"How would you know that?" I enquired.

"Most kids will take photos of themselves using a webcam. They usually have at least one picture from a webcam in their Facebook albums. The webcam pics they post show the background of where the photo was taken. So if you look in the background, you can usually tell what room they're in.

If it's got something like Justin Bieber posters or fluffy toys or a pink bed-spread, you can be pretty sure it's their room. So either they have a computer set up in there or that's where they use their laptop."

Ethan waited for me to soak that one up and bask in his brilliance.

"Like I said before, I'd wait until they posted a sad update or something and then send them a message."

"Saying what?"

"Nothing about their status update. Instead, I'd be normal like, 'Hey, we've been friends for a while now and haven't even talked.' Once we were done with the introductions and shit, I'd say something like, 'Aw, I just saw your status update—are you okay?'"

He was a pathetic human being. "And then?" I asked.

"They would love it. Teenage girls crave that sort of attention-seeking shit, especially from boys, so I'd use it to my advantage. They'd think I was nice and keep talking."

"At what point would you pursue sexual conversations?"

The question seemed to excite him. He was almost rubbing his hands with glee at the prospect that I wanted to take the conversation there. It was also becoming increasingly obvious Ethan had many, many victims.

"That would depend on the girl. If she was a flirty little slut, I knew I wouldn't have to wait long. But it's weird because I actually enjoyed chasing the difficult ones more."

"The difficult ones?" I sought clarification.

He nodded enthusiastically. "Yeah, the ones who wouldn't come across too easy; they played a bit harder to get. I liked the idea of being the one who made them lose their innocence. It also dragged the fantasy out, and I *loved* the challenge. It made me use every bit of cunning in me to get them to do what I wanted."

"How would you do that?"

"Easy," he said as if it was some great accomplishment. "Over time, I'd pay them compliments—tell them I thought they were gorgeous and flirt with them. Like in the middle of a general discussion, I'd type something randomly, like 'kisses your neck softly.'"

"How would they respond?"

"They lapped it up! They would start reciprocating in the same way. It would go back and forth like that for days, even weeks, until one of us would take it to a more sexual level. After you get to that point, it's anything goes every time you see them online."

My facial expression was one of exasperation. I'm sure he took it as an acknowledgement of his genius and efforts. "This was a lot of work," I suggested.

"I loved the chase! It was exhilarating! I'd be jerking off all day and night!"

He was so excited, I was worried he might start masturbating there and then. Normally I would hone in on the fact he was becoming aroused discussing his offending, but this was an information-gathering exercise, a reconnaissance mission.

"Would you have other chats going at the same time? Other girls you were targeting?" I asked.

"No," he said categorically. "I only ever focused my attention on one girl at a time. I wouldn't even look for others until I was finished with the current one."

"What do you mean by 'finished with'?"

"It would eventually get to a point where I'd get bored with them. Or they would want to meet me. Or they wanted more pictures of me."

"How did you get around not having more pictures of yourself?"

He smiled. "That's where the child pornography helped out. I'd find images of a kid having sex that looked somewhat like my profile picture. I'd tell them I was the boy in the pictures, and they believed it."

"So you sent child porn to these girls, and they believed it was you?"

"Yeah, I'd tell them it was me with an ex-girlfriend or some bullshit like that," he chortled.

"How would they react?"

"Most wanted more. But there would come a point where they also wanted more normal shots of me. That's when I couldn't produce the goods because I usually only had one image like that, so I'd have to move on."

"To what?"

"Another girl," he stated as if I were an idiot. "But the webcam thing would also usually pose a problem."

"How did you get around that?"

"I'd tell them I didn't have one. I could only get away with that for a while though."

I contemplated what he was proposing. "So would you ask to see them on webcam?"

"Yep," he said smugly. "I wouldn't do anything untoward to begin with. I'd wait until our chats got a bit steamy. Then once they were at the point of having full blown cybersex with me, I'd manipulate them toward using the webcam."

"And do what?"

"Just get them to turn it on so I could see them. I wouldn't pressure them to do anything sexual on it. I would wait a while."

"How long?"

"Weeks if I had to. Eventually most would come around," he said as if he were some Casanova.

"What do you mean?" I asked.

"I would start off by getting them to turn it on, then type something random like 'undoes your top button.' I'd watch their reaction on the webcam. You could pretty much see straight away if they were up for it."

"How?"

"They would giggle or blush. I'd keep gently pressing, then after a while I'd suggest they actually do what I was saying. Like if I typed 'undoes your top button' that they literally do it."

"And would they?"

"Every single time," he said assuredly.

"You never had a single knock back?"

"Not one," he said as he sat swinging his legs side to side. They would spread open, then close repetitively; it was an unconscious masturbatory practice, as his penis was likely massaged between his thighs.

"I put in the groundwork," he continued. "They believed everything I was saying. Then over time I'd slowly manipulate them to do more and more sexual stuff. I'd start off with getting them to strip to their underwear. Once they were at that stage, I'd move on to them taking their bra off. After that it would be removing their panties, then touching themselves, and so on, until I got them to place objects in their pussy."

Ethan sat delighting in his conquests. "I'd also get them to record what they were doing on their webcam and send it to a phony e-mail account I'd created."

"And they had no idea?"

"Nope."

In a way, I was glad those girls were oblivious.

"I did get busted once," he admitted. "I accidentally turned my webcam on. The girl got a glimpse of me masturbating, and I never heard from her again."

"So even when you got caught, you never suffered repercussions?"

"No," he said cynically. "What the hell was that little slut gonna do about it? Go tell her parents she had been fucking some guy online and sending him nude pics? No teenage girl is going to tell their parents that! Besides, like I said, I screened them *very* well and earned their trust."

I wanted to see just how far Ethan had taken his exploits. "Did your fantasies on the Internet ever transfer over into real life?"

Again, the question had little, if any, impact on him. "If you're asking me if I've sexually abused a kid, the answer is no. I don't go out much. I stay at home and sleep until midday. Once I get up, I'm straight on my computer. Don't get me wrong—if I do go out and see a beautiful woman I feel attracted—"

"Woman, or teenage girl?" I interrupted.

"Both, but I'd never do anything." His voice had changed. He had lost the arrogant edge. "I wouldn't know what to say. I'd be too scared."

Ethan's last comment encapsulates who he is beyond the image he attempts to portray to the external world. His inflated ego, probably implemented by his parents, is a protective measure to conceal the multitude of inadequacies he has no desire to address. This is the very reason he used the Internet in the manner he did: to pretend to be someone he knew he wasn't. He wanted to be "cool" because deep down he knew he was pathetic. That's not to say he would ever agree with my supposition; his ego wouldn't allow it.

HARRY

Harry dressed like Eminem and talked as though he were a "mover and shaker" in the music industry. There wasn't a famous person he didn't know. Of course, Harry was full of shit. He'd never left his hometown—a rural community with a population of fewer than twenty thousand—had never had a job in his life, was an avid collector of Pokemon cards, and spent his days playing X-Box while smoking copious amounts of weed. Not too dissimilar to many small-town kids in the modern age—but the problem was, Harry was forty-six years old.

"How's Jenny?" I enquired, knowing all too well what the response would be.

Harry made eye contact. There was an element of hidden disdain in his pupils. "Why do you always ask me that, bro? It seriously pisses me off."

I relaxed into my chair. "I just like to consider her in our conversations."

"For what?"

I observed Harry remove his heavy gold chain necklace. He began polishing it using the corner of his Lakers basketball singlet.

"To remind you that your girlfriend is sixteen years old, I guess."

Harry continued polishing. I could see he was smiling under his Chicago Bulls cap—oddly, not worn backwards. "I don't need reminding, my man," he said in gloating manner. "I'm not doing anything illegal; she's of age."

"Just."

He ceased cleaning; the chain gleamed. "What do you fucking care? You jealous, bro?" he goaded.

I took a sip of coffee, then faked looking at something in my diary.

"Even if Jenny was the most stunning young girl—notice I didn't say 'woman'—on the planet," I started, "there is no way in hell I'd be with her, given the baggage she carries around."

"What the fuck is that supposed to mean?"

I'd hit a nerve. Harry leant forward to try to intimidate. It might have worked if his skinny tattooed arms weren't lost in the massive sleeve holes of his long, heavy singlet.

"It means she has issues. Major issues," I stressed.

"How the fuck would you know?" Harry was used to dealing with kids. He likely stood over them and was very seldom challenged.

"Well," I started, then paused as I sipped my coffee, "she's hooked up with you, isn't she?"

Harry shook his head. It was a combination of disbelief and disdain. "She's a lucky girl. There's plenty of hot ass lining up to be with me, bro."

I wanted to laugh but refrained. "Lucky? I would say more disempowered and controlled."

Harry removed his wallet from his big baggy shorts, which was attached by a silver chain. He looked ridiculous. I waited, as he felt it appropriate to begin sifting the rubbish from the important stuff, none of which was money.

"Jenny is free to do whatever Jenny wants, bro."

"Bullshit," I retorted too honestly, "she relies on you totally. Coming from a broken home and living on the street for two years, she thinks she needs you and can't do any better. She's too scared to find out if she can."

"Can't do any better?" Harry was affronted. "What the fuck! Are you for real, bro?"

I looked at him oddly. "She's sixteen. Why would a sixteen-year-old want to be with you?"

I was alarmed as he stood up. I wasn't sure what his intentions were until he twirled like a model.

"Um, yeah. As I said, why would a sixteen-year-old want to be with you?"

"You don't see it?" he asked in jest. I wasn't sure if his joke was based on the fact that he knew he looked like a fool or that I earnestly couldn't see the attraction.

"I'll tell you what I see, Harry."

He peeked out from under his cap, cautious of the forthcoming analysis. He'd attended a few sessions by this stage and knew I'd tell him what I truly believed, as opposed to what he wanted to hear.

"I see a middle-aged man acting like he's eighteen—if that—and taking advantage of a young girl's insecurities and vulnerabilities."

"Pfft. Middle-aged. Whatever."

I half-chuckled. "You see, Harry, in that statement all you focus on is the middle-aged part. In that whole statement, that bit offended you most."

He sat fiddling with his skull-and-crossbones ring, picking at its big red-stoned eyes with his fingernail. They were almost as bloodshot as Harry's.

"You're out of touch with reality because you're too damned focused on yourself."

The comment seemed to get his attention. "Get with a young chick sometime, bro. Then tell me you still feel your age." He snickered.

"Well," I hesitated as I prepped him for a blow, "getting with young chicks got you here, didn't it?"

Bang! He was bolt upright and on the attack. "That was Jenny's fault!"

I lifted my coffee mug, pressed my lips to the ceramic, then desisted. "How was that Jenny's fault?"

"It was her idea."

I nodded mordantly and placed my mug on the table. "So let me get this straight. One day—out of the blue—Jenny says, 'Hey, Harry, how about we start stalking young girls on Facebook, make friends with them, get them to come over to our place, and after a while encourage them to engage in threesomes with us'?"

"Yep, that's pretty much how I remember it going down." His assurance was fabricated. He might have believed his crap, but I didn't.

"I don't think so."

"Why's that, bro?"

In asking the question, he'd opened the door for me to challenge his bullshit.

"Well," I dragged it out, "before I answer that I want to clarify something."

"Shoot," he said as he simultaneously made a pistol with his fingers and proceeded to fire a bullet in my direction.

I remained laid back in my chair. I didn't want him aware of the fact I was setting him up. "You believe any young girl would want you, right? As in, they think you're cool, sexy, and all that business, right?"

He smiled knowingly. "One hundred percent, bro."

"Well, I find that very interesting, Harry. You see, if you're so appealing and so attractive to young girls, wouldn't it make sense that you'd be the one on Facebook doing all the interacting instead of Jenny? Wouldn't you—being so hot—attract more girls for your threesomes and therefore cut straight to the chase as opposed to having a middleman?"

He unconsciously reeled back. "Whatever," he said with resentment. "This is bullshit. Jenny did it, but she fucked up big-time by not checking those girls' ages."

"Hmmm, interesting."

"Is it?"

I waited for an extended period. Harry sat staring at me, waiting; he knew there was a "blow" coming, but I wanted to soften him up first.

"So the first time a twelve-year-old girl showed up at your place to 'hang out'"—I made quotation marks with my fingers—"you didn't once think to yourself, 'Geez, this girl looks a bit young'?"

Harry glared at me. "Actually, the first one looked over twenty. She was done up to the max: makeup, tits hanging out, short skirt, the works."

(And here came the right cross). "So the fact she arrived on a bicycle didn't give anything away?"

I could see the panic in his eyes as he strived to keep his lie alive. "Plenty of people ride bikes, man."

"Obviously that's true, Harry. Coincidentally, quite a number of them showed up at your place."

He panicked a little more. "I didn't know how old they were; I never asked. I had no need to ask. Besides, we were just hanging out at first. It was no big deal."

I sipped some more coffee. "Ah, but it was a big deal, Harry. Because the sole intention of inviting those girls over—as Jenny admitted in her state-ment—was to engage them in sexual acts. Which, I recall, she said was your idea."

"That's bullshit!" He was fuming. "That little bitch lies all the time. She only said that to get herself out of trouble." The true Harry was morphing out of his "Eminem" cocoon.

"No, Jenny told the truth after she divulged to the police that you drilled it into her head that it was better if she took the wrap because she was only sixteen and would get treated lightly in court."

Harry was unresponsive. He sat brooding. I could tell he wanted to get up and walk out, but he knew there would be consequences. I continued.

"According to you, this was all orchestrated by Jenny, right?"

He didn't answer, so I repeated the question.

"Yep," he responded brusquely.

"And then she stabbed you in the back by squealing on you, right?"

"Yep."

(Another right cross). "Then why are you still with her?"

Harry feigned being interested in something out the window while nervously and repetitively removing and replacing that hideous skeleton ring.

"I can't shake her, bro," he eventually offered. "She's like this little fucking puppy that follows me everywhere. It's like she's starstruck."

I ignored his reference to his "star" qualities; I had bigger fish to fry. "Are you still having sex with her?"

"Why?" His response was too quick, indicative that he wasn't sure where I was headed.

"Answer the question."

I could tell his brain was working overtime trying to work out my agenda. He'd run out of natural time, that is; the space between the question and his answer had expired. He knew he had to come up with something. "When she asks," he blurted.

"So you don't want her around, but you use her for sex?"

"No, I do it because she says she needs to feel close to me."

"And how often is that?"

Harry paused. "A few times a day—she's a needy little bitch, man. She's like a nympho."

A projection if ever I heard one.

"And you, being the caring guy you are, fulfil her need every time?"

"Yeah," he said, relieved. "I'm actually an okay guy."

I was astounded for a few reasons. First, he'd believed I'd swallowed his story. Second, he believed he'd convinced me he was an "okay guy." But moreover, I was in absolute shock at the strength of his libido. For a man his age, he was going at it like a rabbit. There were obvious issues with sexual preoccupation for Harry, but I wasn't going there just yet. Therapy was down the track; this was information gathering.

He sat watching me finish my coffee. "I'm not what you're trying to paint me."

I swallowed the remnants of the brew.

"What am I trying to paint you as?" I asked.

"Some pedo."

His assumption was odd. I decided to tell him what I thought to see what he'd do with it. "Actually, I don't think you are a pedo."

He was suspicious. The look on his face suggested he knew I had more to add. He waited; I delivered.

"But I do think you are one seriously deluded human being."

Harry looked at his watch—yes, it was ugly—and as he stood to leave, he looked me in the eye, and with as much wisdom as someone like Harry can muster declared, "Reality is what you make it, bro."

I blocked his exit. "No," I said sternly, "reality is reality. People try to force their desires to fit into reality. The more extreme those desires, the more deluded the person gets and the further removed they become from what actual reality is—until they get *so far* removed they believe their cognitive distortions are truth. And that, *bro*, is you."

CONCLUSION

Of course not every cyber offender is in the mold of Ethan and/or Harry. Some are businesspeople. Some are police officers. Some are church pastors. Some are women. This is an important variable to remember when considering the profile of sexual offenders: there is no profile. They are each unique. They come from different walks of life. They have independent reasons behind their actions. Their uniqueness is what makes it so easy for them to blend in.

Generally when I speak with people about their ideas regarding the predatory-type offenders, they equate them to a wild animal, like a leopard that uses camouflage while stalking its prey before the kill. The vast majority of child sex offenders don't need to conceal themselves. They are all around you. Your innocence and trust are their camouflage.

Please take a moment to take in that last sentence. That sentence explains why child sex offenders are solely responsible for their actions: they use the virtuous qualities of human beings as a means to betray, exploit, and perpetrate. Is there anything more cowardly than willingly abusing a person's goodness for personal gain?

CHAPTER EIGHT: THE VOYEUR

"All human beings have three lives: public, private, and secret."
~ Gabriel García Márquez

VOYEUR—NOUN: A PERSON WHO obtains sexual pleasure or excitement from the observation of someone undressing, having intercourse, etc. (Collins English Dictionary)

EUGENE

Eugene entered the interview room wearing his prison "browns." He didn't make eye contact and nervously shuffled his way toward his seat.

"So you were studying engineering?" I asked in order to put him at ease.

"Yeah."

His response was minimalist by virtue of his shyness as opposed to rudeness. His reserved nature meant I would have to develop rapport before cracking him open.

"How have you adjusted to prison life?" I angled in.

He glanced at me, determining if the question was genuine. "Okay," he replied. "It's hard, but I deserve it, so I can't complain."

"What's the hardest part?"

He smiled wryly. "Dealing with idiots. Answering to people who would be trailer trash on the outside, but in here have some credibility—if you can call it that."

"Do you get any grief for your offenses?"

"No." He shook his head with a relieved look on his face. "They don't know what I'm in for. I don't talk to anyone. I figure I'll just fly under the radar and get out of here as quickly as I can."

Smart kid, I thought. "Does your family visit?"

"No," he said ardently. "I've asked them not to come. I prefer it that way."

Many inmates request the same of their families. I asked the obvious question simply to keep the conversation rolling. "Why's that?"

"Two reasons. One, I don't want my head filled with stories from life outside, and two, I don't want my family coming here." He looked at our surroundings. "This isn't a place for good people. This place tortures souls. There is nothing virtuous here. I don't want the people I love experiencing that ambience."

His analysis struck me as darkly poetic.

"So you know why I'm here?" I asked.

"To assess me for placement in a sex offender program?"

I nodded in confirmation and noted his apprehension. "How do you feel about that?"

"A bit uneasy, to be honest—not about the interview. I just don't want to sit in a group of guys I don't know and tell them what I did."

"Yeah, I can understand that. I don't think I'd want to do it either if I was in your position." My answer was sincere. I had never been entirely convinced group therapy suited all offenders.

Eugene seemed appreciative of my honesty. "I know in the programs there is a rule about confidentiality, but in a place like this, you can't trust anyone. If you do, you're a fool."

"Hmm." I agreed. "I guess that's true from both sides of the fence."

He was interested in my comment. "How do you mean?"

"Like you, if I were to trust everyone I met in here and take their word at face value, I too would be a fool."

He smiled knowingly. "Yeah, that's *very* true."

Eugene seemed to be relaxing, so I decided to attempt entry into the dark world he kept private.

"How open are you to discussing your offending today?" I asked solicitously.

"It's not whether or not I'm open; it's whether I have the courage."

His philosophical mind-set was perhaps indicative that he had pursued studies in the wrong field.

"And are you brave enough?"

He grinned. "I'll tell you after we're done."

The atmosphere thickened.

"So how did this begin?"

Eugene's gaze diverted from mine. "Delivering newspapers," he said seriously.

I waited.

"I had a part-time job delivering free local papers," he began. "The money was shit, but when you're a student, money's money."

The comment brought back memories of stacking shelves in a supermarket when I was his age. Back then, I couldn't wait for the day to come when I was able to inform my boss I was quitting that mind-numbingly boring waste of my time. Eugene's clearing of his throat jerked me back to the present.

"I had this paper run in the neighborhood where I shared a house with some other guys from the university. I would walk the entire route with the newspapers in a backpack. It was hard work for fifteen bucks an hour."

"Go on," I requested politely.

"One day I met this girl. She would have been about, oh, I don't know, thirteen." He paused and looked at me earnestly. "She was the most *beautiful* woman I'd ever seen."

Woman?

"She was sublime, just gorgeous. There was just something about her that really spoke to me, like we had been lovers in a previous life, a mysterious connection."

I didn't burst his bubble. "Where did you meet her?"

"She was out the front of her house, in the yard playing with her little brother. I went to put the paper in the letterbox, and she came over and took it from me. We just started talking, and every time I looked at her I'd just melt."

"Was she physically developed?" As soon as I said the words, I wished I could shovel them back in. I didn't want him to feel judged. When people like Eugene feel judged, you force them to lie to you. Luckily for me, his need to be honest took precedence over his pride.

"Partially," he admitted. "It wasn't her body I was attracted to though. It was her face. She was the most heavenly thing I had ever seen, just beautiful."

"What did you talk about?"

"Nothing much, just her school and her brother and where I was from and what I was studying. Just general stuff, but that night I couldn't get her out of my head. I lay in bed thinking about her all night. I thought about all these different scenarios where we could be together. The next week I delivered my papers, and I couldn't believe how excited I got thinking about the possibility of running into her again."

"And did you?"

"Yeah," he said dejectedly. "She was there. But she just waved and left me to put the newspaper in the letterbox. I was distraught. I felt gutted, like I'd been dumped."

I wondered how a seemingly intelligent human being could confuse his thoughts and emotions so profoundly as to believe a brief encounter with a thirteen-year-old child was his destiny.

"Did you think she liked you the same way you liked her?" I tested.

"I felt a connection. I thought she would have felt it too, but obviously she didn't."

"So then what happened?'

"The night before I was to deliver my papers, I'd get so worked up with excitement I couldn't sleep. I was like a little kid on Christmas Eve. I would get disappointed every time I delivered her paper and she wasn't there. I also started walking that route home even though it was out of my way. Once I even had the gall to knock on the front door. I had this plan: I would tell whoever answered that I had lost my dog and ask if they had seen it, but no one was home."

Eugene paused for a while. It appeared he was remembering the girl. As an observer, I felt he didn't seem regretful of his desire for her. Rather; it seemed he was heartbroken at the prospect of losing someone he truly loved. If it weren't for the situation, I'm sure it would have made for a great romance novel in some twisted parallel universe.

"After I hadn't seen her in about five weeks," he lamented, "I just couldn't take it anymore, and that's when I got the crazy idea to go there one night. I got dressed all in black and snuck around outside her house looking through the windows to see if I could see her."

"And did you?"

"Yeah, she was sitting with her family watching TV. I waited until they went to bed and tried to work out where her room was. I peeked in every window until I found her. But it was too late; her light was already out, and she was in bed."

"What did you do?"

"I stayed there looking, just watching her. I couldn't really see anything, but just being there was exhilarating."

Eugene spoke like a besotted, mesmerized teenager discussing his latest pop star crush. If his emotions at that moment were only a miniscule reflection of his feelings at the time of his offending, it concerned me how far his distortions may have taken him. I kept the conversation "in the moment" so as to maintain his intensity and therefore his willingness to disclose.

"Describe 'exhilarating' for me?" I pushed.

"A total adrenaline rush; it's addictive." He paused and took a deep breath. "You know, in the past I could never work out what those adrenaline junkies were on about when they talked about the buzz they got from extreme activities, but I can now."

I pondered his comment. I had never really given much consideration to that aspect of offending. I jotted down a reminder to give it due thought at a later date.

"How long did you stay there that night?"

"About an hour, then I went home and thought about her all night."

(My head said *no*, but my gut said *go*.) "Did you masturbate?"

The question didn't faze him. He was too caught up in the hypnosis of past romanticisms. "No, not that time," he said.

"When did you return to her house?"

"The next night."

Suddenly Eugene's facial expression went from serene to anguish. "That next day I was, like, 'what the fuck are you thinking, Eugene?' But that night, while lying in bed, I found the drag of my desire to return too strong. I got dressed in my dark clothes and went back."

"Did you see her?"

"Yeah, but she was already in bed. It was late. I just looked at her through the window again. That's when I . . ." His body language inferred he felt embarrassed.

"Eugene, I want to tell you something, and I want you to listen closely to what I am about to say."

He looked at me in a way to demonstrate he was attentive.

"Being honest now will keep you honest later," I said. "Honesty helps people take responsibility. Those who own their behavior gain a better understanding of themselves in therapy. And having that insight is paramount in the reduction of risk for future offending. So don't hold back."[2]

He showed he understood my point with a grimace and a nod. He adjusted his posture for the verbal delivery of his inner shame.

"That's when I started masturbating about her—that night."

"Staring through her window?"

Eugene nodded. "I left after I ejaculated."

His forehead furrowed. "My behavior that night scared me. I didn't go back for about a month, but I would still secretly hope I'd see her when I delivered my papers. Then one day I went past her house and there was a

---

[2] Some researchers claim an offender in denial can still obtain full therapeutic benefit. I absolutely disagree with this supposition. There are many details in offenses that are vital for offenders to grasp. The buildup phase to their actions is where the "gold" is to be found in helping them understand themselves. This is also fundamental in helping them rehabilitate and therefore reduce their future risk. To suggest otherwise, in my view, is ridiculous.

"For Rent" sign out in front. I was absolutely devastated. I went into the yard and looked in the windows, and my heart just sank. The house was empty."

He sat reminiscing for a period.

"I lost the plot after that," he continued. "I called the real estate agent on the sign and asked all these questions about the house. I pretended I wanted to rent it. I was trying to get information about where the girl had moved to. I couldn't find out anything. Eventually my sadness turned to anger. I don't know why. It's bizarre, but for some reason I felt duped."

"Why duped?"

He looked at me weepily. "I'd found the person I thought was my soul mate, and in the twinkling of an eye she was *ripped* away from me."

Eugene spoke as if he and his "love" had been conversing about their devotion and longing for each other for years. Somewhere in the mix he forgot he had handed a thirteen-year-old girl a newspaper.

"After that I started scoping the entire neighborhood whenever I delivered papers. I'd carry a notebook and take details about possible places to peep into."

I was confused. "Why was that your next course of action? You said you felt like this girl was your soul mate, she leaves, and then you start peeping in other places?"

"I didn't care anymore. I was addicted to the adrenaline and the risk."

Eugene's response may seem strange, but it is fairly typical of some offenders; they do not cope well with stress, and rather than assume positive, productive action to address a problem, they spiral into behavior that affords them a feeling of sexual pleasure.

"You said you carried a notebook to list potential homes to peep into. What were you looking for?"

"The first thing would be establishing if a teenage girl lived in the residence," he divulged.

"How would you do that?"

"I'd deliver my papers around the time school got out. I'd start at a different spot every week so I could check out where girls lived. I'd also take notice of clotheslines and see what items were hung out: bras and panties and any clothes that looked like something a teenager would wear." He shot a sly glance at me to see my reaction. Seeing it was safe, he resumed his spiel.

"I made sure to spot windows from the street and see what kind of curtains they had—if they were girly, I'd check that room out that night. One of the most important things I looked for was a dog in the yard. If there was a dog, I just didn't go there. I'd also look for lowset houses. Ones that had windows at a level you could stand and look in. That way I could masturbate while peeping and also duck for cover if need be. I'd also check out the surrounding yard for shelter, like shrubs and bushes in case I needed concealment from neighbors."

It was obvious he did his "homework." The "experts" always do.

"How many girls did you discover in that area?" I asked.

"There were about twenty I would visit," he admitted.

"Every night?" My tone must have been one of disbelief because he gave a slight laugh.

"No," he replied, "I was out peeping every night, but obviously I couldn't fit them all in."

"What were you hoping to see?"

He thought for a minute. It seemed an obvious question, but his offending behavior clearly required consideration beyond the blatantly discernible.

"I wanted to see the girls naked, but I saw a lot of things that turned me on. That was the magnetism of it—you were never sure what you would see."

"Such as?"

"Them just doing random things like dancing by themselves, getting changed, trying on clothes, applying makeup, looking at themselves in the mirror, Anything."

"What did you like about that?"

Again Eugene contemplated my question. I respected the fact he gave consideration to what I was asking as opposed to opting for the typical cognitive indolent response of "I don't know." I despise that response in therapy. It is the patient's way of saying, "I can't be bothered thinking too hard, so how about you do it for me."

"I loved being privy to it," Eugene said. "Seeing it but remaining unseen. It's a control thing. It's kind of weird. I liked the anonymity, but at the same time I wanted them to know I was there."

"So would you do things to alert them?"

"Not so much alert them. More arouse suspicion."

I was intrigued. "How did you achieve that?" I asked.

Eugene looked embarrassed. "I started stealing underwear from the clotheslines."

"Their underwear?"

"Yeah, the idea of being in possession of their panties gave me major excitement. I just can't explain the level of exhilaration it offered."

He didn't need to explain it. I could see it in his eyes.

"I always took the best pair: frilly type panties. I would keep them at home and hold them while I masturbated. Depending on which girl I visited that night, I would take her panties with me and masturbate while peeping. When I was done—after I'd ejaculated in them—I'd put them on the front door step. If it was the night before I delivered my papers I'd stuff the panties in the letterbox."

I found his last comment odd. "Why the letterbox?"

"I liked putting the newspaper in the letterbox the next day and seeing if the panties were gone. If they were, I felt excited at knowing they had been discovered recently."

I imagined the shock of a parent checking the mail and finding a pair of their daughter's semen-stained undergarments. I'm sure it would have sent them spiraling into all sorts of assumptions.

"So you like the idea of the panties being found even if they aren't discovered by the actual targeted girl?"

"I didn't think about it like that." His answer was not a statement. It was more a revelation. "In my mind it was *always* the girl who discovered them. Putting the newspaper in the letterbox—whether the panties were still in there or not—made me feel like I was leaving a clue. Like a signature mark that could lead to me if they cracked the code."

I wondered how he managed to return to the scene of the crime after leaving his "mark." The way I saw it, if I discovered that in my letterbox, I'd have a plan hatched to apprehend the offender, and it likely wouldn't involve authorities.

"How did you get caught?" I asked.

"I was at a house and started looking in the window. Then, *whack*! I felt this thud to my back, and I collapsed in a heap."

Yep, that's how I'd deal with it.

"Then there was this barrage of smacks to my face. All I could see was this big dude swinging punches. There was another guy with a baseball bat. I assume that's what the first hit was. I didn't fight back. I knew I deserved what I was getting." His comments trailed off into self-pity. I decided to use his statement as a learning curve.

"That must have been a terrifying experience?"

He looked up, glad that I had acknowledged his suffering. "It was," he said. "I was scared shitless!"

I smiled at him, but it wasn't designed to be a friendly gesture. It was a smile offered as a means of saying "I really want you to get this next bit." I leaned into him for emphasis.

"Kind of like how those young girls would have felt after discovering they were being watched," I said softly.

He didn't comment. He simply closed his eyes, pouted his lips, and nodded purposefully.

ALBERT

There was nothing particularly controversial or splendid about Albert. He was a family man: wife, kids, dog, etc. He owned a moderately successful business working as a handyman doing odd jobs. He was the typical "guy next door."

"Technology has made what I do easier," he said. It was more a confession than bragging.

"Yes," I concurred. "What was the appeal?"

"The thought of invading their privacy, I guess," he said in a depressed tone. "I liked the idea of doing it and them not having a clue."

"Why?"

"I'm not sure really. It just made me feel *alive*, kind of invincible. It was as if I could get away with this stuff right under their noses." He paused in deep thought. "Have you ever used a pair of binoculars or a telescope?" he abruptly blurted out.

I nodded.

"The last time you used them, what did you look at?"

"The ocean," I said. "I was staying in an apartment on the Gold Coast."

"And was the ocean the only thing you looked at?" His manner in raising the question suggested it had deeper connotations.

I scratched my head. "No," I replied. "I also looked at people on the beach."

He sat up instantly.

"Women?" he asked with a touch of anticipation.

My gut said *go*. "Most likely," I admitted.

"And what did you feel when you were looking at them lying on the beach in their bikinis?"

I considered his question and took some time to answer. "A sense of power, to be honest, as in, 'I can see you and watch your every move, and you don't even know.'"

We both sat in silence, then a new thought came to me. "To be *really* honest, I would almost be hoping they did something out of the ordinary— something taboo or socially unacceptable, so I could delight in having witnessed it."

One thing I have learned in this work: you have to be able to think like these guys. You have to be able to go to the parts of yourself you don't want to own or admit. If you can do it, you will be a better therapist because it allows you to walk in their shoes. Not for empathic value but for the simple objective of comprehending how they process information. You also have to be able to adapt to the person you are working with. You have to see who and what they are and morph into the therapist most beneficial to them.

Albert seemed confused by my honesty. It appeared he was not expecting such a direct and authentic response. It caught him off guard. I decided to use the moment to turn things around and apply a little of the blowtorch to him.

"How would you set up your cameras?" I asked.

"Through my work. I'd be in people's homes, doing jobs. I'd suss things out first though."

My honesty had reaped the desired reward. Albert wanted to be truthful too.

"What do you mean?" I asked.

He groomed his moustache with his thumb and index finger. "I'd talk to the customer—usually the woman of the house. I'd ask questions about her family. She'd like it. She'd think I was nice and that I cared. I'd tell her about my family and my kids, so she instantly felt she could relate to me."

I watched as he looked intently at the wall behind me, seemingly recollecting memories of past exploitive behavior.

"What information were you attempting to extract?" I enquired.

Albert eased back from his journey in time. "I was trying to find out if she had daughters. I'd take notice of the photos in her home—family portraits and stuff. I'd usually check out what was stuck on the fridge too. People usually put photos there as well. I'd look for young girls, and if I liked what I saw, then I set up my camera."

"In the bathroom?"

"Sometimes," he said. "Most times I would find an excuse to get in the attic. I'd work out where the girl's bedroom was, drill a small hole, and place a camera there."

I was stunned by his dedication. "I'm guessing you did this more times than you got caught?"

Albert didn't acknowledge the question for fear of incriminating himself. His silence spoke volumes. I pondered for a moment how many young girls had unknowingly been victim to Albert's misappropriations. This was a man in business for many years with access to people's homes on a daily basis. The likely victim number was astronomically huge.

"What would you do with the footage?"

"Store it. I had it all on disk hidden in a safe place. I'd watch it when my wife was out." His head drooped in shame. The realization of sacrificing a life he cherished to fulfil his lusts seemed to be hitting home.

"What about your own daughters?" I asked with interest.

"What about them?" he snapped.

"Would you watch them in their rooms too?"

"No! They're my daughters," he retorted with detest. "I'm not a fuckin' sicko!"

RICHARD

Richard liked to talk. He had a vast knowledge on many topics and an opinion on everything with the exception of one: his offending behavior. He would avoid discussing that subject at all costs; pinning him down was like trying to catch a rat with a set of chopsticks.

After yet another session in which Richard used his subtle powers of interpersonal persuasion, I decided to call him out on his reluctance to venture into understanding the finer points of his "shady side." You see, Richard had been incarcerated at least six times for his voyeuristic activity. His signature offense always took place under the cloak of darkness. He would strip naked to his running shoes, break into a home, and stand masturbating at the foot of a sleeping child's bed.

To my knowledge, no therapist had ever gotten "boo" out of Richard. However, I'd spent enough hours listening to his life stories—which I must admit were fascinating—to have gained his respect. I believe all he ever wanted was to be heard and to feel important; in granting him as much, I was allowed into his world. I didn't realize, however, that entering that world would be venturing into an abyss.

I surveyed the skinny, little man before me. If he were a puppy, he would have been the runt of the litter.

"How many times do you reckon you've done this?" I asked from left field. The question took Richard by surprise; it was a far cry from our typical discussions about his humorous life anecdotes.

"Done what?" he toyed.

"C'mon, Rich," I encouraged.

Surprisingly, his body language altered. He was less guarded and ready to talk.

"I'm not sure," he replied. I believed him.

Richard sat up. "Let's put it this way. If I had a dollar for every crime I've committed, I'd have enough to make bail at my next court appearance."

His joke deserved a laugh for no other reason than to appease him and keep him chatting.

"So what are we talking, hundreds? Thousands?" I pushed my luck.

"I really don't know. I don't keep a logbook. It's not like I can claim it on my taxes or anything."

Again I rewarded him with a chuckle. Sometimes I make myself sick.

"What's the appeal? I mean you never actually physically assault these kids."

I took a swig from my coffee mug—the action designed to mask my probing as opposed to fulfilling any need to sustain a caffeine hit.

Richard's expression changed. He looked at me like I was a potential spy candidate being assessed for a top-secret mission. "The fact you ask that question," he said as he paused midsentence to sip his own coffee, "means you wouldn't understand even if I told you."

"Try me," I suggested in cool monotone. Inside I was praying he would "go there."

He stared at me as if I were a fool. "Why would I give up that secret?"

The answer to his question was obvious—to me at least—and I blurted it out too quickly. "To help you desist from doing it."

Richard went to slurp his coffee, but instead put his cup down and began to shake his head. "See, that's the thing with you shrinks—you all make that one major erroneous assumption about me."

"What do you mean?" I requested sincerely.

Richard sat quietly. I could tell he was deciding whether to commit to continuing the conversation. He latched on to his coffee cup and took a swig before letting out a sigh commensurate with total satisfaction. He held the mug in both hands, then looked at me calculatingly. "I don't want to stop doing what I do," he declared.

I was stunned. "Huh?"

"I like it. Nothing in me wants to stop."

We sat looking at each other, both attempting to determine what the other was thinking. I didn't give anything away. At least I didn't think I did.

"You and I are well aware I'll do it again," Richard admitted. "I'm not going to sit here and deny that. For me, that's all part of the buzz—doing it and getting away with it."

"Ah, so it's like a challenge."

His silence suggested I was onto something.

"Don't you ever worry about getting caught?" I continued.

He looked at me like I was an idiot, again. "Of course," he replied tersely. "I just said that's part of the buzz. If the potential for getting busted wasn't there, what'd be the point?"

Richard certainly had a unique take on his crimes. It reminded me of an article I once read about an armed bandit discussing the banks he had held up, said that he would have an erection the entire time the robbery was taking place. That robber wasn't too dissimilar to Richard; the "benefits" in terms of proceeds stolen were secondary to the sexual arousal. The thought led to my next question.

"So what do you find more arousing—the kids you're looking at or the act itself?"

Richard tapped his coffee cup with his fingernail as he contemplated my query. "I'd have to say the kids are just a means to an end. I'm not attracted to kids in a sexual way. I know that sounds weird, but I'm not. I'd never touch a kid. I don't find them sexually attractive at all."

"What do you mean they are just a means to an end?"

He ceased his tapping and took another sip before staring vacantly at the wall, then turned and looked at me warily. I figured he was concerned how what he was about to say would be received. "Okay, here's an example.

If I broke into your house and stole your TV, would you feel a degree of violation?"

"Absolutely."

Richard nodded and grinned. "What if I took your TV and left your wife's dildo on your bed so you knew I'd been there?"

"Well, uh, yeah," I said, more perturbed by his assumption about my partner's sex life than where he was heading with his "example."

"Okay, so what if I broke in, stole your TV, and masturbated while watching your kid sleep?"

His questions seemed to have a genuine agenda. Pursuing his motive was more exciting to me than getting bogged down in the inappropriateness of a sexual offender having weaved my child into his story. I was simply glad he was talking.

"Hang on a sec," I intervened.

Richard looked nervous. I think he thought I was about to reprimand him for making his example personal toward my family.

"You don't get caught very often doing that stuff, so the parents don't even know you've been there doing your 'thing.'"

Richard nodded. "So?"

"Well, they notice their TV gone, but they don't know the extent of what you've done, unless of course you leave semen behind?"

He shook his head. "I use protection; I carry condoms. If I left semen behind, I'd never get away with a single offense these days. Back in the old days it wasn't a problem—no DNA testing back then."

I ignored his technological-advancement lamenting and continued to press the conversation toward where I wanted it. "So if the parents of these kids are your real target, and they have no clue what you've done, what's the point?"

He downed the remnants of his beverage. "But I know," he declared with a grin.

"What does that mean?"

"I know," he repeated. "For me it doesn't really matter if *they* know, because I know what I've done. I've got a one up on them."

I couldn't believe I'd just heard what I'd heard. I faked another sip of coffee. "So which would you prefer: the parents knowing or not?"

"Hmmm, that's a tricky question." He paused in consideration. "I guess the answer is both. If they don't know, I beat them. If they do know, I beat them."

"Yeah, I get that, but which would you prefer?"

Again Richard took some time to think about his answer. I waited in anticipation but concealed my eagerness.

"Them knowing," he finally said. "But it can't always be that way, because if they know, it increases my chances of getting caught."

"But you said you like that; it generates more of a buzz."

"Yeah, I'm not claiming to understand it completely," he immediately countered. "I'm just saying it's a bit of a paradox. I can't explain it clearly, but in my head it all makes sense."

I had little doubt his ideas made perfect sense to him. The fact they were highly distorted likely made it difficult to explain in a rationale that would make sense to a "normal" person.

"Would you say the basic objective is to obtain power and control?" I asked in the hope he would divulge more secrets.

"Definitely! But not in the same way as a rapist."

"What's the difference?"

"Well, then again"—he hesitated—"maybe it's no different. Maybe a rapist does feel what I feel. Maybe he's motivated by the same reasons but just prefers a different means to satisfy the urge."

"The urge?"

He looked at me as though I should know what he was referring to. "You know," he said, "the feeling of completely dominating someone, having total dominion over them."

"But couldn't you get that same feeling in acts of bondage with a partner?" I tested, attempting to determine if there were any other underlying fantasies.

"No," Richard stated emphatically. "Not unless they weren't consenting."

"So they would have to be at your mercy?"

"No," he again replied categorically. "I wouldn't enjoy that. If I was to go to some sort of sadist-masochist club, it would be pointless because every person there is attending of their own free will."

"Oh, I get you. So you would have to do it in full knowledge that the person didn't want it?"

"I wouldn't do that kind of stuff anyway," he insisted. "But in answer to your question, yeah."

I decided to revisit the original disclosure, given I believed he held no interest in the areas I'd attempted to take him. "So it's not the kids that are arousing you; it's the thought of committing this act in a person's home without their knowledge and consent?"

"Exactly!"

I smiled and simultaneously nodded at him in an effort to suggest we were on the same wavelength, that we'd connected. "And you don't want to give that up because . . . ?"

My question surprised him. He looked up startled. "What am I going to replace it with?"

I think my shock at his response to my question was more extreme than his initial reaction. I'd hit a nerve. "There's nothing that could substitute?" I continued.

"Not a thing."

I sat in a pose of pensiveness. I knew exactly what I wanted to ask him, but I didn't want him to think it had come to me so quickly. Asking what I was about to ask without pretending to have to search deeply into my thoughts would likely scare him off.

"I'm guessing," I finally ventured, "based on what you're saying, Rich, that the ultimate situation for you would be doing this in the homes of people you know?"

Richard looked shocked, then sat staring into his empty coffee cup.

"Yes?" I sought clarification even though I knew I'd hit pay dirt.

"Maybe," he replied.

I maintained my discipline and waited for what seemed like an eternity. Everything in me wanted to ask the forthcoming question, but a rapid reproach might have spooked him.

"I'm curious, Rich, how often do you target people you know?" I finally squeezed out after feigning deep thought once again.

"It's something I do," he confessed with a grin. "The frequency of which is not up for discussion, for obvious reasons."

The "obvious reasons" being if he admitted to anything he hadn't been convicted of, he feared I might inform the relevant authorities. I wasn't as much concerned with that as I was intent on getting to the core of his deviance. I took some time to consider what he'd offered up thus far. Then it came to me.

"These people that are known to you . . ."

Richard looked at me suggestive that I should continue.

". . . I'd hazard a guess you don't like them very much. In fact, you probably pretend you do, but deep down I think you actually despise them."

I didn't know how he would respond to my analysis. I eased back in my chair and waited.

"I can't stand them," he said bitterly.

"Because?"

"They think they're better than me."

"In what way?"

"Most of them are people I go to church with. They all know about my stints in prison; they pretend they don't, but they all know. They all talk about me behind my back—acting as nice as pie to my face then having a laugh at my expense when I'm not around—bunch of hypocrites."

His comment perplexed me because his rebirth as a Christian had only come a few years prior, and his offenses stemmed way back, spanning three decades or more.

"But you were doing this before you became a fully-fledged churchgoer," I protested.

"Oh, I thought you meant recently," he said, unassumingly giving himself up. "Yeah, there've always been other people putting me down, making out they're better than me."

"When did it start?"

"In high school," he said with an expression beyond dejection. For a brief moment, I felt sorry for him. I envisaged he would have been bullied and tormented on a regular basis. He would never have fitted into any clique—a classic social outcast.

"And these kids at school—did you ever break into their houses and do what you do?"

My tone was empathic, but his smile eroded my compassion. "Yep," he said full of glee.

"So I guess you beat them too?" I asked while considering the pitiful means he obtained personal triumph over his perceived oppressors. My thoughts were interrupted by the clunk of his coffee cup hitting the table top.

"I'll never give it up," declared Richard in defiance.

I believed him. It was all he had.

CONCLUSION

These cases, among many things, demonstrate the degree of distorted thinking that occurs for offenders. They take innocuous events and interactions and reframe them in a way that totally misrepresents reality. I often think of this as being analogous to those funny mirrors you see at carnivals: they reflect something that you recognize as yourself, but the image projected back is a distorted perspective. That's why they're funny. They distort what you know to be reality. Offenders gaze into their mirrors of life, observe the distorted image, and believe it represents reality.

As you will read in the following chapters, humans are capable of massive distortions in their thinking. It is these distortions that are in need of addressing in therapy. As a victim of childhood sexual abuse, you are not responsible for how an offender sees you. The distorted perceptions they hold are theirs and theirs alone. There is nothing you did, or could have done, that would alter that distortion for them.

Chapter Nine: The Intra-Familial Offender

*"Stab the body and it heals, but injure the heart
and the wound lasts a lifetime."*
~ *Mineko Iwasaki*

WHEN PROFESSIONALS TALK OF INTRA-FAMILIAL offenders, they are discussing people who commit sexual crimes within the institution of family. As I commented in a previous chapter, intra-familial offenders are the least likely to re-offend. While this supposition is my truth—based on my experience—it only applies to intra-familial offenders as a conglomerate whole.

Remember: all offenders are unique and must be treated as such. Pigeonholing them is a dangerous practice.

Intra-familial offenders may not always be deemed the highest in regard to potential recidivism, but the damage they cause can be second to none. All offenders, in one way or another, destroy families, but intra-familial offenders often obliterate their own. They breach the trust of their victim, partner, and other family members; they often cause a divorce or separation; and sadly, they leave children without a parent.

The above is only relevant to those offenders who assume responsibility for their crimes. There are many who maintain their innocence for the duration of their lives. Consider for a moment how this might affect the child victims. Not only have they suffered sexual abuse, they are further denied validation of their experiences. When this happens, families tend to take sides; subsequently, the victims are often ostracized by those they love.

Typically intra-familial offenders abuse their own child(ren) due to a blurring of parental boundaries. Once the distortions are brought to his or her attention, the perpetrator *generally* does not offend again. In my experience, intra-familial offenders often possess the most significant distortions . . .

PAUL

I waited impatiently in the interview room of the cell block. Finally Paul entered. He wasn't what I expected. For some inmates, prison garb is congruent with their personality and physical appearance, Paul wasn't one of them. He was gangly to the point of gracelessness, and his wearing of plastic Velcro "laced" sandshoes with brown socks did nothing to enhance his skinny white legs.

Paul was a former cattle farmer. He had inherited a massive property upon his father's death and worked the land his entire life. Like most country folk, Paul was very down-to-earth. However, even straight shooters can distort the truth when it comes to themselves.

"Are you married?" I asked.

"Yes, I was," he said, his reply reeking of social correctness.

"No longer together due to this?" I inferred in reference to the reason for his incarceration.

"No, not at all," he stated abruptly. "My wife passed away six years ago."

His tone suggested he didn't like her much.

"Farming accident?"

Paul looked surprised that I had knowledge of his vocation as a farmer. "No, it was a car accident," he replied cautiously. "She hit a cement mixer on the highway. The police said she fell asleep at the wheel."

"Tragic," I said dolefully. "Do you agree that she fell asleep?"

My question may seem strange, but such accidents and many single-vehicle accidents can actually be suicides.

"Yes, she had been up all night with the baby. She would have been very tired. She was heading into town. It's a long drive to town. Our property is a long way from anywhere. Our closest neighbor is forty-two kilometers away," he stated robotically.

"The baby also died in the crash," he suddenly added from nowhere. "Luckily my daughter caught the bus to school that day. Otherwise she would have been killed too."

His words may have been void of emotion, but the thought of that little baby dying in such violent circumstances made me feel as if someone had placed a heavy, flat, cold stone on my chest. I pushed the feeling aside and reminded myself I had a job to do.

"I assume you're talking about the daughter you offended against?"

Paul looked at me gravely. His mood altered. "I don't like that word."

"Which word?"

"Offended," he said corrosively.

"Why?" I asked as I considered the irony of Paul being offended by the term *offended.*

"It doesn't sit right with my situation."

I tried to make sense of his comment. I couldn't. "I'm failing to see how that's possible, given that you're sitting in prison."

Paul rolled his eyes but remained upright in his chair. He was as stiff as a board and unwavering in his intensity. "You don't know anything about how I got here." His comment was a chastisement.

I needed to backpedal to get him onside. "That's true. I only know what I've read. Which is why we are having this discussion—so I can get to know you."

His body language didn't change, but his tone did. "Well, I'd appreciate that," he said. "The police and courts certainly didn't do that."

I found Paul a bizarre man, to say the least. I wanted to dig deeper to see what was really at the core of his offending. "So what is it you want me to know?"

"The reasons behind why I'm here."

"There's always a reason; that's exactly what I want to understand."

His body seemed to become a little unhinged. I presume he relaxed as much as was possible for him. I think it was his belief that I was willing to get to know him and conclude that he didn't belong in prison that won him over. The truth was, I didn't want to understand him to get to know him for the reasons he assumed. I wanted to get to know him to see how he had come to be involved in an ongoing sexual relationship with his daughter.

"I believe this whole thing got out of control after Cindy died," he said. I supposed Cindy to be his wife. "How so?" I asked.

"I was left to run a property and bring up a twelve-year-old girl all on my own. The property I could handle; the girl I had no idea about."

"Your daughter must have taken the loss of her mother and her baby brother hard?"

"Rebecca cried every night for months. She refused to go to school. She would just stick to me like glue. She stayed with me at work all day because she said she was so scared something bad would happen to me and she would be left alone."

There was still no emotion expressed by Paul. It was as if he were reading the instruction manual from a toaster.

"She never went back to school," he continued. "In the end, she was driving me nuts. She would be in my way all day, so I made her a deal. I told her she didn't have to go back to school if she stayed home and did the housework and cooked the meals. She seemed to like that."

"Did she have any friends?"

"Yes, she did before her mother passed away. But because we were so isolated, she wouldn't see them. I used to take her to town with me, and she would make arrangements to visit them, but when we got there she wouldn't leave my side. In the end I gave up."

"Did you have any support yourself?"

"No. I'm a loner. I love my work and that's it. I have employees, but I don't get close to them. They live in a camp many miles from the homestead."

"What about your parents?"

"They are both deceased."

I contemplated his predicament—being entirely alone to raise a daughter whose mother and baby brother had been smashed to smithereens by a concrete truck. I wondered how that child coped, given her father had about as much compassion as a house brick.

"Did you seek counseling for Rebecca?" I eventually asked.

"I arranged for her to attend, but she refused to go. She said all she needed was me and she would be fine. I was at a loss with what to do there. I didn't know whether to push her or not. She had already been through enough."

I didn't believe him. I sensed he enjoyed his daughter's unhealthy dependence.

"So she stayed home doing chores until what age?"

"Until the police knocked on the door, charged me, and took her away."

"Why did they come knocking?"

"They got tipped off by one of my employees."

"I thought they didn't live near you."

"They didn't. Rebecca used to drive around on the property; she could drive when she was eight. She would do food deliveries to the employees' camp and bring me my lunch. The employee saw us having sex in the car in a place we thought was private."

"How old was Rebecca when they took her away?"

"Almost fifteen."

I figured he must have been given a lengthy sentence since he had already served about three years. I quickly glanced at the inside cover of the file in front of me. His information sheet stated he had been sentenced to nine years. Three years inside to consider his crime, and this is all he had come up with? He obviously believed his version. I decided to pursue a new path.

"How do you feel about everything that's happened?"

"Angry," he said with vigor.

"Angry?"

"When Cindy died, Rebecca and I became very close. We were there for each other day and night. People just don't seem to get how that can bring a father and a daughter closer."

I wondered just how close. "Did Rebecca sleep in the same bed as you?"

"Yes, of course. She started doing that the night her mother passed away. She refused to sleep alone because she would have nightmares. I figured it was something she would get over in time, but she never did."

"So she slept in your bed, with you, until she was fifteen?"

"Thereabouts." There was no thought on his behalf that this was remotely problematic or abnormal.

"What about you? Did you need her sleeping there?"

"Yes, who wouldn't?" Paul stated as if I were a fool.

"Why did you like it?"

"Comfort. I missed my wife, and having Rebecca there helped."

I was beginning to wonder who needed whom more.

"Did Rebecca keep in touch with her school friends online?"

"No," he said staunchly. "I didn't allow her to have Facebook and that sort of thing. You hear too many stories about that stuff, and she was just a shy, gullible country girl with no real understanding of the big, bad world."

"Did you think it was unhealthy for Rebecca to spend all her time isolated like that?"

He frowned at me. "No. I grew up on that farm in the same way, and it didn't do me any harm."

I thought his point was highly debatable and wondered how on earth he'd ever met his wife.

"Where did you meet Cindy?"

"She was my stepmother's daughter."

What!?!

"Sorry," I said, in need of clarification. "She was your stepsister?'

"If you want to put a label on it, yes."

"So the woman you call Mom is actually your stepmother?"

"Yes, I disowned my birth mother. She left Dad and me on the property for another man. So when Dad married Mom, I accepted her as my mother."

I thought if Paul's father was anything like him, his birth mother had made the right decision.

"So you accepted her as your mother, but you didn't accept Cindy as your stepsister?"

"Yes. But Cindy was only a child when Dad married Mom. So she was my sister then, but I didn't see her as that in later years."

He was doing my head in. "What do you mean?"

"When Cindy and I became lovers, I obviously didn't see her as my sister then. I saw her as my girlfriend, then my fiancée, then my wife."

I had a morbid fascination with his incestuous story. I was intrigued, and it took everything in me not to get too pushy in wanting him to disclose more.

"How old were you when Cindy became your girlfriend?"

"I was twenty and she was thirteen."

What!?!

"And your parents were aware of this situation?"

"Not at first. We kept it secret for a while until we couldn't anymore." He chuckled. To Paul, the retelling of his relationship with Cindy was like reliving some humorous event that took place down on the farm where Billie-Jo and Bobby-Sue once knuckled it out over who was to blame for a burnt pot roast.

"What happened when they found out?" I asked.

"I broached the subject over dinner and told them how it was. Dad said I was old enough to make my own decisions, and Mom said it was fine but that we weren't to have sex before we were married."

"And did you?"

He looked at me incredulously as if I had asked the most stupid question possible. "Of course not! I respected my parents' wishes. Cindy was a virgin until the day we were married."

I loaded a bullet. "I wonder if they would have approved of you being with Rebecca?"

"My parents were not alive to make any stipulation about my relationship with Rebecca."

I didn't know if he was being serious. More to the point, I hoped he wasn't serious, but I knew he was. I must have spent a good few minutes going over what he had just said. I hadn't really noticed the silence until he spoke up.

"There was only the four of us at the wedding. We had it on the property, and a celebrant came and it was done. After that night we shared the same room in the house. Dad gave his blessing, and we all lived together until Mom and Dad passed away."

"How did they die?'

"Dad was diagnosed with cancer a month after the wedding and was gone within three months. Mom went about a year after. The doctors say it was a heart attack, but Cindy and I thought it was because her heart was broken. She loved Dad to bits."

I was perplexed as to what his definition of love entailed.

"So how old were you and Cindy when they passed away?"

"Cindy was eighteen and I was twenty-five."

"And when did Rebecca come along?"

"The very next year, 1995."

"Then it was just you, Cindy, and Rebecca for how long?"

"About twelve years, until little Bradley came along. He wasn't planned. Cindy and I only wanted one child, but I must admit it was good to have a boy. I could leave the farm to him, and he could keep the legacy going."

I didn't want to get into the details of his farming history so kept the train of conversation going in the direction I knew the juicy bits were lurking.

"Did you ever consider anything strange about being married to your stepsister?"

He reacted as if affronted. "I told you already, she wasn't my stepsister. She was my wife. Dad always said that love knows no boundaries, and he was right."

Maybe he was, but I don't think dear old Dad meant for Paul to take his words of wisdom quite so literally.

"I was just wondering: Did you love Rebecca as a daughter or a partner?"

"A partner."

"And she saw you as her dad or a partner?"

"Her partner."

"And you believe that's normal?"

Again he hackled up. "I don't care what you or anyone else thinks is normal. We were in love. We still are, and nothing you or anyone else says or does will alter that."

I found his comment delusional, given he hadn't seen or heard from Rebecca in three years, and with age she had probably come to recognize her father's abnormality.

"How do you know she still loves you as a partner?'

"She told me."

"When?"

"The last time I saw her."

"But that was the day the police took her away."

"That's right."

My attempt to show him reason proved futile. His brain had set his distortions in stone, and I pitied the poor bastard who had to deal with him on a program in the future.

"Do you think it's fair that you're in prison for having a sexual relationship with your daughter?"

"People just don't understand. They have been brainwashed to think that love in that situation is not possible, but it is. When I get out of here, Rebecca will be waiting for me."

"How do you know that?"

He held his fist to his chest in similitude of feeling the truth of his delusion in his heart. Of course *he* didn't see it as a delusion. Paul earnestly believed what he was saying. His inability to grasp reality outside of his own little bubble reminded me of people caught up in religious cults who shut down anything that challenges their belief system. Paul's ingrained notions about life were the legacy of his upbringing. If not for Rebecca having escaped, this too would have been her understanding of "life."

"What do you think Cindy would make of your relationship with Rebecca?"

He shot me an odd look. "Cindy doesn't make anything of it; she's dead."

"So you believe Rebecca will become your wife one day?"

"Yes," he replied resolutely.

"And children?" I asked.

"That's up to her."

I started to consider what Paul made of the people he was now surrounded by, given that he saw nothing wrong with himself. He resided in a cell block designated to sex offenders. The fact he didn't identify as one sparked my interest.

"How do you feel about participating in a sex-offender program?" I asked.

"I'll do it if it means I get out of this place."

"So you understand you will have to talk about your *offense*?"

I watched his body tense up. "People can call it what they like. I know how it is."

Paul's thinking was entirely skewed, distorted, and way left of center. With that in mind, how would you address his thought patterns? I'm a therapist and I would struggle.

Now consider what chance Rebecca had.

THEO

Theo was a miner—a divorced father with two boys. He met his partner, Sally, at a singles' site online. Sally had two daughters. After a period spent dating, Theo and Sally decided to move in together; they chose Theo's house. It was only partially built but had four bedrooms. The couple decided it was best if the girls had their own rooms, and subsequently, after much protestation, Theo's boys were forced to share a bedroom.

Fast-forward a year, with Theo now sitting before me in prison . . .

"What the hell was I thinking?" he asked. The question wasn't directed at me; he was talking to himself in the hope that he might find some reason that explained away his behavior in a rational sense.

"Why would I do this?" he asked again. I didn't respond. The answers were in him, not in me.

"I'm an idiot," he said. That was my cue.

"That's the easy way to think about it." I intervened in his self-deprecation.

"Huh?" My lack of pity toward him wasn't expected. He must have been one of those people who think psychologists are always supposed to make them feel better. Little wonder really, when the majority of psychologists think their job is to "fix people" as opposed to help them grow out of their issues.

"Calling yourself an idiot is a cop-out. You don't have to think or explore the issue once you say that."

He attempted to pull me into his victim mentality. "But I've got no idea why I did it. I really don't," he pled.

I wasn't prepared to play his pity game—the one in which I allow my ego as a therapist to overrule his needs and let him manipulate me into making him feel better. I wanted to test how sincere he really was about developing an understanding of his behavior.

"Let's go back to the beginning of your offending and see what you can gain from that," I said, fishing.

"Do we have to?" he immediately whined.

"No, we don't have to. You're quite welcome to continue to do nothing about it and not understand it, if that's what you want."

He was aggravated that I'd countered all his attempts to try to suck me into his self-pity vacuum, but it didn't stop him from trying again. "I guess I don't have much of a choice," he bemoaned.

Theo didn't really bother me. His negative, pessimistic, self-pitying attitude is typical of many sex offenders. I'd seen and dealt with it before, but I wanted him to think I was pissed off. In one fell swoop I gathered my paperwork and stood. "You have a choice. So decide what you want."

I headed for the door.

Theo panicked. He knew he needed my recommendation to get in a program. He called me back. "Hang on, hang on."

I sat back down across from him at the desk but ensured my body language suggested I might leave at any minute.

"It started when Sally and the girls moved in," he revealed.

I made myself more comfortable. "How old were the girls?"

"Rhiannon was six, and Frances was ten."

"Did you offend against both girls?"

"No," he said aghast, "only Frances."

His being adamant he only offended against one child was probably true, but working with liars and manipulators makes you doubt everything people say—not just offenders. It's one of the drawbacks of the work. You become cynical and dubious of the good in people. In that environment you cannot survive any other way. If you don't doubt, you get chewed up and spat out. I've seen it happen time and time again.

"Why only Frances?" I asked.

"I don't know," he whined.

"You didn't think long enough to say you don't know; answer the question."

"She was older, I suppose," he replied immediately.

"Was she physically developed?"

He looked at me as if I was the odd one. "No, she was just a kid."

I kept firing questions so he wouldn't have time to lapse back into his old patterns. "Do you like the bodies of developed women?"

"Yes, of course."

"You say 'of course' like it's a strange question, but you committed sexual offenses against a prepubescent child."

He didn't seem to like where I was taking things. "What's your point?" he half-demanded.

I feigned being confused. "It doesn't make sense."

Theo's body suddenly drooped. He wasn't completely limp, but I could tell something about what I said disturbed him. I assumed it was just more of his "woe is me" routine until he looked up. "Am I a pedophile?" he asked sincerely. "I'm worried I might be a pedo."

For the first time, I felt some compassion for him, simply because his request was a genuine yearning and reaching out for help. When you've been in this game long enough, you learn the difference between forced and true emotion. Theo's was the latter.

I looked at him for some time as he sat willing me to wipe away his fears. "For me to answer that question you are going to need to be more honest with yourself than you've ever been in your life." I allowed Theo to soak that statement up before getting him to commit. "So do you want me to answer it?"

He seemed apprehensive but put himself in the firing line. "Yeah," he said hesitantly. He moved backward in his chair as if bracing for impact.

"Have you ever felt sexually attracted to any other child besides Frances?"

"No, never. Well, I don't know," he stammered. "It depends on what you mean by 'attracted.' I've seen girls around that age and thought they were pretty. I've thought they'd be stunning when they're older."

I shook my head. "No. Not like that. I mean, do you feel sexually attracted to them? Do you like them as they are, in their undeveloped physical state?"

He reflected on the notion. His deliberation lent more credence to his proceeding answer. "No."

"Then you're not a pedophile," I stated boldly.

He looked up. "How can you be so sure?"

"Trust me; I'm sure. The question is: Why are you so unsure?"

"Because of what I did," he said preposterously.

"But you said you're not attracted to prepubescent children; pedophiles are. So if you're not attracted to prepubescent girls, what we need to work out is why you sexually abused one."

He sat more upright in his chair. I could see what I had presented made sense to him, and he immediately became motivated to find answers for himself. I refrained from speaking as Theo sat earnestly going over his past. "I felt close to her," he finally said.

"How?"

"It was like an emotional connection."

I nodded. He was a far cry from piecing the whole puzzle together, but it was a solid start. "Did you have the same connection with your wife?"

"No."

"Why?"

"She's a career woman. After we were together for a while, I saw why her previous marriage had broken down. She's all about her. I looked after the girls, and she spent every minute entertaining her clients."

Strange how easily people see selfishness in others but rarely in themselves.

"Where was Frances's dad?" I asked.

"The girls never saw him. I have no idea where he is. Sally never says much about him."

He failed to grasp the obvious and forced me to ask the evident question. "So it would be fair to say that after a while Frances saw you as her dad?"

"It was never said, but I think so."

The outer edges of the jigsaw that was his offense were beginning to take shape. "I'm guessing she would get close to you and want to be around you?"

He nodded. "She was always in my pocket."

I took it a step further. "Would she be affectionate toward you?"

"Yes," he said with seemingly no clue where I was headed. "She was very cuddly."

It was time to pull the trigger and unload. "How did you feel in those moments?"

Theo reeled back as if my imaginary bullet had struck him in the chest. He took his time to answer. "Totally uncomfortable," he eventually said.

I wasn't about to ease up. "Why?"

"Because it just felt wrong."

"A child expressing love toward a person they see as a father figure is wrong?"

He ran his hand over his forehead to the back of his skull and reversed the action until his palm covered his eyes. "No, not when you put it like that."

"So why did you feel it was wrong?"

I knew he didn't want to answer that particular question, because if he did, and if he was honest, there was no more dodging and weaving of responsibility. He would be in the midst of the storm and would have to wait it out. This was a healthy position for him to be in; it is where he needed to be to understand himself.

"I suppose it felt wrong because of the way it made me feel. It felt sexual."

I didn't respond at first. I let him rest with his own words because in all likelihood it was the first time he had openly acknowledged the truth. The silence didn't seem to bother him. Not in an uncomfortable way, at least. It appeared as if the burden of a long-held, repressed secret had lifted from his shoulders and lightened his load.

I wasn't done yet. "If you had a daughter and she was affectionate with you in exactly the same way, would you still see it as sexual?"

"No," he said.

"What's the difference?"

"Frances wasn't my daughter," he argued.

"There's your problem, right there," I said as I pointed at him. "You want to understand why you did this? Analyze that comment."

He looked confused but knew by my reaction that it was important for him to dissect his previous statement. "I see what you're saying. Not seeing her as my daughter meant I was able to do the stuff I did."

I smiled at him. "Yes, that's part of it," I offered gently. "But you did still manage to sexually abuse her even though you knew she was a child, and that has nothing to do with whether she's your daughter or not."

Theo became entranced by his own thoughts. "I think that's the next problem," he stated after some time.

I waited.

"I didn't see her as a child either," he declared.

"Explain that to me."

"Don't get me wrong, I knew she was a child, but I stopped seeing her as that."

"Why?"

"It was because of the way she acted toward me at the end. She would engage in the acts freely with me." He repeated his previous action: running his hand from his forehead to his skull before resting it over his eyes. It was perhaps an unconscious desire to wipe his memory.

"Did you ask her to keep it secret?"

"Yeah," he said ashamedly. "I told her we would get into trouble and that we would hurt her mother's feelings."

"What did she say?"

"She agreed. I think she liked what was going on between us. Yes, she definitely liked it because she would enjoy it."

His reply highlighted yet again his level of distortion.

"She enjoyed 'it,' or she was a lonely little girl without a parent to love her?"

Theo didn't respond. He didn't need to. The gloomy look on his face said it all. I allowed him time to recover from his unstated admission.

"So let's go back to the start of this conversation, the part where you have no clue why you committed these offenses. Now you tell me. Theo, why did you do what you did?"

"Because I misread things. I misconstrued them deliberately to be what I wanted them to be and not what they were."

"List for me some of the things you misconstrued."

"Her affection, her love, her need for a parent, her innocence, her willingness, her company . . . I can't think of any more off the top of my head," he said in a way that insinuated he was unsure if the quantity he had listed was to my expectations.

He needed to be rewarded for his efforts. "Not bad for a guy who was calling himself an idiot because he didn't know why he did it."

My comment seemed to open Theo up further. He shifted forward on his chair and appeared motivated.

"I need to get honest with myself. I just remembered something that I had previously tried to block out."

"What's that?"

"My house was only partially built. I was building it myself. Inside, I had only put the walls up. There were no doors. I don't think it was a coincidence that Frances's door was the last one I hung. Before any of this started, I used to see her changing after she came from the bathroom. I guess at some level even back then I had sexualized a ten-year-old girl. I used to think that because she never tried to hide her nakedness from me that she wanted me. How screwed up is that?"

I didn't acknowledge his question. He was right. It was totally screwed up.

"Where did you think all this was heading with Frances?" I asked.

"I never really stopped to think about it. I blocked it out. I knew it wasn't going to end well. I knew she would grow up and realize what I had done."

"And you kept going?"

"Somewhere deep down I think I had this fantastical idea that we would be together when she grew up and matured. That I would leave her mom and be with her. Then there was this other part of my brain—the reality part—that would remind me it just wasn't going to be that way."

Theo sat thinking about his disclosure. "I enjoyed the emotional connection."

"But it was the connection of a child in need," I countered.

"I'm aware of that now," he said sternly.

"So what have you learned?"

He inhaled excessively. "I have the ability to bullshit myself beyond belief."

EDDIE

Eddie was quite a confident fifteen-year-old lad. In fact, *confident* was an understatement; his self-assuredness was arrogance personified. In his mind, he was very special. He lived with his parents in a close-knit community— a small town where everyone knew everyone's business. Well, almost . . .

"It started when I noticed my sister got boobs," said Eddie unreservedly. There didn't seem to be too much embarrassment attached to his disclosure.

I remained silent to see if he would continue.

"I started looking at her through the keyhole to the bathroom when she'd have a shower," he revealed.

"Weren't you worried your parents would catch you?"

"They did a few times." He half-smirked.

"And?"

"And what?" His question was framed as a demand. It was designed to make me look small for asking. He wanted to project this as being a pointless investigation on my behalf. However, his aggressive response alerted me this was not a topic he wanted to discuss. Naturally, I pursued it.

"What did they do about it?" I asked.

"Nothing. They didn't really do anything."

"So they didn't sit you down and talk to you?"

"No, why would they?" he said, belittlingly. My ensuing silence and lack of reaction to his intimidation tactics made him uncomfortable.

"Geez, man!" he said in frustration. "It wasn't that big of a deal! I was just looking through the keyhole."

I remained silent and calm. Eddie sat glaring at me with his arms folded.

"No big deal," I said softly as I played with my pen. Then I shot my gaze directly at him. "But it did turn into a big deal, didn't it?"

He balked. He didn't like the question and broke eye contact.

"I don't really care what you say," he suddenly spewed at me. He waited for a reaction; I didn't give him one. "I don't want to talk to you anymore. Pastor David was right about you."

I knew he wanted me to ask who Pastor David was. I didn't.

"Pastor David said you wouldn't see it from a Christian point of view and not to be too bothered by what you say."

I smiled at him. "It seems to me you aren't implementing Pastor David's advice too well."

Eddie looked confused. "What the fuck are you on about?" he scolded.

"Pastor David said not to be too bothered by what I say; however, you seem *very* bothered, and I'm not even really saying that much."

He looked flustered. I imagined Eddie was used to getting his own way and being in control.

"Just get on with it," he demanded as he scrunched his face up.

You asked.

"Tell me about the night your mother walked into the lounge room in the early hours of the morning and found you and your sister having sex."

He recoiled as if he had been hit with a sledgehammer to the stomach. For a fleeting moment, he looked like a scared little boy. It didn't last long.

"We weren't having sex, you idiot. I was only touching her privates."

"Only?" I asked, pointing out his obvious minimization.

"Yeah, *only*," he said sardonically. "Big deal. Pastor David said all kids go through an experimentation thing."

Pastor David would be best sticking to what he knows.

"Anyway, Pastor David said Kylie was as much to blame as me."

Kylie was Eddie's twelve-year-old sister—the subject of his sexual abuse. His statement stirred my interest. I wanted to leap in, boots and all, and had to literally force myself to wait. I sat thinking of a way to present a question that he didn't feel threatened by and would allow him to offer up the information I sought.

"Did Kylie get in trouble with Pastor David?"

"Yep, and Mom and Dad," he said somewhat delightedly.

"What did Pastor David tell her?"

"That she had committed some sins that caused me to sin too."

"Such as?"

"Not dressing to church standards. Not telling me to stop what I was doing. Not going to Mom and Dad and telling them what was going on, and not praying for forgiveness," he rattled off.

"And what did Pastor David tell you?"

"The same as my Mom and Dad. He said I needed to stop doing what I was doing because it was wrong."

This Pastor David is a real genius.

I considered Eddie's comment more earnestly. "But you already knew it was wrong."

"Not really," he said innocently.

I got the impression that he had likely been schooled by Pastor David that his behavior toward his sister was the act of a child with no understanding of the moral and legal implications.

I leaned into him. "You knew it was wrong," I posited firmly.

"How the fuck would you know?" he attacked. His response surprised me. I didn't expect a boy in his position to be challenging me.

I remained leaning forward and continued meeting his eyes with mine. "I know you knew it was wrong because you would meet Kylie late at night when everyone was asleep. It was only by chance your mother discovered you. If you didn't think it was wrong, you wouldn't have been sneaking around."

He knew I'd cornered him. He folded his arms and pretended to be disinterested.

I took a chance at conning him with a stab in the dark. "Kind of like that time your parents discovered all that porn on your computer," I bluffed.

He suddenly looked up. He must have been perplexed how I knew about the incident. "That was Dad's porn, not mine!"

"It was on your computer."

"No it wasn't, you retard. It was on the family computer. It was Dad's stuff, and he blamed me when Mom found it."

Eddie seemed to be telling the truth. "Fair enough," I said, "but you still used to look at it."

"So what? Pastor David said it's normal to be tempted by that stuff at my age."

I wondered if dear old Dad got a reprimand from Pastor David. I also wondered what I might find on Pastor David's computer.

"I'm guessing you started doing things with Kylie soon after discovering your Dad's porn?" I wasn't entirely convinced what I presented was the case, but I wanted to give Eddie an "out." I wanted him to continue to give himself up by getting him to talk about his offending from a position of not being accountable.

"Yeah, that's true. That's when I started noticing her boobs, and that's when I'd sneak into her room at night. But she liked it too. So it wasn't like I was really abusing her like some freak you see on TV shows."

The kid was way off. "So you also snuck into her room? I thought you would meet in the lounge."

"That was later. We only used to go there to watch porn together."

"What porn?"

Eddie laughed snidely. "Dad's pornos. That moron has a hiding spot in his shed. He keeps them in a box in an old fridge. I found them and started watching them with Kylie. That's when stuff started happening."

"Your mom never mentioned that to the police when they asked her about what you were doing that night."

Eddie scoffed. "Mom's an idiot. She pretends our family's perfect. You should listen to her at church—you'd think our family were already angels in heaven. She sweeps every problem under the carpet. To her, none of us can do any wrong—especially Dad. He's like her hero or something. They're fucking weird."

I found his analysis of his parents quite astute. It got me thinking how difficult it would have been for the police to obtain the information they did from Eddie's mother. It suggested to me that his mom and dad likely knew a great deal more but simply covered it up for as long as possible.

"What did your mom do that night she found you and Kylie?"

"She walked over, turned the TV off, told us to put our pajamas on, and went back to bed."

I was now beginning to understand how Eddie had become an arrogant, precocious brat; he never had to face any consequences. The picture was now becoming crystal clear.

"I'm guessing you knew you could get away with doing this even if you did get caught?" I tested.

He tried to conceal his smirk and sat looking at me.

"What are you thinking?" I asked.

"How me and Kylie would probably still be doing it if she hadn't blabbed to one of her friends. I always said she had a big mouth."

It was obvious his parents' lack of intervention and complete ineptness in addressing his sexualized behavior had distorted Eddie's beliefs to the point that he thought he could get away with anything. To him, it was merely an inconvenience that the situation had come to the attention of authorities.

"What did you think when your mom turned the TV off and went to bed?"

He looked at me oddly. "I didn't think anything."

"Did you go to bed?"

"No. We turned the TV back on and kept doing what we were doing."

Eddie's mom's preference to live in a fantasy world made me realize what little chance Kylie had.

"Do you think your mom's behavior is odd?"

Eddie burst out laughing. "Have you met my mom?" he asked excitedly.

"No."

"She *is* fucking odd! Put it this way: she thinks when Dad tucks Kylie in at night, closes the door, and stays in there for an hour it's because he's praying with her!"

CONCLUSION

As you can see from the cases presented, each offender is only a risk in a certain type of situation—in the environment of their own family. In other words, they are highly likely not to commit crimes outside of the predicaments they created. In saying that, I'm not entirely sure I won't see "Eddie's" name in the news in years to come.

The legacy of the breaching of familial trust lingers for years after the "bomb" drops. Think of it like the atomic blast that hit Hiroshima. After more than half a century, the aftermath of the impact is still visible today. It's no different for victims of intra-familial sexual abuse. The family is never the same again. Love and trust evaporate, and this, for the victim, often spills over into their future relationships.

Sadly, many victims believe they contributed to the breakdown in some way. It seems to me that blaming themselves is easier to make sense of because many simply cannot understand how a person they loved and trusted came to exploit them. Whenever one is emotionally attached, it's easy to lose objectivity.

This is why it is essential for therapists aiding both victims and offenders during intervention to help them stand on the outside and look in. To free themselves of the emotions that hinder their ability to see the truth. The victim in accepting any part of the blame is paradoxically a reflection of the offender; they have lost objectivity because of their emotional attachment.

CHAPTER TEN: THE EXTRA-FAMILIAL OFFENDER

JUST AS THE LABEL OF intra-familial infers "within the family," the term *extra-familial* means external to the offender's family. In other words, extra-familial offenders target children outside his or her family system. Generally, such offenders have an understanding of the boundaries that exist with their own children but allow that line to become blurred when interacting with children they are not related to. That is not to say an offender is either one or the other. Sometimes they are both, depending on the level of distortion.

KELVIN

"You don't like me very much, do you?"

The accusation took me by surprise. I hadn't consciously set out to make him think I disliked him.

"What makes you say that?"

"I can tell. You look at me like I'm a piece of shit."

One thing I remain very aware of during session is how I am being perceived. If I think it works to look at an offender like he's a piece of shit, I will. As I've said, I'll do whatever it takes to get the information. However, on this occasion, Kelvin was way off. This was simply his means to derail my attempt at challenging his thinking.

"I find it interesting you ask me that question when I'm on the verge of delving into the detail of your offenses."

Kelvin's eyes darted to the right. "I'm not asking for that reason," he lied. "I just don't think it's very objective of you. How can you do your job well if you have opinions like that about people?"

I looked at him for a while before answering. He was well groomed and brandished a thoroughly maintained moustache. I figured he spent lots of time in front of the mirror.

"Maybe instead of worrying about my flaws, you should focus on your own?" I offered.

"I knew it. You don't like me."

I rocked back and forth in my chair. "See what you're doing there, Kelvin?"

"What?" he snapped.

"Making it all about you. The heat's about to get pretty intense. We're going to start discussing your offending behavior, and when we do, I'll bet you do what you just did."

Kelvin looked puzzled.

"I'll bet you try to turn things around and make it all about you," I explained. "Do you see how you do that?"

"No."

"Well you do, and it's probably how you came to offend against a nine-year-old girl for a period spanning five years."

"What the hell are you on about?" Kelvin raised his voice.

Gut says go.

"I'll show you what I'm on about—"

"Get on with it," he interrupted.

Kelvin folded his arms and leaned back—my cue to lean in.

"I don't know the ins and outs of your crimes," I began. "All I know is you maintained a sexual relationship with a young girl. I have no idea about your attitudes and beliefs pertaining to your offending. None. But I'll bet you a million bucks you believe this child seduced you."

He immediately sprang forth in his seat. "She did!" he declared, his voice staunch in his conviction. He didn't seem perturbed at all by how I had deduced this correct assumption, so I forced him to engage.

"You know how I know that, Kelvin?"

He was stubborn. A real hardhead. I could see how he would have convinced himself his actions were aboveboard. He sat there feigning disinterest, playing with a paper clip he had retrieved from the floor. He bent it into various shapes and sat back admiring his abstract sculptures. He wasn't giving an inch, so I decided to move in.

"Well, I figure I need to tell you how I know, Kelvin. You need to hear it. I know it because you'll take a situation in which it's obvious to others you act immorally, but you twist it on its head so that you're in a position of indignation. Then, once you've achieved that, you use a kind of reverse morality to make others believe they are doing something wrong toward you, when in fact it's you doing something wrong toward them."

He didn't bat an eyelid, remaining fixated on his paper clip. "Fucking psycho-babble," he mumbled.

He shouldn't have muttered; I knew he was paying attention.

"That being true, I'd say you probably allowed the victim to think she was to blame."

"She was."

"You just proved my point. Explain to me how this child is responsible for what you did."

Kelvin bent his clip into a straight length. "Easy," he replied aggressively.

"Then explain it to me. Start from the very first time she seduced you."

The fact I'd colluded with the possibility he was actually the victim engaged him, albeit on his terms.

"It was when she came to my swim school. We were in the pool. I was teaching her freestyle. I was holding her around the waist, and every time she moved her arm she brushed my penis."

"Did it occur to you she was brushing your penis because she was intent on learning how to swim and didn't even notice?" My delivery was soft; I wanted to suck him in.

He thought for an instant. "No, she knew she was doing it."

"Okay, let's say she did know. Let's say you're spot-on, that she was highly sexualized for her age and was intentionally brushing your penis. She's still nine years old. Why aren't you getting out of the pool, or at the very least moving away? I mean, that's a potentially dangerous scenario."

"I told her many times she was too young to be interested in me." It was an effort to convince me he was a man of integrity.

"But you stayed in the pool. She did it over and over again. Why didn't you get out or move away?"

"I was a bit confused at the time," he said.

I pretended I was in deep thought. "Were you erect?"

"No!" he shot back with too much protestation.

"So this girl is brushing against your penis with every stroke and you're not erect?"

"No, who would get erect from that?"

"Most men. It's a physical interaction with a part of their body that becomes stimulated by touch. So in knowing that, when it comes to a nine-year-old girl, the vast majority would get the hell out of there."

The way he looked at me, I could tell he thought he was onto something. "So you're admitting you would be aroused by a nine-year-old girl brushing your penis?"

He sat smiling victoriously; it didn't last long.

"No, Kelvin, I wouldn't hang around to find out. But you did."

"Well, I think you're way off there," he backpedalled.

"About?"

Suddenly his paper clip was fascinating again. "My motives—you're way off. I don't see it that way at all."

"Of course you don't. Like I said earlier, you twist things so you come out smelling like roses."

"Well, explain this one, then." His statement was matter-of-fact. He obviously thought he was onto a winner. "Why would she send me a text asking me to meet her on her morning jog so we could have sex in my car?"

"When was this?"

"When she was about thirteen."

"You mean after you'd groomed her for four years and manipulated her to believe she loved you and that you were going to be together forever?"

"I didn't groom her to believe she loved me."

I opened his file and hastily flicked through the content until I found the police transcript of the victim being interviewed. "Let me just read this for you."

I made sure to hold the page up for his full viewing pleasure. I began to read.

"Kelvin told me that I loved him. But he would say it's not like the same way you love your mom and dad, not like your swim coach. You love me like your boyfriend."

He had no answers, and consequently his paper clip became highly intriguing yet again.

"Then there's this," I declared, "where the victim says in a text message: 'Do you think we'll ever get married, baby?'"

He looked up eagerly. "That's what I've been telling you. *She* seduced *me!*"

"She was eleven at that point."

"And?"

"Show me an eleven-year-old that seeks out a thirty-seven-year-old man in the hope of getting married."

"Well, she did. You just read it."

"Yep, she did, based on the shit you fed her."

Kelvin looked perturbed. "Not true. She loved me of her own accord."

I backed off a little, allowing him some breathing space before I headed back into battle. I could tell he earnestly believed what he was saying. He actually believed this child loved him, seduced him, and had eventually played him. Just when he seemed settled, I dug in for another skirmish.

"I'm just thinking, Kelvin, if you weren't responsible, and it was all her doing, why did you have to hide everything?"

"I wasn't hiding anything."

"So when you bought her a mobile phone and told her to keep it hidden from her parents, that wasn't you hiding anything?"

"That was me being nice; it was a birthday present."

"So why tell her to hide it?"

"I didn't know if her parents would approve."

"Isn't that hiding it from them?"

"I don't think so."

He went back to his paper clip, and I went back to my corner of the metaphorical boxing ring. I figured I'd wait some more and then go in hard.

Ding! Ding!

"You didn't like it when she got a boyfriend, did you, Kelvin?"

"She was too young."

"What?" My response was more emotive than I intended.

He looked up from his paper clip modeling. "She was too young, way too young to understand what that boy was trying to get from her."

"But she was old enough to consider marrying you?"

"That was different. It was her idea. I simply went along with it. I didn't want to break her heart."

"If that's true, why would you be concerned? I mean, that boyfriend gave you an out."

"She was still in love with me."

His distortions were a serious problem. I tried a new angle. "You were jealous, so jealous you actually confronted him like a jilted lover, in the middle of a shopping mall."

"He was going to hurt her."

"It wasn't a real bright thing to do, given he didn't know about you at that point."

"See?!" he exclaimed. "She kept it hidden because she loved me!"

"No, she kept it hidden because she was incredibly ashamed."

Kelvin's face scrunched up. He was truly confused. "Ashamed of what?" he asked.

"Herself," I raised my voice. "Up until that point she had no concept of the degree you had manipulated her into a sexual relationship. She was hardly going to tell her boyfriend about it."

Kelvin became attentive to his paper clip once more. "I told you, she seduced me," he muttered under his breath.

"No," I said in harsh tone. He looked up. I made him keep eye contact. "That girl was learning to swim, Kelvin. And in your screwed-up head you took an innocent, accidental event to mean something entirely different."

He held onto his paper clip for dear life but didn't respond. He didn't go into his shell, and he didn't get angry. I hoped I'd gotten through. I continued, ensuring to keep my tone gentle.

"Think about what I just said for a minute, Kelvin. Just consider how much a man's thinking would be skewed to believe a child was responsible for all this."

He stared at me. For a fleeting moment I perceived he was seeing logic. "See, I knew you didn't like me."

And then it was gone.

TONY

"So you believe everything the police say, do you, John?"

He waited impatiently for a response. I probably would have offered something if he wasn't so demanding.

Tony was tall and thin, but not in a wiry way. He was gangly and soft–looking—the type who wouldn't be able to open a jar of tomato paste for his wife. He wasn't effeminate, but he wasn't what you would describe as manly either. He was elderly—about seventy—and had a crop of thick silver hair. He wore sneakers with brown trousers, what you might buy at a thrift shop when attending a '70s-themed party. His pants were pulled up high, very high—to the point his family jewels were visually unavoidable. He also wore an old flannelette cowboy shirt that capped the ensemble off "superbly."

"I can't believe a man of your supposed intelligence can fall for that." He was draining. "Don't you look at that crap and think 'this can't be right,' John?"

He was truly tiresome. "I trust my intuition," I replied unenthusiastically.

"Have you ever been wrong?" It wasn't so much a question as it was intended to insult me.

"Not when the feeling that I'm onto something is coming through loud and clear."

He scoffed and rolled his eyes. "You base my guilt on your feelings?"

"Pretty much," I lied. The evidence was irrefutable.

"That's unprofessional," he reprimanded.

"So I've been told." That part wasn't a lie.

"So you think I actually touched that little girl like some deviant, sick pervert?"

"Yep."

"You're a clever man, but you're way off on this occasion."

The oldest trick in the book: the reverse compliment.

"Nope."

Tony was getting frustrated with my lack of engagement.

"How can you be so sure to the point of arrogance?" he insisted.

That was my cue.

I smiled at him. "How can you be so delusional as to think I'd fall for your story?"

"Because it makes sense, it's logical, and it's the truth." He delivered the statement with the fervor of a patriot singing a national anthem.

"Yeah, the way you present it certainly makes it appear that way; however, the police version is quite a different proposition altogether, isn't it?"

"I was set up!" he yelped. Tony composed himself. "Surely you can see I was set up, John? Surely?" His voice now lowered for emphasis so as to try to instil doubt, to convince me that he may be the one case in a thousand the system got completely wrong.

I sat up in my chair. "Okay, let's go through the details of that day, and then you can explain to me this supposed setup?"

"I don't need to go over it again, John, I know what happened."

"Just humor me."

Tony rolled his eyes. He knew no amount of protesting would stop the forthcoming dissection.

"On the day in question," I started, "a father and his daughter arrive at your place to pick up a dollhouse they purchased from you on eBay?"

I looked at him to ensure he was paying attention and to gain confirmation so as to keep him accountable.

"Yes," Tony said with a degree of attitude.

"A dollhouse you had built?"

"Yes. I build lots of things."

"But mainly dollhouses."

He was wary. "Yes, and Joyce, my wife, makes the curtains and little bedspreads, and mats and things for them."

"So this little girl comes to your shed, where your dollhouses are stored, and her daddy carries it out to the car while you show this child all the other magnificent treasures you've created." I looked at him intensely. "How am I doing so far?"

"A little sarcastic, but otherwise all true to this point."

I nodded. "Anyway, after her daddy returns from the car, he collects his little girl and they head home."

I paused.

"*However,*" I accentuated, "Daddy does detect something wrong with the child, but he can't quite put his finger on it. He thinks, 'Gee, for a little girl who just got the dollhouse she begged for, she doesn't seem too happy.' He doesn't think too much of it and figures once he gets her home and she starts playing with it, she will come good."

"I presume," he said, somewhat grudgingly.

"However, the little girl is only visiting Daddy for the weekend, and then—out of nowhere—demands she go back to her mother's house. No amount of consoling or comforting works, so Daddy drops her at her mother's, unable to explain what the problem is."

Tony sat upright and nervously wrapped his fingers on the knee region of his brown trousers. I paused; he went to speak, but I held up my hand, gesturing that I was intending to continue.

"Mommy—being a police officer and bitter over her ex-husband's affair—suspects Daddy has done something untoward. She questions the little girl indirectly, but the child withdraws and won't talk."

"I wasn't there, so I'll take your wor—" he interrupted. I spoke over him.

"So Mommy decides to leave the questioning until bedtime, all the while having panic attacks in the belief that her ex-partner molested their daughter. Mommy eventually calls the child for a bath, and as she helps her daughter undress, notices bloodstains on the child's underwear. Mommy, understandably freaking out, calls her ex-partner to inform him he can expect her workmates to be on his doorstep within the hour—along with some other choice words and derogatory labels."

Tony jumped up from his chair just enough to be taller than me. "See! Right there!" he yelled as he pointed his finger. "There's the sting! It was him!"

I ignored him. "Upon hearing the ramblings of his ex-wife, and out of concern for his daughter, Daddy thinks back over the day, and in particular, his daughter's unexplainable mood alteration after visiting *you.*" I pointed at him for weight.

"Daddy then puts two and two together and recognizes you as having been the perpetrator. Without uttering a word to his current partner, he grabs a crowbar from his garage, jumps in his car, promptly smashes your door in, confronts you in your own home in front of Joyce, and proceeds to beat the shit out of you."

"Yes, covered his own arse very well there, didn't he?"

"Now, because you plead not guilty, you forced the child to testify. That brave little eight-year-old girl had to go through cross-examination, during which she undeniably and positively gave testimony that you inserted your fingers in her vagina while her father took the dollhouse to the car."

Tony sat back rigidly and folded his arms. "Don't be daft, John. He planted those ideas in her head. She was coached what to say in court."

Again, I ignored him. "The evidence from the expert at the hospital said, and I quote, 'An examination of the child revealed tearing of the hymen.'"

"Yes, I remember that. I watched her father look at the ground when they read that. He was so ashamed he—"

I continued. "The prosecution went on to say you had sold more than ten dollhouses online."

"Yes, it was a nice little sideline for Joyce and me in our retirement. Not that I can do it anymore. I'm not allowed."

I think he may have expected sympathy.

"But the police could not trace the purchasers, with the exception of one."

"Yes, I remember that lying bit—"

"A woman who claimed you showed a little too much interest in her child. So much so, she refused to take the dollhouse to the car on her own. Instead, she pretended it was too heavy, so that you would help her. But you insisted Joyce help her and the little girl stay with you to look at your other treasures." I looked at him squarely. "Sound familiar?"

Tony quickly broke eye contact, resumed his folded arm pose, and let out a patronizing sigh as he waved me away with his old, wrinkly hand.

"Luckily that woman had her intuitive radar working—kind of like me—and saved her little girl and herself a lot of heartache."

Tony sat brooding. "Pure speculation," he mumbled.

"Where there's smoke, there's fire," I immediately countered.

He assumed a less-defensive posture and reengaged. He liked that I'd answered him and was no longer ignoring his involvement.

"What a mantra to live by in your profession," he chastised. "Aren't you supposed to be scientific in your approach? Aren't you supposed to work with facts?"

"I am. The fact is simple: you've been found guilty in a court of law."

Tony sneered at me and went back to his arm-folding position. This time he crossed his feet too. He then produced a comb and slicked his hair, making sure to pay me no attention whatsoever. As he returned the comb to the pocket of his Western-style flannelette shirt, he gave it one last effort.

"Just so I know where I stand with you, can you tell me if you honestly think I'm guilty? I mean, using all logic and reasoning, you can honestly sit there and say, unreservedly, without any doubt, this man is guilty? Because I don't want to work with someone who thinks I'm guilty."

I let some time pass in order to ensure he paid the utmost attention to my answer.

"I'll go one further, Tony. I'll say you're not only guilty of this offense but most likely plenty of others."

"You can't say that!" he yelled, jumping to his feet.

I remained calm. "You insisted I tell you exactly what I think. So there it is."

My inaction made him return to his chair. "Well, I don't want to work with you if you believe that."

I looked at him quizzically. "What's to work on?"

"You're supposed to help me!" Tony demanded.

"With what?" I responded calmly.

"All this bullshit!"

"How am I supposed to help someone who doesn't take responsibility, who doesn't own up?"

He tried to stare me down. "I'll *never* own up," he said determinedly.

"I know."

He threw his hands in the air in exasperation. "So what's the point of all this bloody crap?"

I leaned forward into his space.

"Sometimes, Tony, it's not about what you get out of this. Sometimes it's about what I get out of it."

CHAPTER ELEVEN: THE SERIAL PEDOPHILE

"I never wonder to see men wicked,
but I often wonder to see them not ashamed."
~ Jonathan Swift

HENRY

"AND THAT'S IT," SAID HENRY as he folded his notes, put them in his pocket, and waited for feedback from the group.

His "disclosure" presentation had affected everyone in the room. The other offenders, my co-facilitator, and I sat in mesmerized silence with our jaws on the floor.

Henry remained awaiting some feedback, but I don't think anyone really knew what to say. Finally one of his fellow participants kicked the proceedings off. Kevin was an outspoken member of the group. A tall, muscular man doing time for a break-and-enter "gone wrong."

"Do we have to listen to this fuckin' shit?" he yelled, his eyes glazed over like a raging bull.

Henry turned quickly to look at Kevin. His facial expression suggested he had no idea why his fellow participant would have issue with what he had just presented. I motioned Kevin to direct the question to Henry.

Kevin told him, "Seriously, dude, that was fucked! I'm not gonna sit here and listen to bullshit like that when I had to bare my soul to everyone in this room."

Henry looked at Kevin, then at me, and then back at Kevin. He was at a loss as to why he was being targeted in such an aggressive manner. I didn't intervene. I wasn't going to rescue Henry. It was time for him to sink or swim.

"Sorry, Kevin, I don't know what you mean," Henry said in a soft tone. He was quite an effeminate man. He wore his graying hair in a long ponytail. His skin looked soft, especially around his eyes. He looked a peaceful, gentle soul and spoke with a certain articulation to his words that suggested he may have attended allocution lessons as a child.

"That's the problem," said Kevin in a manner suggesting Henry was an imbecile.

Henry still wasn't getting it.

"I agree with Kev on this one." The support came from Terry, an older gentleman incarcerated for the sexual molestation of his granddaughter.

Henry again looked at me to come to his rescue. It wasn't going to happen. He then turned his attention to Terry.

"Well, I must have *really* said something wrong because no one else has been reprimanded like this in here," he whined. He was trying to play the victim to manipulate me into becoming involved.

"You do that every time," said Kevin distastefully. "Do you know you do that? Every single time you get confronted about anything to do with your offenses, you turn it around like you're the fucking victim. I'm over listening to your bullshit!"

"My offenses? What are you talking about?" Henry seemed lost.

"Forget it; you're a dickhead. You'll never get it."

I intervened. "Kev, I think you need to explain it to Henry. It's obvious he's not getting your point, and I think it would be highly beneficial for him to understand."

Kevin sighed and shook his head as Henry sat waiting for an explanation.

"Look, dude, just before when I told you I was sick of listening to your bullshit, you immediately started on about how you were reprimanded."

Henry still looked blank. "Well I *was* reprimanded. The way you spoke to me after all the effort I put into writing and presenting my disclosure was quite frankly insulting."

Kevin looked at me and rolled his eyes. "What's the point?"

"To help him, he needs it. He needs to get your point because you are spot-on," I urged.

Kevin turned his attention back to Henry. "Look, it's like this: whenever anyone has something to say about you that you don't like, you take it as criticism and turn everything around so you seem to be the victim."

"I don't think that's very fair," replied Henry.

"You just did it! Right there!" shouted Kevin emphatically. The rest of the group began laughing. It was obvious to everyone but Henry. He took their jest as derision and got even more defensive.

"Oh yeah, all of you, just laugh. That's really helping. You call this therapy?" he asked me.

I didn't have to reply; Kevin did my work for me. "You just did it again!"

I could see Henry becoming flustered. He wanted to speak but feared that opening his mouth would give Kevin further ammunition.

"Kev," I said, "perhaps it might help if you use an example from Henry's presentation. If you could link what you're trying to tell him to something he said in his disclosure?"

"Pfft, how many fucking examples do you want?" said Kevin as he laughed with the participant sitting next to him. "Okay," he began, "here's one for ya. You said during your presentation that you were charged with sexually interfering with fifteen different boys all around eight years of age?"

"That's correct," Henry confirmed.

"Yeah," said Kevin, nodding as he prepared to deliver his knock-out blow. "And then you went on to say—and I quote—'I can honestly say, I never once initiated the sexual contact with my victims.' What a load of shit!"

The room went silent. Henry sat thinking about Kevin's comment. He looked confused, as if he were waiting for more, a possible punch line.

"And?" he asked.

The group began laughing.

"Are you seriously *that* dense?" Kevin responded. He looked at me. "Seriously, John, seriously, he can't be that dumb?"

"It's not that he's dumb, Kev. What you are witnessing is *exactly* how he was able to commit his offenses." My words seemed to be somewhat of an epiphany for Kevin. He suddenly became quiet.

"Henry," said Terry, reinvolving himself, "you show me an eight-year-old kid who initiates sex with adults."

"I could show you fifteen of them!"

"No, Henry, that's complete and utter bullshit. Kids don't do that." Terry's approach was a little less confronting for Henry, and he seemed to be at least attempting to understand.

Terry continued. "All right, watch this, Henry." Terry looked at the rest of us. "Put up your hand if you think eight-year-old boys willingly seek sex with adult men."

All hands remained lowered. Terry reached over to Henry, grabbed him by the wrist, and put his hand in the air. "Now, Henry," he said, "there are ten people in this room. Nine disagree with what you're saying. Do you honestly think all nine of us can be so far off the mark?"

Henry, possibly for the first time in his life, didn't defend himself.

"I can see why all of you think that," he said sincerely, "but it's just not my experience."

The group let out a simultaneous dejected sigh. It was as if they were waiting in expectation that Henry would suddenly have his eyes opened. When it didn't happen, they collapsed in disappointment.

"Let's go back to the start, Henry," I suggested.

"Why do I have to go back to the start? No one else has had to do that after their disclosure."

"You're doing it again," said Kevin in frustration. "Fuck me, it's like talking to a brick wall."

"If other people have the distortions you have, they too will be going back to the start," I said firmly. "Now, the most recent boy you offended against. Tell me how you came to engage with him sexually, right from the beginning. How did you meet him?"

Henry was annoyed. "I just went through all that." He looked at the other group members for support; it didn't come.

Kevin put his hands to his face. "You're doing it again," he said as he slapped his forehead. If it wasn't for the situation, it would have been comical.

Henry gave in. He looked at me. "The boy was in the soccer team I coached."

"Does anyone want to take things from here?" I threw to the group.

"I will," said Wayne enthusiastically. He was around forty years old and had a massive reputation in the prison system as a heavyweight. He had committed some horrendous crimes and personally considered his latest offense, a rape, "a blight on his criminal history." He loathed sex offenders. Wayne was a tough man. Up until this point he had not said much during his participation in the program. I think I was more surprised than Henry when he offered to give some input.

"Go ahead," I said half-wincing at what might be forthcoming.

Wayne turned to Henry. "I'm guessing you're not married?"

Henry gulped. "No," he said, as if it were an odd question.

"And I'm guessing you don't have kids of your own?"

"No, no, I don't." Henry was nervous.

Wayne looked at him with suspicion. "Then why the fuck are you coaching a kids' soccer team?"

It was certainly a good point. Why would a man of Henry's age with no attachment to any child in a sporting team want to coach little boys and submit themselves to such stress?

"I just love kids, and I wanted to help out," said Henry in his soft, gentle tone.

Wayne nodded. I could tell he didn't believe Henry. His next question proved it. "You don't look very athletic. You look as soft as butter, to be honest. I can't imagine you ever played a sport in your life."

"I didn't," Henry admitted.

"So you never played the game in your life, you have no kid on the team, and then you go and coach a bunch of brats out of the goodness of your heart?" Wayne chided.

Kevin tacked on to Wayne's comments. "Yeah, he's right," he said, pointing at Wayne. "I know I wouldn't go and coach a bunch of kids if I didn't have one of my own playing in the team."

"Oh, so I do something good, and it's twisted to be evil," said Henry as he fell freely back into his victim stance.

"Doing it again," said Kevin.

Wayne waved his finger at me as if asking permission to involve himself again. I returned a hand gesture implying he didn't need to request my approval to speak.

"Oi!" he said to get Henry's attention. "You just said we tried to make something good you did into being something evil. Right?"

"Yes, well not you. Him," Henry said, pointing at Kevin.

"Whatever," said Wayne. "The fact is, you took advantage of being the coach of those kids. In my book, that's wrong."

"Coaching them is wrong?" Henry scoffed.

I could see Wayne becoming angry at the perception of having been disrespected. "You fucked one of them, didn't you?" The words were delivered with venom beyond any poison known to man.

"No, I never *fucked* anyone," responded Henry. It was interesting to watch two people from opposite ends of the prison hierarchy go toe-to-toe. I attempted to simmer the situation.

"Let's try to stay on track here, guys. Let's ditch the insults. Henry, I want to ask you something: If coaching that boys' soccer team was all about your good heart, why did you choose them?"

"What do you mean?"

"Why didn't you coach the under-fifteen girls?"

Henry began to squirm. He didn't like the question, and he certainly reacted to it with a certain uncomfortableness that both Wayne and Kevin picked up on. Henry reeled back in his seat while the latter two sat forward waiting for a response.

"Just circumstance, I guess," he reluctantly answered. "There was no one else to do it, so I offered."

"And how did you find out about the position being vacant and no one wanting to take the role on?"

"From one of the boys' fathers at Naval Cadets."

Kevin burst out laughing. It wasn't a genuine laugh; it was a disbelieving jeer. "What the fuck?!" he stated.

Henry looked at him oddly.

"Isn't Naval Cadets where young kids go to learn about being a sailor?" asked Terry.

"Yes," said Henry.

"How many associations were you involved with where there were young boys around?" Terry sought suspiciously.

"Just the soccer team and the cadets."

"So if that father had said there was a position vacant as a coach of the under-fifteen girls' team, would you have volunteered your services?" asked Terry.

Henry feigned being thoughtful. He put his index finger to his chin and looked toward the ceiling. It was truly a pathetic attempt. "No, I don't think I would have. I don't relate as well to teenagers as I do younger boys."

"More like you aren't attracted to girls," stated Kevin with sarcasm.

"So you're saying I was only involved in kids' soccer and naval cadets because I was attracted to young boys?" Henry asked Kevin. His question wasn't a sincere effort to understand himself. It was stated with an intention to somehow highlight how far removed Kevin was from the truth.

"Fuck, dude, that's not just what I'm saying; that's what everyone in this room is saying!"

"He's right. That *is* what everyone in here thinks," Wayne added. "I wanna know where you molested this kid."

"Why's that important?" asked Henry.

"Because you left it out of your presentation," replied Wayne.

I found his thoughts insightful. I have always believed the details offenders leave out are the most important variables because they are the parts they don't want you to know. They are the factors that potentially have the most value in regard to rehabilitation.

"It happened in my home," said Henry, in a way designed to suggest he had nothing to hide.

"How does an eight-year-old kid come to be in your home?" asked Kevin.

"There were always kids at my house on the weekends. We would have a blast!"

"Doing what?" asked Wayne.

"Playing Xbox and other games," replied Henry.

My co-facilitator smiled at me. "Yes, Henry, can you please tell the group about some of those other games?"

Her input roused the other participants. They waited with bated breath for Henry's response.

"Just normal kid's games. Hide-and-seek and stuff like that."

"Well, I wouldn't exactly say it was a 'normal' version of hide-and-seek," said my co-facilitator.

"We were naked," said Henry. "Big deal! Human bodies are nothing to be ashamed of."

"Dude, seriously, you're really fucked up," said Kevin.

"There's no point telling him he's fucked up. You need to help him understand," I directed at Kevin.

"He's beyond help," argued Wayne. I agreed. It seemed to me Henry was an exclusive pedophile through and through. The best we could hope for was to help him see he was a threat to children. We were never going to get him to stop being attracted to them.

Terry took up the challenge. "When you had this kid over at your house, and you were running around naked playing games, how did it come about that you touched him up?"

"We were lying on my bed," said Henry.

"Naked?" asked Terry. I was relieved Wayne and Kevin were silent. They had done their job.

"Yes."

"And then what happened?"

"We played another game. I would tickle a certain spot on his body, and then he would do the same to me. He liked it. They all liked it."

"Then what would happen?"

"I would eventually become erect and, I don't know, the children would be fascinated, and it would go from there."

"So a short version of the story is something like this. You met this particular kid at Naval Cadets. His dad told you about a coaching job on a soccer team for boys of the age you like. You took up the position, had the kid over for a weekend, played your games with him, got naked with him, lay on the bed with him, played your tickle game with him, then molested him?"

"I didn't molest him, per se. He touched my penis first."

Henry's inability to own the more overtly sexual part of his offenses left Terry gobsmacked. He seemed unable to process Henry's capacity to remain rigid in his beliefs in spite of the fact he had done everything to challenge as much.

"That short version of your offense Terry just gave you," I said, "what do you think about that, Henry?"

"It's an accurate account of how I came to be involved with boys."

"Would you describe it as grooming?"

"Grooming to what end?"

I needed to take him away from the emotion attached to his thought processes surrounding his offending. "Let's imagine for a minute that the children you offended against didn't initiate the sexual contact. Let's imagine that it was actually you who did that; you were the one who initiated it right back at the start when you became involved in Naval Cadets, etc. etc. etc. If that was the case, what would you think then?"

Henry looked at me strangely. "God," he said, "that would make me a monster."

The room went deathly silent. Not a word was spoken as Henry sat contemplating his own definition of his own behavior. No one rescued him.

I'd hoped it would be the beginning of a paradigm shift. It wasn't. He left the program no further progressed than when he started. His attraction to boys and his uncompromising need to remain fixed in his belief that he was a loving man with a heart of gold means he will forever remain a risk.

MICHAEL

Michael had been married for forty-five years. He was a retired police officer and took up residence in a small coastal caravan park. He and his wife leased a cabin and were extremely well liked by the other residents, until they discovered his secret . . .

"From what I've read, I'm guessing there are a lot of offenses of which you've escaped detection," I stated. I never really expect an offender to offer up more information in making such comments—although, it has happened. I am simply attempting to ensure they're aware I'm not the type of psychologist to willingly accept every word they offer. I find they often get nervous and begin to give away many "tells" when engaging in the game. As I've said, I'll do whatever it takes to get the information.

"No, that's it. Just the ones I've been done for," replied Michael. I could tell he was lying. I kept staring at him in silence. He was uncomfortable, and I wanted to wait and see what his next comment would be.

"Best to be honest about these things," he said.

"Why's that?" I asked.

The question took him by surprise. "Huh?"

"Why would it be best in your position to be honest? I know I wouldn't be. I'd be lying through my teeth."

He swallowed hard. "Uh, I don't know. I just think honesty is the best policy."

"I find it interesting you say that."

"Why's that?" he asked confidently.

"Because if you truly believed it, you wouldn't be here."

Michael shuffled his weight in his chair. He was obese and obviously diabetic judging by the clots in his legs. He gave a nervous cough and wiped his mouth with his handkerchief; the job was insufficient, as he left residue spittle at the corners.

"I used to be a police officer, you know."

I looked at him strangely. I supposed he wanted me to think him a decent person at one point in his life. However, from what I had read in his file, I suspected Michael's offending dated way back and that he had likely been interfering with young girls as a policeman. His comment made me think I had adopted the wrong approach with him. He needed his ego stroked, not to be challenged. I adapted.

"Did you like your work?" I asked respectfully.

He looked relieved I hadn't pursued the prior statement about his integrity. Little did he know I was buttering him up to squeeze as much information out of him as possible.

"Yes, I loved it. I had to retire though. I was injured on duty."

He wanted me to know he was some kind of hero. "What happened?"

"I was shot during a robbery." He lifted up his T-shirt to reveal a scar on his large abdomen.

"Looks nasty."

"It didn't tickle." He laughed. I pretended to be engrossed in his tale.

"So, how does a person go from being a hero to being here?" I said in reference to his incarceration.

Michael looked at the floor, then he glanced at me slightly to reveal his glum look—the one unremorseful offenders give to show you how sorry they are. "I don't know," he said with a sigh. "I just lost the plot a little, I guess."

His offenses indicated he had far from lost the plot; he was a specialist at his craft.

"What happened?"

"I just started drinking too much," he said with a look of despair. The entire act was designed to make me feel sorry for him, to perceive him as a fallen star.

"Well, yeah, I suppose the stress of being a police officer would drive anyone to drink."

"Yes, for sure, it's a tough job at times." He liked that I was colluding with his rationalization that alcohol was a determining factor in his offending. The reality is, alcohol is rarely ever a cause of offending. You get the odd case in which someone has absolutely no clue what they were doing and commit a sexual offense, but in most instances, it is merely a means to lower inhibitions to engage in secret desires.

"How did you like living in the van park? I'm sure you would have run into some of your old 'customers' in a place like that?"

Michael laughed falsely. "Not where we were. It was quite a nice place. There was the odd riffraff that would come through, but mostly I enjoyed it there."

"Do you still keep in touch with anyone?"

"No, not now. Not since all this."

That was my sign to slowly integrate his offending into the discussion. "I noticed in your file all the victims were children who resided in the van park."

He nodded. I remained quiet so as to maneuver him into being the one to bring up his past.

"Poor old Margaret, she's had to go through all this." Margaret was his wife, but he had no concern for what she was going through. He simply was trying to manipulate me into discussing his pitiful existence.

"Did Margaret know the children too?"

"Yes, very well. They were always over at our place. She would bake for them and give them things," he said chirpily.

That's how you earned the trust of the parents; a nice old lady baking for all the kids was the perfect ruse.

"Would they ever come to visit you—as in, only you?"

"Oh sure, all the time. The kids called me 'Vandad.' It was my nickname around the park. Margaret was 'Vanma,'" he recalled with fondness.

"I noticed in the police transcripts they mentioned that the veranda railing of your cabin was lined with toys?"

"Oh yes, they were just McDonald's Happy Meal toys. I kept them for my grandson."

"Why would you keep them on the railing?"

"It was just easier to keep them there. The cabin was quite small, and I didn't want to upset Margaret with clutter."

"But if they were for your grandson, why didn't he take them home?"

"His mother wouldn't let him. She said that because Grandad had bought them, they had to stay at Grandad's house."

"Yeah, I can understand that. When you've got kids, things can get pretty untidy around the house in the toy department." I pretended I'd swallowed his story.

"I bet the kids at the van park loved them."

"Yes, they'd all want to stop in and play with Vandad's toys." He laughed jovially.

"Did Margaret go out much?"

"Oh yes, Margaret is quite the social butterfly. She and the old girls at the park would go to bingo at least twice a week. I'd drive them there and pick them up after they had finished their afternoon tea."

And therefore be fully aware she wasn't going to show up in the middle of molesting a little girl.

I needed to deliver my next comment tactfully. Subsequently, I masked my intent with a dejected facial expression and sadness in my voice. "I guess that's when the offenses took place? When Margaret was at bingo?"

Michael nodded his feigned remorseful nod.

"So you would be drinking, and that's how it happened?" I knew he hadn't been drinking. I said it so he would latch on to an excuse and give me more information than he intended.

"Yes, I'd be pretty drunk and wouldn't really know what I was doing," he said as he shook his head in what can only be defined as a B-grade acting attempt.

"Like when you would bring the child in the cabin and show them pornography on the television?" I asked in my dejected tone.

He nodded.

"Where would you watch it?"

"I'd lie down with them on our bed and watch kid's television shows. Because I'd be drunk, I'd forget the girl was there and put a 'rudey' on. By the time I remembered the little girl was still in bed with me, it'd be too late."

"What do you mean by 'too late'?"

"They would have been watching it for a good portion of time."

I looked at him like he was the victim. "What would they do?" I asked woefully.

"Just sit and watch, and because I'd forgotten they were there, I'd be naked and having a bit of a feel of the old fellow downstairs."

"Yeah, I can see how that could happen," I lied, making myself nauseated in the process. "So I assume you would start touching them?"

"Yeah, I often got it in my head that I was touching Margaret. You know? Like it was our bed, and because I was so drunk I'd forget it wasn't her."

"You must have realized at some point that it was a child?" I offered gently.

"Yeah, I'd shit myself," he said, clearly feigning.

"I can imagine!"

We both sat for a time "lamenting" his lost life as a hero due to the natural course of progression to his alcohol abuse. "Would you ask the children to keep it quiet?"

"Yeah," he said miserably. "I never threatened them or anything. I'd just explain that Vandad had made a big mistake."

"Oh really? I thought I read you actually told a couple of them you would stop being their Vandad if your secret ever got out." I couldn't help myself.

"Oh yeah, well, I was really drunk on those occasions, so I could have said anything."

"You must have really liked to drink to offend that many times."

"Yeah, I did. I'm quite ashamed of how much I used to drink, and I've told Margaret that when I get out of prison, I won't be touching another drop ever again."

I had by now ascertained that Michael's level of distortion relative to his sexual offending and desire for little girls was extreme. I decided to terminate the interview, as I wanted to wait for him to begin participating in a program before challenging him head-on. I did, however, want him to know he wasn't dealing with a novice.

As we were waiting to exit through opposite doors, I turned and looked at him. "Hey, Michael," I said.

"Yes?" he replied, leaning on his walking stick and looking at me through the bottoms of his granny goggles.

"I was just thinking. You said you were really, really drunk every time these offenses occurred, right?"

He nodded.

"As in blind, rotten drunk? Barely able to function?" I clarified.

He nodded. "Blind," he said with enthusiasm. "Absolutely rotten, all right."

As he finished his sentence, the buzzer on the doors went off, indicating the magnetic force had been released and we could exit. "Yeah, I thought that's what you said," I stated. "Makes me wonder how the hell you were able to pick Margaret up from bingo."

ROY

The best way I can describe Roy is to liken him to a snake in the grass. Interacting with him was trying—not only due to his cunning and deceit but also because he was highly intelligent and convincing. Roy was the type of offender who loved playing the game as much as I do. He was always trying to outsmart and outmaneuver me.

Roy had hundreds of offenses, possibly even thousands. He was a virtuoso and would literally spend months formulating his modus operandi. He admitted to me that he would prey on vulnerable children by selecting the ones he thought were easy pickings. These were the children with problems at home and no friends. He showed them what he defined as "love," and in return he got sexual favors.

"How can you say you know you won't offend ever again?" I asked as I held up page after page of Roy's criminal history.

"I've turned my life around. I'm a Christian now," he said, smiling as he tapped his pocket Bible.

"And?" I moved right along. I'd heard that one many times before.

"What do you mean 'and'?" he retorted defensively.

I liked the fact I had got under his skin a little. "How does being a Christian preclude you from future risk of recidivism?"

"That's pretty obvious," he said smugly.

"Is it?"

"Yeah, if you're a Christian, you can't sin like that. It's against the rules."

"Really?" I asked with a touch of sarcasm. "I see plenty of cases in the newspapers about priests who sexually abuse kids."

"They aren't Christian, then, are they?"

"I'm sure they'd identify as Christian if I were to ask them. They'd just see themselves as sinners."

Roy sat glaring at me. "Why are you attacking my religion?"

His question awakened me to the prospect that I was "winning." He had reverted to morally based arguments to hide from my probing. "I'm not attacking it. I just don't see how it lowers your risk."

Roy became angry. "Of course it lowers my risk. If I live by the principles, then I'm absolutely no risk."

"Yes, exactly, Roy, *if* you live by the principles."

"What's that supposed to mean?"

"It means there is no guarantee you will always live by the principles of Christianity."

He made a snorting sound and simultaneously rolled his eyes. "I can guarantee you I will always live by the principles."

"Really? You can guarantee me?"

"Yes," he nodded. "One hundred percent."

I knew what he was saying was untrue. It was too idealistic. I needed to think of a way to show him he wasn't deceiving me with his newfound fundamentalism.

"When was the last time you masturbated?" I asked.

He looked suspicious. "Why?"

"Just curious," I lied. I was setting him up.

Roy eyed me dubiously. "About three weeks ago," he said. I thought he was probably lying. His past suggested his sex drive was incredibly high, and

I perceived he would be masturbating more often than once every three weeks. However, the quantity was irrelevant in terms of the point I was about to make.

"So, given that we have established you are exclusively attracted to pre-pubescent boys, what did you think about while you were masturbating?"

"That's different." He panicked. He knew he had been snared.

"How?" I demanded.

"We are all, to some degree, tempted by our desires." The manner in which he delivered his philosophical repartee seemed to make him think he was wise, like he was some ancient seer.

"But isn't masturbation a sin?"

"Yes, of course," he admitted with poise.

"So then you sinned. You didn't live in accordance with the Christian principles you claim you will one hundred percent always maintain."

"I didn't say I was perfect. That's the blessing of God's grace. He gave his only-begotten son to atone for our sins."

"I'm fully aware of the design of the plan. It's just counter to what you were saying before. Anyway, you didn't answer my question."

"Which question are you seeking an answer for?"

I couldn't believe his phrasing; he had seen too many Charlton Heston movies.

"I want to know what you were thinking about when you were masturbating. It can't have been a woman; you don't find them attractive."

"What does it matter what I was thinking about?" he asked warily. "I sinned in masturbating. The content matters not."

"It matters in the context of what you are saying about your perceived future level of risk."

He thought for a moment, then shook his head. "I don't see the relevance." His answer wasn't the result of analysis of his thinking; it was the result of trying to escape the trap I had set.

"Your reluctance to answer the question leads me to believe you were thinking about a past offense. Which one was it?" I knew he would go for the least "damaging" of his crimes—the one he thought was the least incriminating of himself as a deviate. He would most definitely overlook the offenses involving the abduction and rape of boys.

"The boy who lived with me," he offered slyly.

"I don't think you've told me about that one. How old was he?"

"Fourteen."

Minus two, I thought. Roy liked them a tad younger.

"And this boy, he lived with you?"

"For a while; he was a street kid I took in. I met him at my dealer's house. After a while he came to trust me."

"How?"

"I'd spend a lot of time with him talking about the problems he had with his parents and stuff. I gave him a shoulder to cry on occasionally."

I was envisaging how Roy would have masqueraded as the cool, caring, adult friend. He would have played the role expertly. That's why when you deal with "the best," you have to be an expert at subterfuge yourself.

"So basically you exploited him?"

"If you want to put it that way." He shrugged.

"I'm not putting it any way. I imagine if you're now a Christian, you would have to own your past in order to repent of it and obtain forgiveness?"

"Yeah, of course."

I'd trapped Roy again. "So did you exploit him or not?"

"Yeah, I guess so, but that's all in the past." His response was void of any empathy, remorse, or shame.

"So when he came to live with you, how long did it take for the situation to turn sexual?"

"Not long," he said, dodging.

"How long?" I demanded.

"I don't know," he said indignantly. "About a week."

"Where did he sleep?"

"With me, in my bed."

There was little evidence to suggest Roy had even considered how he'd likely made a mess of this child's life. He appeared oblivious to the possibility that the child might not look back on the experience with fondness, if it even mattered at all what the child thought or felt.

"So you saw the situation as if you two were a couple?"

His silence was indicative that the answer was in the affirmative.

"How did you convince him to stay?" Roy wasn't exactly the best-looking of men, and I assumed there must have been something in it for the boy.

"I gave him an endless supply of drugs," he said blithely.

"So it wasn't a relationship at all. You manipulated him through his addiction."

Roy turned away from me, folded his arms, and crossed his legs. "Why do we have to go over this? I've moved on in my life since then."

"So you think you can just get baptized, announce Jesus as your Lord and Savior, and all is forgiven?"

He looked up with a smile. "That's how the miracle of forgiveness works," he said. "Besides, how long is a man expected to feel bad about himself?"

"I wonder what all your victims and their families would say to that."

He looked at me as though he had never considered their perspective. It was highly likely Roy had never felt bad about his past. His next comment proved his callousness. "My personal relationship with God is not their concern or yours."

"That's where you're wrong," I hit back. "It is my concern. You don't want to discuss your past, which means you can't have a sound understanding of why you did the things you did. Furthermore, if you were to quit Christianity tomorrow, the fact you have nothing to fall back on puts you in the high-risk category."

He refrained from responding to my statement. He didn't like that I wouldn't settle for his faith-based strategy to end his sex crimes. While Roy might have had faith in his turning over of a new leaf, I certainly wasn't prepared to put my faith in Roy.

"Are you still attracted to boys?" I asked.

Again he was cautious of the motive behind my question. "Yes, but I control the temptation."

"How do you control it?"

"I rebuke the thoughts in the name of Jesus Christ."

"So what if you don't have Jesus?"

He shook his head at me condescendingly and gave a little chuckle. "I will *always* have Jesus."

I started giving deeper thought as to why Roy might be embarking on a new life. His past was littered with instances whereby he would weave in and out of different lifestyles to gain access to children. It was possible church was yet another disguise.

"Do you attend church?" I asked.

"Yes, every week. I also attend Bible study class midweek, and I fellowship with other members as often as possible."

"Are there any boys of interest to you at church?"

"Not really," he lied.

"'Not really' isn't an answer. Is it yes or no?"

"Not in the way you're thinking." He paused. "You think I'm sexually attracted to them."

I decided to be honest. "Yeah, I do."

He looked at me as if to say I didn't know what I was talking about.

"Do you talk to them?" I asked.

"No, I avoid them."

"Why?"

"Temptation. I don't want to be in that predicament."

He knew he was already *in that predicament* simply by being in their presence. I designed another trap. "So you do it to avoid potential sin?"

"Yes."

I smiled. "But you're already sinning by masturbating and thinking about your past victims."

"But I'm not hurting anyone," he shot back.

He was conniving. He would have run rings around the people in his program, quite likely inclusive of the facilitators.

"Like I said before, Roy, it's contrary to your ideals about living a guaranteed Christian principled existence. The way you talk, you think your pedophilia can be changed, that it's a choice."

"It is!"

"Really? So you think that you will eventually find adult women sexually appealing?"

His face had a slight repulsed air about it. He was in no way known to be attracted to females. "No," he said after some time, "but I will be able to make an emotional connection."

"Without sexual intimacy?"

"Yes. Relationships aren't all about sex, you know?" he said in his sagely way that was designed to make me look like an ill-informed heathen.

Got ya, I thought.

I waited a little while to gain composure. I was excited by the prospect of where my next question would lead. "So then, Roy, how would you get your sexual needs met?"

"I wouldn't need them met."

I couldn't wait to get the question out. "Then why do you still masturbate?"

He may as well have begun looking under the table for an answer because the expression on his face was priceless with regard to searching his brain for a response that could get him out of this one.

"It's a progressive thing. I will get there eventually," he said, trying to convince me.

There was an ensuing silence. His brain was working overtime in an effort to find an answer that would cover his tracks. I could tell he thought he'd come up with something of worth as a subtle smile leaked across his face.

"It's no different than being an alcoholic," he said. "You don't have to drink even though the temptation exists."

The look on his face suggested he thought his analogy held some brilliance.

"But alcoholics understand they have an addiction," I explained. "Even after twenty years of non-drinking, they still refer to themselves as alcoholics. Will you still refer to yourself as a pedophile in twenty years?"

"No," he stated emphatically.

"Why not?"

"Because I won't be one in twenty years."

"But everything you say about your offending—your sexual attractions and your fantasies—involves young boys."

"So?"

"Doesn't that infer you're a pedophile? Doesn't that imply you will always have those attractions, and if so, doesn't that suggest you will always be a pedophile?"

"Not if I'm refraining from sex with children."

"So in your view, if you were heterosexual but didn't have sex with the opposite gender, that means you aren't heterosexual?"

His face went blank. He was running out of hiding spots. "I wouldn't know," he said. "That analogy doesn't apply to me."

I looked at him distrustfully. "C'mon, Roy, you understand my use of it."

"I guess," he grudgingly admitted.

"So answer the question."

"I guess you'd still be heterosexual," he replied testily. "I don't care what you say; I'm a changed man."

"How? You still fantasize about young boys. You even fantasize about past offenses! Where is the change?"

"So I can't change?" It wasn't a question of a man feeling helpless; it was an accusation intended to make me feel guilty for my lack of faith in him. I wasn't falling for it.

"You can reduce your risk, but you won't change your attractions. The thing that concerns me is that you try to repress and conceal those attractions. By doing that, they aren't open for discussion. So let's take Christianity out of the equation for a minute. Let's say you don't have it. How would you stop from re-offending?"

"But I do have Christianity," he replied pretentiously.

"Hypothetically," I insisted.

"I can't say because I don't think of my life outside of my beliefs."

"So in your mind you don't think you need intervention, you just need God?"

"Hallelujah!" he shouted. "He finally gets it."

"I'll tell you what I get," I said quietly enough for him to pay the utmost attention. "You'll always be high risk."

ARTHUR

Arthur was a small man; he stood no more than five feet high. He had snow-white hair that was as coarse as a wire brush and a blotchy red face that was likely the result of years of drinking top-shelf spirits. Arthur was approximately sixty-five years old when I met him. He was in prison and had already served ten years of a fifteen-year sentence.

I found Arthur to be strange—not in an eccentric way; he was just plain peculiar. In hindsight, his strangeness was possibly the result of him appearing somewhat normal in general conversation, but as soon as the discussion centered on his offending, he morphed into a different person. He became unable to repress his thoughts. There was nothing off-limits in respect to discussing his offenses. I never got the impression Arthur became aroused during the sessions. At least he didn't get off talking about his "feats." He seemed more excited by gauging my reactions to what he was saying.

Arthur had an extremely long history of offending against little girls. His age range was anywhere between three and six years old. His victims included grandchildren, nieces, the children of his friends, and on the odd occasion a child he had no connection to. I presume he had hundreds of victims spanning decades. When the whistle was finally blown, family members came out of the woodwork recounting their childhood abuse at the hands of Arthur. In all, he was convicted on 212 charges. What interested me most about the old man was his modus operandi; it was different from any offender I'd ever encountered . . .

"So let me get this straight," I said, stunned in response to Arthur's revelation. "You would commit your offenses in the presence of the children's parents?"

Arthur sat clasping his hands together and grinning like a little goblin. He nodded enthusiastically in glee that he had managed, yet again, to make my head spin.

"No, seriously, Arthur—are you bullshitting me or what?"

"Nope, no way, John; it's the truth. I swear. That's how I would do it."

There was no game-playing with Arthur. He wanted me to know everything. I sat dumbfounded resting my head in my hand. "How the hell did you get away with this?"

He scratched both his cheeks at once. Every movement he made was rapid; he was like a terrier hunting rats. In a blink his arms were back resting in his lap, his hands clasped again and his eyes darting all over the room. Arthur also spoke fast. I had to pay close attention to understand what he was saying because he talked as though periods and commas hadn't been invented.

"Easy, John, it was easy. Doing it in front of the parents actually made it easier to get away with."

"How do you work that out?"

"They wouldn't suspect a thing. I could sit at the kitchen table with them and have a coffee and a chat. Then I'd pick their little girl up and put her in my lap. I would sit there talking to her mommy or daddy while touching her vagina," he said with delight.

"Would they do anything? Say anything?"

"The parents?" he asked. Before I had time to clarify, he was off and running with his next sentence. "No, John. They wouldn't say anything; they wouldn't know. Oh, you mean the little girls. No, John, they wouldn't say anything. Sometimes they would squirm a bit when they felt my finger touch their vagina."

I was still reeling from that mouthful when Arthur started up again.

"The little girls didn't think I was doing anything wrong because most of them knew me very well and they trusted me, so I was pretty confident they wouldn't say anything because they wouldn't really be thinking I had sexually abused them. I think most of them liked it anyway."

"What?" I asked before he could launch into his next spiel.

"Yes, John, most of them liked it," he repeated as he sat watching me intently.

"How do you work that out?"

"They never stopped wanting to sit on my lap. If it was my granddaughter, I could touch her anywhere between five to ten times a week. If she hadn't liked it, she wouldn't have come back for more."

"Maybe they simply had no clue what the hell you were doing?"

Arthur giggled like a naughty sprite. "Oh, I don't think so, John. I'm pretty sure they liked it."

"Do you like the idea they liked it?"

"Yes, John, I would be highly aroused by the thought. Sometimes I would even blow a load in my pants sitting there talking to their parents."

"What did you like about it?"

His answer took longer than normal. He seemed to be sincerely reaching into himself to explain to me the delight his offending gave him. "It was a few things, John. It was the feel of their bald little vaginas, the smoothness," he said as he demonstrated with hand movements. "It was also the idea of doing it in front of their parents, and what I liked best was seeing what they would do. How they would respond to what I was doing. Whether they would squirm and like it."

His last revelation made sense. His interest in their reactions intrigued him, and our current conversation was a similitude of those moments. Arthur loved watching my reactions.

"But the parents were your own flesh and blood." I reasoned in the hope there would be an inkling of remorse.

"I liked it too much to care, John. I liked that they had no idea. That was all part of the buzz, the arousal."

Arthur sat wide-eyed waiting for my response. I found him repulsive yet interesting. I had to collect my thoughts because he spat out so much information in such a short time that I was confused as to where to take things next. I decided to revisit his earlier comment.

"You said before that the girls all liked it. Did they ever do anything to you?"

He smiled in his evil elfish fashion. "Yes, John, of course. They would grind me."

"Define grind?"

"Wriggle around. Rub themselves against me while sitting in my lap."

"Isn't that just kids being kids?" I asked, wanting to see just how demented his thinking was.

"No, John," he replied as he waved his bony index finger from side to side. "It's different. They would feel my hard penis on their little bums. They knew."

"They were kids; they didn't think anything of the sort," I half-reprimanded him.

He liked my emotive reaction. "Kids these days are far more sexual than you think," he teased.

"What, at the age of four?" I felt myself reacting again. He was playing me well. I took some time to regain composure.

"Was there anything else these children would do that made you think they wanted you to touch them?" I asked.

"Sometimes they would sit with their legs apart and flash me their snatch." He lunged forward waiting to see if his crudity would affect me. I kept calm.

"Isn't that what kids do? They're innocent to social appropriateness."

Arthur shook his head and waved his finger again. "Noooo," he said in a drawn-out manner. "Many times they would look at me like they knew it turned me on. They would make sexy eyes at me. They did it to get me to pick them up and rub their vagina. Why else would they sit there with their legs spread? My own wife never did that once in our married life. If a girl spreads her legs in front of you, it means she wants you. Sometimes it's an unconscious strategy, John."

Arthur earnestly believed the drivel he was spraying. I began to wonder what his marriage was like. "How was your sex life with your wife?"

Arthur looked less mischievous and more bilious. "I didn't have sex with her, John," he stated nauseatingly. "I refused to. She was fat and ugly, and we slept in separate rooms most of our married life."

"You obviously had sex a few times, given you had children?"

"Yes, but that was early on because she was skinny then." His delivery was apathetic and missing the intense edge.

"So you preferred her skinny, like a little child?"

And in one single question Arthur was back to his devilish, excitable self. "Yes, John," he said, beaming. "They're beautiful!"

He sat waiting in anticipation, hoping I would continue to converse along the train of thought he preferred. "What makes them beautiful?" I asked.

He was almost in rapture. "Their little bodies, their perfectly rounded little bums, their smooth vaginas. They're just so soft and lovely."

"Did you molest your own children?"

"No, John, I had three boys," he said disappointingly, as if I had built him up then spoiled his party.

"Do you masturbate in prison?"

"Yes, every day." His melodramatics had returned.

"What do you think about when you masturbate?"

He liked the question. "I look at pictures," he radiated.

"Of?"

"The children's underwear section from advertising pamphlets."

GREGORY

Gregory was a self-confessed pedophile with an exclusive interest in prepubescent girls. He also hated my guts—namely because I would never give in to his attempts to deceive me during therapy. I would continually hound him for the truth, and if I couldn't get it one way, I'd try another. He loathed me for it.

Gregory was convicted for possessing thousands of child-exploitation images. I was absolutely positive he had many undetected physical offenses that he'd managed to bury. He was extremely cagey, full of bravado, and a narcissist in the truest sense of the word. On this particular day his arrogance was unprecedented . . .

"You know," he started, in a tone that implied I was his employee.

I waited for his "prudence."

"They can never totally police the whole child porn thing on the Internet. You do get that, right?"

His words were delivered with the authority of a high-court judge passing sentence.

I decided to enter "the game." "Why? Because it's too prevalent?"

"Well, yeah, there's that," he said as he rested his boots on my coffee table. "But there's also another problem."

"What's that?" I asked as I motioned for him to remove his feet; he begrudgingly complied.

"Last night I masturbated to images of little kids," he conceitedly blurted out.

The statement unnerved me, and he knew it. More to the point, he was rejoicing in having rattled me. I was at a loss as to why he would confess so brazenly. The look in his eye was boastful. He looked too comfortable, even for him.

"You seem a bit flustered." He smirked in full knowledge that he was currently streets ahead.

Because he was an egotist, he couldn't help himself—he had to push that little bit extra to ensure I knew he was cleverer than me.

"You know what I was looking at while I was smacking off?" he said, mocking me.

I sat silent. I figured he couldn't wait to tell me. I wasn't going to give him the satisfaction of soliciting the information. Besides, I was now aware what he was doing—the entire conversation had been premeditated.

My silence eventually got the better of him: his gluttonous lust for instant gratification disgustingly overruled his patience.

"I was online looking at semi-naked kids."

The tone of his statement pissed me off more than the content. It was designed to belittle me as a professional, but that's not what bothered me. His blatant disrespect for encroaching upon innocent children did. I composed myself and began to think about what he'd likely been viewing.

Nudist camp websites.

I was wrong.

"Interesting how I can go to the kiddie's underwear section of a global clothing retailer's website and feel perfectly safe," he said, gloating.

I glared at him. "You're proud of that?"

"Not illegal," he answered. He was like a tormenting bully. Worse than that—he was like the weakest kid in the schoolyard hiding behind a protector while he picked on the kid above him in the pecking order. It was likely a reflection of his offending style; he was probably a sadistic bastard.

"You like doing that, don't you?" I honed in.

"What's that?"

"Riding the razor's edge?" I tried to conceal the condemnation in my voice. I failed miserably.

Gregory smiled his smug smile. "It's fucking stupid. All these dumb rules about what is and isn't pornography. Besides, what would you prefer, as my therapist: me going to child porn sites or going to the Target homepage?"

It was a difficult question to answer. While his viewing of children on the Target website was immoral, it was by no means criminal. My back was against the wall—which, of course, was exactly what he wanted. I did the only thing I could think of. I made it *his* question to answer.

"It seems you're trying to paint me into a corner."

Gregory grinned like a winner.

"So I'll ask you this: If your little sister was a model on that Target website, and a pedophile was using her for masturbatory stimulation, how would you answer your question?"

I thought I'd snared him, but he didn't bat an eyelid. He was better rehearsed than I'd given him credit for.

"You have to go with the greater good," he replied. "The greater good is the non-offense. My sister being some guy's jerk-off material is irrelevant."

I raised an eyebrow. "So it wouldn't be an issue?"

"Well, I wouldn't even know it was happening, now, would I?" His words rang with condescension.

Gregory waited eagerly for a response; I feigned disinterest. However, he couldn't help himself. Again he pushed the issue in an effort to ensure that the euphoria that comes with victory was maintained.

"So if I don't even know some guy's jerking off to my baby sister," he said leaning back conclusively and stretching his legs, "what the fuck does it even matter?"

He had me again. I felt he was going to cry "checkmate" at any moment.

"Okay, I concede the point," I said.

Conceding didn't feel good, but based on Gregory's least-collateral-damage theory, I had no argument. In any event, I wanted to see what he'd do when I submitted.

Gregory looked pleased with himself, too pleased. Pleased beyond content, his little victory ballooned an already overinflated ego to the point of explosion. It took his arrogance to new heights.

"Ya know what my favorite place on the Internet is?" he chided.

I kept quiet. I knew he'd tell me; in his pitiful little existence, this moment was going to be one of his greatest triumphs.

"YouTube!" he exclaimed, gazing at me and looking for overt signs he'd hit a nerve. Having him scan my body for an indicator made me feel like one of his victims. I felt violated.

Gregory sat tugging on a loose thread in the cuff of his dress shirt. It appeared his script had run its course. He eventually yanked the thread hard enough to detach it and held it up to peruse his tailoring prowess—yet another victory. He was having a good day indeed!

When the silence became too much, he discarded the piece of cotton to the floor and attempted to engage me again. "It's amazing, you know?"

I remained distant as he gawked at me like I should be interested. Upon coming to terms with the fact I was unlikely to seek clarification of his question, he persisted regardless.

"Yeah, anyway, it truly is amazing how little girls post their personal videos on YouTube," he declared with glee. He was off and running in pursuit, once more, of ego-gratification. He truly was a self-centered asshole.

He scoured me for a hint of interest.

"People are such dumbasses," he said, testing me. "How the fuck a parent can allow their kid to post a gymnastics routine online is tantamount to negligence."

I tried to keep my poise, but I'd seriously had enough.

"You know, Gregory," I said, emphasising his name somewhat patronizingly, "most people who post stuff on YouTube do so in complete innocence. They don't for a minute think someone like you is out there utilizing it for seedy, distasteful, ulterior motives."

I let him take that hit before following with another blow. "Do you know why they don't, Gregory?"

He shrugged in a manner suggesting that I was boring him.

"Because normal people don't think like you. The way you think is a very, very serious problem."

I could see I'd made him angry. He didn't like that I'd personalized the issue. Suddenly he looked at me with contempt. "Well, what are they gonna do?" He snickered. "Start arresting people for possession of YouTube clips?"

It was his attempt to take the conversation back to a place where he'd previously been a champion. Unfortunately for Gregory, he was now having to adlib; he'd overplayed his role and run out of script.

"A very, very serious problem, Gregory," I repeated. "So serious, that rather than come here and use these sessions as a means to better yourself, you prefer to boast about how you fulfil your perversions."

His eyes had lost that winning zeal. He looked at me scornfully. "You're not supposed to say shit like that. You're supposed to help me."

"I can't make a horse drink."

"As if I'm gonna talk to you and tell you everything when you act the way you do. You call yourself a psychologist? You're not a psychologist's asshole!"

I smiled at him. "But, Gregory, you do tell me everything," I said softly. "Don't you see you do that? All your silly little games in here—they all tell me things about you. I don't even need to ask; it comes freely because you have to feed your ego. And with that information I ask myself one question: Does this guy want to help himself? After today's performance—and it truly was a performance—I'll let you figure out where I think you're at."

CONCLUSION

Having read the five case studies presented, you may well be inclined to believe they are extreme in terms of the distortions projected by the offenders in question. In reality, this is far from true. That is, most, if not all, offenders have faulty perceptions about reality that divert so far from acceptable modes of thinking that I never cease to be amazed.

Certainly, there are similar themes that crop up from time to time that remind me of past cases, but on the whole, there are generally new twists in the stories that forever fascinate me. It has truly enlightened me to the power of the mind and its ability to create a "reality" the individual desires. This is not only true for sexual offenders but people in general. The mind is so powerful, a person can use it to justify sexually abusing little children. That's some serious force.

The power of the mind is also the factor most detrimental to victims. As I said in the concluding section of Chapter Nine: victims are bound by their emotional attachments left as a legacy by those who abused them. They create "stories" in their heads to explain their abuse as simply as possible. Many never come to fully comprehend the psychology of their abusers. Subsequently, the simplest means to make sense of the abuse is to integrate a blaming of the self. If a victim can overcome this powerful conditioning, they can heal. They can move from victim to survivor.

All too often the term "survivor" is used to describe people who have suffered sexual abuse. Most may have lived through the experience; a sprinkling deal with it productively. In my view, and with all due respect, the term "survivor" is reserved for those brave souls who venture into the unknown to begin a conscious journey to heal. It takes pure courage to step out of your comfort zone, to challenge your long-held beliefs, to decide you will no longer settle for the "role" forced upon you. In my view, "survivors" are those who cope well in spite of their past. True survivors have healed. The scar remains, but it is no longer sore to the touch.

CHAPTER TWELVE: SURVIVING—ACKNOWLEDGING THE WOUND

"Let your tears come. Let them water your soul."
~ Eileen Mayhew

KIRSTEN BLEW HER NOSE. "I can't believe how many tears I've shed in this damn office."

I offered another tissue. She accepted graciously.

Kirsten's journey through therapy had been emotionally arduous. In the depths of her soul had sat dark secrets that fed a form of pain that covertly smothered her spirit—the legacy of being raped as an eleven-year-old girl by a "friend" of the family.

Kirsten had never told anyone of her experience. Not even her parents or—up until a month ago—her husband.

"I'll probably cry again when I finish up with you today. I have to be consistent," she joked.

It was good to see her smile. I respected Kirsten; she was a courageous and strong woman. Outside of my office, I would likely have assumed her to be your average middle-aged mother going about life, nothing exquisite (I guess that's why we should always get to know people before we judge them). In therapy, I saw the real Kirsten: a woman with vigor and a steely resolve to expose and rid herself of the shackles that kept her chained to the past.

She looked at me tiredly but happily. "This whole process has been so painful, yet so empowering. I feel I've reclaimed my life from the inside out."

I was busy reminiscing about some of our past sessions. They were enjoyable as much as they were painful, namely because Kirsten had a great sense of humor. The phrasing of her last comment caught my attention.

"Your use of the term 'process' is interesting," I said.

She looked at me bewildered. "Why's that?"

Gut says go.

"I don't really have a process," I replied honestly. "The way I work is entirely based on what happens in front of me."

She looked somewhat surprised, as if I had robbed her of a belief that I was some form of sage who had an absolute and definitive understanding of everything that took place during our interactions.

"So you don't follow a method?" She sounded disappointed.

"Not really."

She eyed me curiously. "How does that work then?"

"You tell me." I shrugged sheepishly.

Typically Kirsten would have replied with a half-smart quip. On this occasion, I watched as she drew into herself. "It felt like a method," she said softly. "It felt like a process: raw wound to healing scar."

I remained quiet; I have always struggled to explain the way I conduct therapy. Personally, I *totally* understand the feel of how I work. Putting it in words is a whole other story. I am entirely intuitive. I focus on what is presented and search the maze until I find the chamber I feel leads to something of substance. While that, in and of itself, may be defined as a process, it is entirely driven by the client. I have no clue as to where they are taking me. I simply follow their lead.

The intent with which Kirsten suddenly looked at me made me wonder if she was about to abuse me for being a fraudster of some sort.

"Something just occurred to me," she said in the most serious tone I had ever heard pass her lips.

"Yes?"

"Many years ago when my husband and I were first married, we went on a camping trip to a remote place in Western Australia. It was in the Kimberley Ranges. Have you ever been there?"

I shook my head.

"You should; it's beautiful. Anyway, on this camping trip I developed this terrible boil under my arm, right in my armpit."

She subconsciously felt the spot and briefly went silent. After a few seconds she snapped out of her thoughtful gaze.

"I relate this process—therapy—as being similar to that experience. Except, in the case of my boil, the wound was physical. This was entirely emotional, almost spiritual."

I was engrossed by her analogy. "Explain that to me? I'm really interested in the connection for you."

Kirsten felt under her arm again. The look in her eyes suggested there was something deeply connected to the forthcoming story that was a learning curve for her, me, or both of us.

"When that boil first appeared, it wasn't painful. It was just like a small pimple that I really didn't take much notice of. But after a while it got irritable. It stung a little, as if to say 'I'm here.'"

She looked up at me. "You know, kind of like my past? It was there, but I didn't pay it any attention until it began to sting a bit."

I nodded supportively.

"After a while that boil began to get sore. I mean *really* sore. It was the result of the pressure of the pus building up beneath the skin. It's as if all this poison appeared from nowhere in my body and came to rest in one place."

"Kind of like the poison of shame?" I posited.

"Yes, and the more that pus compacted, augmented, and built up, the more pressure there was. What I hoped I could ignore got to a point that I could no longer deny it. I couldn't deny it because I could actually see it. But worse, I felt that throbbing, relentless pain. I knew it was going to get a whole lot worse before it got better. And I just knew with everything in me that there was no longer a means of avoiding the inevitable."

"Such as coming to terms with your past?"

Kirsten nodded. "Yeah, in fact it became so painful I wanted it out. It was not only hurting me, it was poisoning me."

I sat silent, contemplating her words.

"How did you deal with the boil?" I asked, in hope that her metaphor might provide even further insight for us both.

"Once I acknowledged it was there and the pain became too much to bear, I realized I had to take action."

"Similar to coming here?"

"Uh-huh," she said. "It's a tough decision, that one."

Kirsten sat back in a reflective pose.

"You have to be brave," she emphasized as a means to convince me, but she was preaching to the converted.

"You have to be really brave to decide that you need the poison removed. Deep down you know the only way that's going to happen is by relieving the pressure. I knew that boil had to be lanced, but Russell, my husband, and I were in the middle of nowhere!"

I shuddered at the prospect of where her story was leading.

"The only one who could lance it was Russell. He had a really sharp fishing knife, and I knew it was going to hurt beyond belief, but I recognized and preferred the idea of a short burst of intense pain as opposed to the constant suffering I was being subjected to."

We both physically reacted in a subtle startled manner in response to her last sentence—recognition of a type of déjà vu.

"I remember in our second session you said exactly those words to me! You said exactly the same thing about the rape," I offered enthusiastically.

"I know!" she said, nodding in agreement. "I just remembered that too!"

There was a brief pause as we mused over the recollection.

"Anyway," she eventually declared, "I went to Russell and showed him my armpit. It was red and swollen, as if I'd been stung by a bee the size of Godzilla. I held up his fishing knife and said, 'I want you to lance this.' He looked at me like I was crazy. I said, 'Russell, you don't understand the pain I'm in. I want you to slice it open and remove the crap in there.'"

I felt myself grimace. "How did he respond?"

Kirsten laughed. "I'd like to say he was all macho and ready for action, but the truth is Russell shit himself. He refused to do it at first. He wanted to take me to a hospital or doctor. I said, 'Russell, are you serious? Look where we are. There isn't any form of civilization for days. Deal with it!'"

Kirsten sat back again as if remembering the intimate details of the occasion. Before long she embarked on the next chapter of the tale.

"I knew that lancing that boil was one thing, but squeezing all the pus out was another. That part was going to be a hundred times more terrifying than having my skin sliced open with a fishing knife. Russell eventually agreed and boiled the knife in a pot of water over the campfire to sterilize it. I sat watching that water simmer, and I can honestly say I was scared out of my wits. In the end, I couldn't handle sitting there waiting for the big event any longer, so I went searching."

"For?"

"A stick."

I gave her a puzzled look.

"You know," she said. "To chomp down on when the time came. I found a nice round stick and downed a bottle of wine in ten minutes flat. That was my preparation: wine and a stick."

"Thank God for alcohol."

Kirsten laughed, then her face changed. "The big moment finally arrived. Russell pressed the knife to my skin and asked if I was ready. I had the stick between my teeth and nodded. I bit down as hard as I could. I didn't watch, but I felt the knife slide across the boil. It was agony!"

Immediately a thought sprang to mind from our therapy. "Much like that session when you opened up for the first time about the rape," I advocated.

"Yep," she agreed instantly. "What leaked out of me that day was similar to the toxic residue from that boil."

She relaxed into her chair and gazed off distantly. Although it was still too raw to discuss, I could tell Kirsten was relieved. Even though she was emotional, she was more at peace than I'd ever seen her. I could tell she felt it too. A faint smile made its way across her face. She looked serene and content. I didn't interrupt; she had worked hard for this moment.

"We didn't prepare as well as we could have," she said after some time.

"How so?" I asked, thinking she was discussing our sessions.

"Russell, the silly bastard, forgot to have a cloth ready to wipe away the pus; it was running down my side. Mind you, at that stage I didn't really care because the pain was just ultra intense."

Out of nowhere she gave a giggle. "I remember he looked frightened at that point. I think he was more scared than I was about the next part. He asked me if I was okay. I couldn't talk because I had that stick in my mouth. Lucky for him—if he had heard what I was thinking, he probably wouldn't be married to me anymore."

"You never had a stick in here." I laughed.

She looked at me mockingly. "Lucky you can't read minds."

"So what happened next?"

Kirsten repositioned herself in her chair. "Well," she started, "I must have glared at Russell with a frenzied look on my face because he knew instantly he had broken the preset rule: *Whatever* happens, don't stop!"

I didn't share it with Kirsten, but I was thinking her last comment was very similar to my own thoughts about her early on in therapy. My intuition told me in the first session that everything in her wanted to heal. That she had the fortitude to see therapy through to the end. I made a decision there and then to keep going no matter what.

Kirsten squirmed and contorted her face in a manner that implied she was recalling the worst part. "Russell began squeezing. He squeezed, and squeezed and kept squeezing. The side of my body was literally wet with pus and blood and whatever other ungodly fluid was in that festering abscess. But the pain—oh God, the pain!"

Kirsten sat shaking her head. "Russell didn't stop until it was all gone. He told me he couldn't leave any pus in there. He said he had to get it all out because it would get infected. Those moments he was squeezing were so intense, I actually thought I was going to pass out."

I sat considering her comments. It was amazing how the experience overlapped with therapy. "That's like getting rid of the shame when you attended here. I too couldn't leave any poison in there, otherwise the potential to heal would not have been complete."

She nodded with a smile. "Yeah, you actually made me realize there was no use in withholding anything about the rape. You made me see that if I didn't speak about the whole thing from go-to-woe and all the encompassing thoughts and feelings I had about the event—including my thoughts and feelings about that bastard, and myself—then it would still be in me after I had finished here. Because in reality, I could never truly 'finish' here if I didn't off-load the lot."

That's pure courage, I thought.

"Eventually Russell stopped squeezing. It literally seemed like he was doing it for hours, but to this day he swears it was a matter of minutes. It was weird because after he was done I was still in pain, but I felt utter relief. It was a type of pain that made me aware that the worst was over. It was almost a nice pain, a rewarding pain."

"Did you experience that 'nice pain' in here?" I asked, genuinely curious if such a pain existed.

Kirsten thought for a moment. "Yes," she said. "I felt it after I got it all out, after I told you everything."

I watched as she bit her lip and frowned. "No. No. That's not true. It wasn't then. I first felt it during that discussion with you, but in hindsight I realize I still had some poison in me when I left. It was the residue of knowing I hadn't shared this with the person I love most, and that by hiding it from him I had done nothing to help him understand me. Because the truth is, when you suffer a trauma like that as a child—or even as an adult, I guess—and you do everything in your power to conceal and hide it from the person closest to you, they don't really have all of you. It's also not really fair to them, in a way."

I looked at her quizzically.

"I mean, there are various issues I have, not just sexually but in general day-to-day living," she explained. "Russell couldn't comprehend those matters because he didn't know my history. I think I felt that nice pain after I told Russell everything. He was so supportive. I felt he loved me even more, not less."

I sat overwhelmed with emotion.

Kirsten looked at me sternly. "The thing about you is you didn't settle for anything less than what I needed. You wouldn't allow me to escape it. You were relentless in helping me off-load all that stuff."

She was right. If I latch on to something I perceive is of substance, I refuse to let it go.

Kirsten could see my brain ticking. She looked at me inquiringly. "You knew I needed to get it out, didn't you?"

Her question was presented in a way that suggested she thought I knew exactly what she needed at that particular time in therapy. I lied by omission. I didn't answer her. The truth was, I had simply followed my intuition. I trust my gut over *everything*—always. My silence seemed to satisfy her preconceived notions and infer she was correct.

"So anyway," she went on, "after that, Russell got the first-aid kit and cleaned me up. He tended to the newly opened wound with disinfectant and swabbed it. That was painful too, but it was pain I more readily embraced. I knew the worst was over. I knew I was on my way to healing."

There was a long pause. I assumed she was done. "That is a really great analogy, Kirsten. One I am going to steal and use in the future."

She shook her hand at me as a friendly sign she wasn't finished.

"I took a look at the hole in my underarm before Russell dressed the wound. It was massive! A part of me had been removed. A part I wanted removed. A part that induced in me nothing but suffering."

Kirsten looked at me soulfully. "I will forever be grateful for your help in removing that part," she said as her eyes welled with tears.

"My pleasure," I offered genuinely.

Kirsten reclined in her chair and slowly closed her eyes. "There was a dull ache in my arm for a couple of days where that boil once was, but it was nowhere near the same intensity. I gradually felt like my old self. That poison was no longer affecting my bloodstream. In time it healed over."

Suddenly her eyes opened and she lifted her arm. "You see that scar?" she demanded, pointing to her armpit.

I nodded. It was large. Certainly larger than any scar I've seen left by a boil.

"That scar reminds me of that camping trip. Funnily enough, I don't really focus on the boil trauma. I remember the beauty of the Kimberley Ranges, the sunsets, the time Russell and I shared, and the trust we showed in each other during that ordeal. The pain is a distant memory. And the scar—well, that's my mark of courage," she declared proudly.

"Of course," she continued, "I thought I was the bravest person on the planet putting myself through that. At the time I believed I had endured more pain than anyone. Then I experienced childbirth."

I laughed.

"So," said Kirsten, looking at me seriously again, "the lancing of that boil is exactly like this process in every way. The only difference being that, in this case, my spirit has healed. It's clichéd, but the scars will remain. There's no denying or getting away from that. But I don't care that I have scars. They aren't sore to the touch. They are healed. They are like my boil, my soul's badge of honor. I'm a survivor."

CONCLUSION

As I said in the concluding section of the previous chapter, the term "survivor" is bandied around too frequently by therapists and the like. I understand their sentiment in using the idiom; they just want to make people feel better. It's a good thing to want to make people feel better. Unfortunately, telling people what they want to hear instead of what they *need* to hear is not conducive to productive therapy.

Productive therapy is not evidenced by the patient leaving the therapist's office every session feeling on top of the world. Productive therapy is difficult, for both patient and therapist. The former is dealing with past trauma; the latter has to be highly attuned to the process of healing. And healing does not entail protecting the patient from the demons that need to be expelled. Colluding with them to conceal their inner fears does nothing to help them, period.

Consider for a moment a person with a victim mentality. What are they like? Blame others? Preoccupied with the past? Preoccupied with their problems? Self-pitying? Helpless? Self-abasing?

Most victims who attend my office are none of the above with respect to their past sexual abuse. They might demonstrate those symptoms in other areas of their lives, but rarely—if ever—do they present in that manner with regard to their sexual abuse. This is because they don't want to talk about it. If they don't acknowledge it, they don't have to deal with it. For this reason, when a therapist throws the label "survivor" out there, victims will readily attach this descriptor to themselves. "I'm a survivor" sounds a lot more enticing than "I'm a victim."

Being a victim has negative connotations. It implies the individual has lost his or her power and been denigrated. The problem is, when you jump to the application of the label of survivor without addressing your needs, you are deceiving yourself. To survive implies one has outlasted; one is still alive. However, it is possible to be alive yet dead inside. Existing as opposed to living.

A person has not outlasted or gained victory if the very toxin from their trauma still clings to their soul and controls their life. Often that control is not readily linked by the victim to their current problems (e.g., substance abuse, eating disorders, anxiety disorders, depression, problem gambling, domestic violence, etc.). Instead they perceive these matters have simply arisen from thin air. As such, they often attend therapy in the hope the therapist can wave a magic wand and make their lives better without them addressing a single issue or changing anything. In productive therapy, that never happens, ever.

The people who move from victim to survivor are those who understand their current problems are the legacy of past wounds. This is more or less true of all psychological suffering. It is interesting that people will readily attend therapy for, say, an anxiety disorder, fully aware it's a problem, yet not want to pinpoint how it possibly came to be. Some clients even instruct me to just give them a pill. Medication has its place, but doesn't it make sense to first understand the genesis of how the problem came into being?

It's similar to taking a car with a leaky radiator to a mechanic and the mechanic telling you to simply keep filling it with water. The hole has not been repaired; in fact, you don't even know where it's located. You just keep filling the radiator up and never address the problem. One day that leak will get so bad that no amount of refilling will suffice.

Similarly, those who self-medicate with substances are virtually undertaking the same avoidance techniques in order to forget and avoid the shame and hurt. If a man uses alcohol to hide from his past, is he a survivor? Not in my mind. I can respect that he has suffered and I can empathize with him, but I cannot consider he has survived his abuse when he has never dealt with it. His spirit is still broken. He is the living dead.

Suffering sexual abuse makes no person an instant "survivor." I relate the word *survivor* to courage. Sufferance doesn't necessarily equate to courage. Courage is when you stand up for your beliefs. Standing up for your beliefs includes reaching into the depths of your soul, acknowledging what's there (no matter how vile), bringing it to the surface, and making a statement that you refuse to carry the toxic waste that isn't yours. Courage is when you consciously put yourself in a situation that removes you from your comfort zone and you choose to change regardless of how frightening it feels. Courage is when you know the right thing to do but are not guaranteed an easy or desirous outcome. There is nothing more courageous than a person who enters therapy and is determined to change through acknowledgment that a problem exists.

In my view, survivors are those who crush the legacies of their abusers by no longer using them as excuses to explain the aspects of their lives or themselves they do not wish to own. That statement may seem harsh; however, it is imperative to accept that you will not achieve "survivor status" by clinging to the very place your perpetrator designed for you to remain in. Your abuser not only planned for you to be a victim, he intended for you to remain one (few offenders would ever admit that, but it's the truth). Your abuser hoped you would never speak up, so she could continue to do what she was doing and avoid detection. The person who abused you doesn't want you to speak up, ever!

Even if your perpetrator is one of the few who gets caught, he or she would still prefer you kept your mouth shut. Your abuser wants you to be silent. Not just when you were a child, but even now! He wants you to keep your secret because your secret is actually his dirty secret. Your voice is muted by shame—shame that isn't even yours. It's hers—and this allows her to keep her freedom, reputation, integrity, and public image intact.

If you say nothing, if you don't acknowledge the past, if you allow the shame to rule you, if you avoid, ignore, and cover up your suffering, you are still a victim. You must address your wounds. As the great Carl Jung said: "We cannot change anything unless we accept it."

Chapter Thirteen: Fear of the Unknown

"To conquer fear is the beginning of wisdom."
~ *Bertrand Russell*

The Group

"**P**ERSONALLY, I THINK THAT'S AN absolute load of shit," said the small rotund man. He was one of seven offenders in the sterile, drab prison room participating in therapeutic intervention.

The group appeared collaboratively alarmed by the statement. Not because of the aggressive undertones but more due to the unreserved contemptuous tenor. It begged my attention, and ignoring the statement would have been negligence.

"Why's that?" I asked staunchly.

Charlie made a derisive scoffing noise while rolling his eyes; he ignored my question.

"Are you fucking serious?" The demand came from Kirk—an offender convicted for the rape of his ex-partner. Kirk had sexually assaulted "the love of his life" when she finally showed the courage to exit the marriage after years of being his personal punching bag.

"Serious about what?" asked Charlie. His tone was pompous, and his body language reminded me of a lord in a far gone British era tossing a penny to a street beggar.

"Serious about what you just said, that it's a load of shit." Kirk sneered.

"Yes, absolutely," replied Charlie as he folded his arms. "It's total bullshit."

"You're a fucking idiot!"

BOOM!

Kirk's words hit the elderly man like a tracer bullet. His rage was like a drag car; it had the capacity to go from zero to a hundred in an instant. Civility needed to be restored.

"Instead of calling him a fucking idiot, Kirk, tell him why you disagree," I said.

Kirk looked at me like a fuming bull would a matador. "I'm not telling him. Fuck him! Someone else can tell him. He pisses me off."

I waited a while. I could tell others wanted to speak up but they were reluctant; the atmosphere was thick with fury. I was gaining insight as to how Kirk's ex-wife lived a life walking on eggshells. One thing I don't do is desist from challenging offenders because it's uncomfortable.

"Isn't it what you're doing right now, Kirk, what we determined was your problem in life: An inability to communicate because you get too aggressive?"

Kirk's body collapsed a little. "Point taken," he conceded. The other group members exhaled; the steam from the pressure cooker had been safely dispelled.

Kirk turned his attention back to Charlie. "Look, I didn't mean to offend you. I just don't get how you can think that way. I mean, basically what you're saying is that no kid—when they become an adult—has any problems as a result of being sexually abused. You say that's complete bullshit, but I reckon it's you that's full of shit."

"Why?" Charlie became defensive.

"Look at how many kids you abused!" And in a solitary moment, the human time bomb was ready for detonation. "You fucked all their lives up!" Kirk yelled.

"Ha! And what about you, Kirk?" he countered, refusing to take a backward step.

"What about me?"

"You hurt your ex-wife. You actually flogged the shit out of her and violently raped her. In my view, that's gonna fuck a person up more than me having a sexual moment with a child."

"A sexual moment? Are you fucked in the head?"

Charlie looked smug. "I didn't hurt my victims, Kirk. But you did," he stated matter-of-factly.

"You fucked their lives up! They're better off dead!"

Charlie scoffed his patronizing scoff and rolled his eyes; it was designed to incense Kirk further. The human inferno's inability to control his temper, in Charlie's view, only served to prove his point—that Kirk was a more despicable human being than he.

"So you honestly believe those kids you fucked aren't affected by what you did?" Kirk attempted to belittle his opponent.

"Nope, I know for a fact all my victims lead productive lives." Charlie's comment was almost filled with pride, as if he had somehow contributed to these people's success.

Kirk had become less enraged and more miffed. He couldn't seem to grasp the level of Charlie's distortions. He leaned back into his chair and made a waving gesture toward the elder gentleman in a signal that he could no longer be bothered. At this point, Tom—a younger man with child pornography Internet offenses—spoke up.

"I was sexually abused as a kid." Instantly he had everyone's attention. "Personally, I think you're both wrong."

Kirk became attentive. "How the fuck am I wrong?" he demanded, and in recognizing his aggressive tone shot a quick glance at me so as to demonstrate I need not point out the obvious.

"Because you think a person can't recover. You actually said they would be better off dead. Even though I've fucked up and done what I've done—and in my view what I've done has a lot to do with what was done to me—I don't consider I would be better off dead."

"Yeah, well, I don't get that either, to be honest," Kirk stated abruptly.

"You don't get what?" asked Tom.

"You. I don't get you," Kirk trailed off. It seemed he had deemed the entire debate futile. Then, like a dog who can't relinquish a bone, he was back. "How the fuck can you be sexually abused as a kid, then go and look that same shit up on the Internet? Like, what the fuck is that about?"

Tom was unperturbed. His lack of emotive response frustrated Kirk.

"Surely you knew how bad it was when it happened to you?" Kirk ordered. "Why would you want to see other kids suffering the same shit?"

Tom took his time and looked at Kirk sincerely. "That's the thing," he started. "Sex became so confusing because of what happened to me. When I was a kid, I didn't know that what was happening to me was wrong. Fuck, man, it's hard to say, but most times it felt good."

Kirk looked shocked. Charlie sat basking in the glory that his earlier assumption had been proven correct. His gloating didn't last long.

"When you're a kid, you don't know someone is using you," said Tom as he turned to directly face the old man. He wanted Charlie to know unreservedly his forthcoming comments were directed at him. "Kids are innocent, naïve, gullible, and vulnerable," he continued. "For a grown man to overlook that obvious fact to satisfy his own sexual desires—to me—suggests that individual is nothing but a selfish c***!"

Tom's angry tone was followed by a change in his facial expression. You could literally see the emotive shift from anger to shame in an instant. He broke down and sobbed.

I didn't say anything. I let him cry. The group sat stunned and silent. I think they were waiting for me to console the lad, but it would have been counter to his needs. The impact of his statement was of too much worth. This was his time.

"Sorry," he said after several minutes.

"Please continue," I replied forcefully.

Tom looked surprised by my response. He picked up the ball and ran with it. This was quite possibly the best lesson this group of men were ever going to get.

He turned his attention back to Charlie. "How fucking dare you imply for a second that your victims have no adverse life circumstances due to your actions? Do you know how arrogant and disrespectful that comment is?"

"I'm only basing it on what I know about my victims' current life circumstances," Charlie replied conceitedly.

Tom leaned closer to him. "You wanna know the truth?"

Charlie shrugged.

"Answer me: yes or no?"

"Yeah." Charlie was wary. He seemed more spooked by Tom's controlled anger than Kirk's explosive rage.

"Your victims are only pretending to lead functional lives. Inside they're tormented souls confused with their identity, especially their sexual identity. If *any* of them have come to terms with what you did, it will only be by virtue of some serious inner searching. They probably even needed the help of a therapist. Do you fucking get that, Charlie?! If they are okay, they wouldn't need a therapist! That means they are—or were at one point—seriously fucked up!"

Charlie remained still and quiet. Something had shifted; he seemed different. Then it dawned on me: he was actually paying attention.

"Think about that for a minute, Charlie," Tom continued. "Think about how fucking hard it would be for a person to go and see an absolute stranger and tell them the deepest, darkest secrets of their lives in the hope it's going to achieve something. And if you think about that properly, *you*—of all people—should understand how hard that is because it's exactly what you're going through right now! In this program you're telling your secrets to people you don't even know, and look how hard that is!"

The group seemed to have a collaborative "aha" moment.

Tom continued. "And just like you with your bullshit, Charlie—that claim you made about people not suffering if they were abused as kids—when a victim enters therapy, they don't want to tell all the sordid details either—especially the worst parts. So they twist the story, water it down, and basically present it in a way that makes them feel better, which of course results in them not getting proper help because they are too ashamed of telling the story in its entirety. That's you, Charlie. That's you, you're the bullshitter. You use that crap about your victims leading functional lives because it helps you justify your fucked-up behavior. It helps you justify what you did. It keeps you from tapping into the prospect that you actually *did* fuck them up. It keeps you from having to live with the guilt of what you did! And worse still, Charlie, is that by continuing to bullshit yourself, *you* don't get the help *you* need."

The old man sat solemnly; he seemed sorrowful. After a while he became teary. "I don't know what to do." He broke down, his words enveloped in desperation.

"I'm sexually attracted to children," Charlie sobbed.

No one said a word. The old man remained still in his chair, tears streaming down his cheeks. Suddenly Kirk got up; I thought he was leaving the room. He walked over to Charlie and offered his hand. Kirk used his strength to draw the old man up from his chair and embraced him. I didn't question the sincerity of the action; everyone in the room who had the capacity for expressing emotion felt it. The old man collapsed into Kirk's arms and cried.

Charlie eventually returned to his chair. It was an interesting circumstance: the raw wounds of a victim helping reveal the raw wounds of a perpetrator, in turn finding comfort in the arms of an offender with serious anger issues.

Tom placed his hand on the shoulder of the older man. "Charlie," he said empathically, "I want to show you how I know people don't recover well from sexual abuse. Don't get me wrong—some do if they have the guts to deal with it."

Tom then turned and faced the rest of the group.

"I've put my balls on the line by saying I was a victim. I'm dealing with it just as I need to deal with my turning into an offender," he said. "And I think you can tell I'm in no way using it to excuse what I did. If we are gonna help Charlie, we all need to get honest. Right here, right now. So, how many people in here were sexually abused as a kid?"

Slowly the hands were raised. One after another, until every offender except Charlie had his hand in the air. "You see that, Charlie. We are not functioning people. We all have issues. We are all victims who aren't functioning. Not everyone deals with sexual abuse. Some do, but most don't."

Charlie nodded, then he too raised his hand. I wasn't all that surprised by the numbers, but I was astonished that Tom had managed to create an atmosphere for the group conducive to respecting honesty. Even the most resistant person in the room, Charlie, was being truthful. (Much research has been presented to suggest most sexual offenders have suffered no abuse themselves. I'm not saying the statistics are wrong, it's just not my experience; the majority of offenders I've seen over the years were sexually abused at some point.)

"Do you consider yourself dysfunctional, Tom?" It was strange to see a man of Charlie's years seeking counsel and wisdom from a young man.

"I'm human, Charlie. It goes with the territory. But if you're asking if I'm dysfunctional because I was sexually abused, I would answer, yes, I was for many years. But the wounds have healed since coming to jail. Of all places, this is where I made my peace with it."

"Why in here?" asked Charlie.

"Take a look around. This is where society says bad people come to pay their dues. I did a bad thing. When I got here, I decided I needed to get honest with myself. I don't like what I did, but I refused to ignore it or pretend in some way I was justified. I don't want to let what happened to me control me anymore. So I decided to take my power back, to cease bullshitting myself. I decided to stop buying into the lie that I was looking at child porn because of what happened to me."

Tom breathed in deeply. "For some people, all this shit in them—all this bad shit—builds up, and they react in different ways. For us, sexual offending was a reactive response. Maybe that's because we gave up on trying to deal with it. I don't know. I think it's different for everyone. But what I came to realize is I have to separate my abuse from my offenses. Yes, it is a factor, but never an excuse. So in order to address my crimes, I discovered I needed to address my abuse because there was a link. And maybe that link existed for my abuser too—it's certainly possible—but I don't care about his shit; that's his to deal with. Just like all of us, he has to get real with himself, if he ever has the balls. So in order to understand me, and get to a point where I can accept me, I need to acknowledge all of me. Every single bit. Even the bits I don't like. There's no other way."

The group was luckily made up of men who had the intelligence to listen and embrace young Tom's profound truth.

"Tell me," I asked. "You've obviously done some real soul-searching with respect to this, Tom. How did you come to acknowledge you were wounded?"

He thought earnestly before responding. "I guess the obvious answer would be when I started accessing child porn on the Internet, but it was before that. It was little things, little things that added up over time. Little things I pretended weren't there."

"Such as?"

"Mainly feelings of worthlessness. Feeling like I was unclean and dirty. I rebelled, and my parents could never work out why. I only recently told them about the abuse when I decided I wasn't going to hide anymore. I was just a big festering ball of anger for many years."

"Like me," said Kirk in a tone I'd never heard from him—grief-stricken.

"I was the exact opposite," said Dean, a heavily tattooed man with no teeth and long hair. "Don't get me wrong. I felt those emotions too," he clarified. "But mainly I felt sad all the time. Depressed. I didn't rebel. I became very compliant, isolating myself. I hardly spoke to people. I was always scared someone would discover my dirty secret. It's the same feeling I would get after I committed my crimes."

"Do you think all victims become offenders, John?" asked Charlie.

"No. But no one can tell how a victim will respond." I shrugged. "One thing's for sure though, Charlie—it won't be initially positive."

"What do you mean, 'initially'?" asked George, a middle-aged Greek man with offenses against a teenage girl.

"At some point, the victim recognizes they've been wronged. For adult victims that's pretty much straightaway. For some child victims, that can take years. So when all the pieces of the puzzle start to fall into place, the wrestling of the demons begins."

Tom piped up. "Yeah. And that's generally when people want to hide. They want to ignore it. It's usually make or break at that point as to whether they fall off the rails."

"But what is 'it'?" asked George. "I get that it's important for people to acknowledge they are wounded, but—let's say—we had to explain to someone what to look for. How would we do it? What actually is the wound?"

It was a reasonable question. The more I sat thinking about it, the more complex it became.

"I think it's a violation of someone's dignity," said Tom.

George shook his head. "It can't be just that. For kids who get abused, not all of them are gonna feel like that at the time. Maybe they do later. But at first it's more a violation of their innocence. But that can't be true either, because a lot of kids don't even know it's wrong when it's happening."

"Yeah, I guess that's true," admitted Tom.

"No, that's different," chimed in Daniel, "'cause we're talking about awareness. So the suffering starts for the person when they gain awareness," his input more a question than a statement.

"I suppose so," replied George.

"Then if that's true," continued Daniel, "how come people wait so long to do anything about it? I mean, when I look back on my life, I know I started using drugs after what happened to me—which I'm not gonna talk about—but I know I used drugs for that purpose."

"For the same reason none of us seek help," said Tom, pointing to the room full of offenders. "We don't want to admit to every aspect of our crimes because we're ashamed of them."

"That's a pretty big assumption," rebutted Daniel. "I mean, there's some assholes in prison that don't feel a single bit of shame about what they've done."

Charlie's eyes darted. I perceive he took the generalized comment personally, which said a lot about him. A lot more than he wanted us to know.

Tom nodded. "Yeah, I guess. I don't know, man, I can only speak for myself, but to me, it always felt like I was worth less than everyone else. That I had no value. Were you like that, Dan?"

Daniel looked up. "I felt scared, to be honest. I was always on edge. Drugs were my escape from that shit."

George chimed in. "For me, it didn't come until later in life, when I kind of just had this memory of stuff happening. But I don't think it had anything to do with my offense. I was already knee-deep in that shit when I started remembering my past."

I waited until the discussion had run its course before attempting to revisit Daniel's prior comment—in particular, his phrase "which I'm not gonna talk about."

Eventually he made eye contact with me. "Why don't you want to talk about it?"

"What?" said Daniel, but not because he hadn't heard me. He seemed to find the question contextually misplaced.

"Earlier you said you didn't want to talk about your abuse. I'm wondering why."

"Let's just drop it."

He was vulnerable, very vulnerable. I needed to tread carefully, so I took a long pause. "Something just occurred to me, Daniel."

He looked receptive.

"Aren't you doing the very thing right now that we've been discussing?"

"What's that?" he asked.

"Avoiding the wound?" I said gently.

He looked forlornly at me. "Hmm."

I paused again. "Let's talk about the actual wound. What does it feel like?"

Daniel was on the edge of a metaphoric cliff. Looking over the horizon and down into the valley where he could see a safety net at some distance and hoped to God it was strong enough should he decide to leap. I knew he would jump if I'd built enough trust.

"The wound." He pursed his lips, closed his eyes, and leapt. "It's in the details. It's all the details, man."

"Can you explain that to me?"

He closed his eyes tighter. "It's like this: I can sit here right now and say to all of you that I was sexually abused as a kid. I wouldn't have been able to do that years ago, but for some reason, sitting here, I can. However, when it comes to the details, as in discussing the details of what happened, geez, dude, that's a whole other story!"

"Why?"

He thought for a while. "Because it's fucking scary as all fuck! It's the same as the fear I had in having to disclose the details of my offending—you worry what other people will think."

"And did you disclose everything to do with your offenses in here?"

Daniel opened his eyes. His head drooped. "No."

"Why not?"

"I was too ashamed," he said dejectedly. "It's like Tom said. People cover up and leave out the worst bits so they don't have to deal with it. I guess it's a trust thing too. When you have your trust abused, you find it difficult to trust others."

"Do you mistrust anyone in here?"

"Not after today. I did before. Prior to today I didn't trust you, Kirk," he said, looking at the man he was discussing. "Sorry, mate, but that's the truth."

"How come?" Kirk asked, half surprised, half crestfallen.

"Because you're fucking harsh, man. You judge people harshly—like you did to Charlie—and when I see stuff like that, I don't want to tell the nitty-gritty of my story. But then when I saw you hug him today, I thought differently about you. I thought, 'Maybe this guy isn't such an asshole after all.'"

Kirk didn't respond. I could tell he didn't like what was being said; it stung him in the heart, but he didn't flare up. Perhaps he was learning that anger was not an appropriate response to every hurt in life.

I intervened. "I just want to point something out to you, Daniel. You just said you didn't disclose everything about your offenses because you didn't trust people in here, correct?"

He nodded.

"Yet you also said after today's interactions you now trust everyone in the room?"

Again he nodded.

"Okay, so here's my question: When we just went to discuss your own abuse as a child, you asked if we could just drop it. Why did you still feel the need to hide when you, by your own admission, now trust everyone in the room?"

The enquiry appeared to perplex him. The group sat waiting for a response. I could tell he wanted to offer them something of worth. However, what was also obvious was that it was an answer he was seeking deep within himself, probably for the first time ever.

"Fear," he eventually stated.

"Of?"

"Rejection, being inferior. That something's wrong with me."

It made sense. It certainly resonated with his peers as they all sat nodding in agreement.

"So you hang on to it so you don't have to find out if there is something wrong with you?"

He looked me straight in the eyes. "It's fear of the unknown. Fear of finding out for sure that I'm inferior."

"I can see why you used drugs," I offered. I wanted him to think about the connection.

"Fuck, man, that's true. Drugs always kept me from finding out. They were my escape. My means to never confront my fears."

"I think that's why I used child porn," Tom offered. His intrusion didn't take me aback as much as his comment.

"Explain?"

"I accepted that I was inferior. I accepted being inferior to others because I was sexually abused. I accepted that notion for the entirety of my teenage years. So I eventually proved to everyone how inferior I was. First I rebelled, then I became what I hated—an offender. I think I took that path because I feared being anything other than inferior. Being anything other than inferior was an aspiration that seemed unattainable to me."

"So you feared reclaiming yourself?"

"No, I feared finding out. I couldn't reclaim anything. I never knew who I was; it was fear that stopped me from finding out."

Kirk piped up. "So did I use anger to hide my fears?"

"What are your thoughts on it?" I asked.

"I can see that I did in my offense. I was always scared of her leaving. I lived in fear she would abandon me, so I was controlling in the worst possible way."

"What about in regard to your own sexual abuse as a child?"

"I've been angry my whole life. Well, my whole adult life at least. Deep down I know what my problem is."

I wondered if he had the emotional intelligence to truly know what his problem was.

"And what is your problem, Kirk?"

"I'm incredibly insecure. So much so that anger has been my means to stay on top. I use it to keep power over others. Deep down I feel like a worthless piece of shit. So if I keep control over people through my anger, then I can avoid dealing with the stuff that causes the anger."

Wow!

"So if that's true, Kirk, what have you come to realize is the real poison in you? The real toxin that keeps you from developing into someone you desire?"

"Until today I thought it was anger, but that's just at the surface. It's really fear. I guess I've discovered that deep down I'm actually a very fearful person."

"Me too," stated toothless Dean enthusiastically. "I've just learned that too."

"Go on?" I encouraged.

"If I look back, I went into my shell after I was abused because I too felt worthless, but rather than get angry at people, I just became really submissive. I didn't think I was worth anything, so I figured if I just became a wallflower I could fly under the radar in life."

"Can you think of somewhere recently you've adopted that tactic?" I asked smiling.

"It's what I've tried to do in here." Dean laughed. "Say as little as possible in order to stay out of harm's way. I do it to avoid putting myself out there; like these guys, it's also fear of the unknown."

The degree of insight on offer was astonishing. It truly was one of the best sessions I have ever been involved in. Not just because of the progress of the participants but also due to the understanding *I* had gained. I had come to appreciate just how much fear plays a unique (and saboteur) role in people's attempts to heal.

"Seems overcoming fear of the unknown is paramount in dealing with abuse?" I threw to the group.

Everyone gave a signal of some kind that they agreed, except for Martin. He shyly raised his hand to speak, his gesture leading to finally involving himself and in turn overcoming a fear there and then.

"Yes, Martin?"

"The trauma is the wound," he mumbled. "The poison we allow to eat our soul is the fear—fear of the unknown. And in most of our cases, it's also the toxin we have passed on to others."

CONCLUSION

Some groups leave a lasting impression. This was one such group. From that day on, they supported each other in eradicating as much toxin as possible by acknowledging their wounds and those they had caused. They removed fear from the process and, as such, gave themselves every opportunity to heal. It must be stated: this was not your typical group of offenders. They were easy to work with because they were all motivated toward change. As such, they wanted to heal. Typically, most don't. Like most victims, most offenders want to hide.

The most difficult step to venturing down the journey of healing is the first one: seeking help. For offenders, once caught, they don't really have a choice. This of course means they are motivated for different reasons (if at all). Thus, the decision becomes a more difficult one when you are a victim and have options. Typically, things get to the point where the individual cannot cope any longer. As such, they enter therapy in the hope they can change in the shortest space of time by disclosing as little as possible.

It doesn't work that way. Simply showing up isn't enough. It's like going to work and expecting to be paid at the end of the week just for being there. If you decide to attend therapy, you must commit to confronting your fears. It's the only way to heal.

CHAPTER FOURTEEN: ACCEPTANCE

"Acceptance is not submission; it is acknowledgement of the facts of a situation. Then deciding what you're going to do about it."
~ Kathleen Casey Theisen

ONE THING I HAVE NOTED IN conducting therapy of any kind is that when the client accepts the situation in need of resolution, they are on the path to healing. Those who resist, those who cannot bring themselves to accept what has occurred, struggle to get free from the mire that gets deeper and deeper, until the individual is so stuck, no amount of struggling matters.

As stated in a previous chapter, if you are a victim of childhood sexual abuse, no one has the right to tell you how to feel. How you process the trauma is a personal journey. All I can reiterate is what I have stated in the previous paragraph: *those who move on and develop are those who accept their circumstances . . .*

CRYSTAL

"Even though you tell me it's not my fault, it just never feels that way," she said in obvious frustration.

Crystal was in her sixties. She had grown up as a ward of the state in a girls' orphanage run by Catholic nuns. She had never told me the details of what happened to her other than to say she was "beaten, mistreated, and sexually abused."

"What's the feeling?" I requested calmly. I made a point of not feeding her demands for "magic wand therapy," whereby I am supposed to "make it all go away" with a single wave.

"The feeling? I just told you. It just doesn't feel right." She was annoyed at my unwillingness to provide her a "Band-Aid" solution.

"What is the actual feeling though?" I continued.

"I don't know," she stated, somewhat incensed. "Guilt, I suppose."

"You sure it's guilt, Crystal?"

She paused. "No."

I could see she wanted answers, but she wanted them now—without the work, without the pain.

"Then rest with it until you're satisfied you have an honest understanding of what it is." I leaned back in my chair and relaxed. It was my demonstrating that I wouldn't move beyond the current topic until she came up with something of substance.

Crystal sat looking at her cheap costume jewelry adorning her fingers and wrists. Suddenly she made eye contact. "It's more shame."

I remained silent in my relaxed state. The answers she needed were in her, not in me.

"Shame," she continued. "Now that I think about it, it isn't shame because I think I did something wrong. It's shame because it happened. You know? As in, I feel ashamed because it happened to me."

"Why do you find that difficult?"

She found the question affronting. "Who would want to accept it?"

"Accept what?"

"What they did—those nuns. How they used my body for their own lusts. Who would want to openly accept that?"

"So you don't accept it?"

"No!" she said in a raised voice.

I waited, using the silence as an invisible buffer to tread softly into my next point. One she might be too timid to rest with.

"But it happened," I said softly.

"So?" she stated scathingly. "I shouldn't have to think about it."

The ice was thin. I had to tiptoe and attune my intuition toward potential cracks or else I would surely plunge into the deathly cold. "What happens when you do?" I offered cautiously.

"My whole body has a reaction," she said with emphasis. "I shake it all from my mind. Shake it like a horse banishing flies."

"Have you ever tried not to do that?"

"Not to do what?"

"Have you ever tried to just let the memories come back?"

"Why would I want to do that?" The question was sarcastic in tone. It was time for me to "get real."

"Not allowing them to be part of your conscious world hasn't helped," I challenged.

The suddenness of my intensity jolted her.

"It's just too scary," she said, shaking her head. "Besides, why would I want to relive that?"

"You aren't."

She looked at me crossly. "I didn't mean literally. I know they're just memories."

"Then what's to fear?"

She refused to answer the question. I could tell she thought I didn't get "it." I needed to draw her back by demonstrating I understood.

"I know these memories are painful, and they flood you with emotions you don't wish to bring on by choice, but what you are currently doing—repressing them—isn't working."

She played with her plastic jewelry while forlornly nodding in agreement.

"These memories have played a major role in shaping who you are."

The statement sparked her interest. I could see she was wishing to explore that idea. It was a means to get back into the center of the frozen pond, the area where the ice was thinnest and most vulnerable to cracking under pressure.

"What do you mean 'shaped who I am'?" she asked.

"The abuse, Crystal. It would have impacted on you in a myriad of ways. Ways you probably aren't even aware of. Ways that may or may not be helpful to you in the present day, but you don't know which because you don't accept the recollections. If you don't accept the memories, how do you expect to heal?"

"Isn't that your job? To help me heal?"

"Yes and no."

She glared at me in a way that demanded an explanation.

"I can't make you accept your past, Crystal."

"Do I need to?" she said in attack. I could feel the ice starting to give. I committed myself to posing the following question as kindly as possible.

"Isn't that a question you need to ask yourself?"

Crystal sat staring at me. "Yes," she eventually responded. The ice had held. "I need to. I feel it in me. It's as if I've been directed to accept them for a long time but I keep ignoring the call."

"Why?"

"Fear. Total fear." I could see the terror in her eyes.

"Of?"

"Being trapped in those thoughts forever."

"But hasn't shunning them made them more prevalent?"

"Yes," she agreed hopelessly. "It makes them come to mind, and I have to force them away. Bundle them up and lock them in some distant room down a deep, dark corridor where I can just forget them for a while."

"But they always find a way to escape."

She nodded despondently. "They sneak through crevices and cracks and slowly ooze their way back. Then the fight starts all over again."

"When they do escape, maybe they actually want to escape entirely."

"What do you mean?"

"I mean, they leave those deep, dark places to go toward the light. To become fully accepted through illumination. To be completely owned so as to no longer be enshrouded in darkness. To exist in the light and therefore have their power destroyed. Their power is the fear."

"It's just so scary." A glimmer of hope became lost in an ocean of anxiety.

"Why?" I demanded.

"Because if they are brought out into the light, then they are 'out there.'"

"Yes?"

"That would mean I have no control over them anymore."

I smiled. "I'll let you in on a little secret: You don't control them now, Crystal."

"But I do. I can force them away," she said unreservedly.

"Yep, and then they come back."

Crystal sighed. I could tell the conversation was draining her. Which of course was exactly a reflection of her problem: Wasting energy on a battle she couldn't win.

"Don't you get tired of the fight?" I asked.

"Yes," she replied in a tone caught between despair and relief. Relief that in some capacity I understood her plight.

I leaned in; it was time to test that thin layer of ice. "Crystal." I got her attention. "Isn't it time to for you to let the flow of life take you where it wants to take you instead of swimming upstream, wasting your energy on a fight you can never win when it could be invested in areas that would fill your life with joy?"

She looked at me with a flicker of optimism in her eyes. "So just let go?"

"Yes. Acceptance."

I waited in anticipation at the potential promise that this may be *the moment.*

"No," she said, frightened. "No, it's just way too scary."

I wasn't sure if the ice had cracked and I'd plunged. In due course I found out. A month later Crystal attended her final appointment. She was a changed woman.

"Have you ever seen *Forrest Gump?*" she asked.

"Yes."

"Did you like it?" She seemed to need me to relate to the movie before offering up where she was headed.

"Yes, I loved it."

Crystal smiled. "I had a dream about that movie."

I overtly relaxed as a means to tell her I was waiting for the information she wished to deliver.

"Well, not about the movie as such; Forrest was in my dream. He was a prominent figure. So much so that when I woke up, I couldn't remember anything about the dream except Forrest."

"What do you make of that then?"

"I wasn't sure. But I kept thinking about it all day at work. When I got home, I looked for the movie in my DVD collection; I dusted it off and watched it."

"And?" I asked, intrigued as to where the conversation was going.

"Do you remember the character Lieutenant Dan?"

"Yes. Forrest's commanding officer who got his legs blown off in Vietnam."

She nodded enthusiastically. "Lieutenant Dan helped me 'let go,'" she said excitedly.

I looked at her curiously. "How so?"

Crystal sat up straight in her chair. "Well," she started, "I was watching that movie, and he—that Lieutenant Dan—was seriously pissing me off." She laughed. "It was frustrating to watch because it's like 'Man, your bloody legs are gone. Can't you see that, you idiot? Start dealing with it, man!'"

I felt warm within; I knew what she had learned.

"Then it occurred to me," she continued, "Lieutenant Dan was so bitter and self-destructive and hating the world because he hadn't accepted what had happened. He kept denying it and pushing it away."

Crystal looked directly at me in an effort to say "like me."

"Sounds familiar," I acknowledged with a smile.

"Then that night on the shrimping boat, when Dan called on God to give him his best shot during that intense storm, it was like he came to a decision. That he would either live or die—God's choice. Whichever evolved, he ultimately had to accept. As in, he had to find a purpose if he survived, in spite of having his legs blown off."

"And he lived."

"Yes. And thereafter he was able to embrace life because he accepted his legs were gone. Through acceptance he obtained peace. He made peace with God, the world, and himself."

"But he had to let go first."

"Exactly!" she stated with enthusiasm. "He had to give over!"

Crystal became a little emotional. It wasn't sadness; it seemed like joy at embracing freedom. She composed herself as she smiled at me.

"So I decided I would give over," she continued. "I'd let my memories do what they needed to do. Go where they needed to go. I made a committed decision there and then to stop trying to control them."

"And what happened?"

"They came, and then they went." The last part of her sentence entailed a distinct measure of bliss.

"Once I let them come, John, they just sat resting in my mind. I didn't feel too much about them, to be honest. I just remembered without prejudice. Without judgment. I didn't care."

I sat thinking about the value of synchronicity. The offering of 'Forrest' to Crystal in her dream had led to a momentous shift. Of course, those who do not believe in Jung's theory simply rely on that unthoughtful paradigm of coincidence.

"Surprisingly," said Crystal, interrupting my thoughts, "the memories had little effect on me. It's like you have this monster caged all your life and live in constant fear it may escape. So you work your ass off to ensure it's always restrained because you fear what carnage it could cause. You think this even though you've never actually seen the monster; you just assume the worst. You just assume it's this dangerous beast. So once you get the courage to take a peek inside the cage and realize it's a nothing—like the equivalent of a mouse—well, you kind of chuckle because all this time you've been frightened to death of releasing what turns out to be a tiny critter incapable of being ferocious at all. It makes you realize something."

"What's that?"

"That the idea of fear is just a big pile of bullshit that keeps you from accepting reality."

AMBER—PART ONE

"I shouldn't have to go through this," she said, weeping.

Amber was a young single mother of two, and the elder child—five-year-old Carly—had recently "shared a secret": the man in the apartment next door had been "touching her privates."

I didn't respond. She was right; she shouldn't have to go through it.

"Fuck him! Oh God, my little girl!" she shouted, alternating between rage and despair.

I left her to cry.

"God!" she wailed between her tears. "Yes, God! Fuck you! Fuck you!"

Again I let her be. Eventually she became more attuned to her surroundings. Amber looked at me in agony and desperation. She wanted me to say something, anything, that might give her a millisecond of relief. I didn't. It would have been pointless. Nothing I could say would matter. So I sat staring back in sympathy. That was our first session.

I didn't see Amber again for about a month. When she returned, she had become increasingly bitter. Her daughter had revealed in subsequent police interviews the full extent of the abuse; it was more prevalent than they initially believed.

"I hope you're going to say something today," she instructed me scornfully.

I didn't react.

"I guess that's a no?"

I composed myself. "What would you like me to say?" I pressed gently. "That I have all the answers to your problems?"

Amber looked offended. "That's your job, isn't it?" she patronized.

I took a moment. I wanted to her to get the full impact of my response. "I think that's what a lot of psychologists pretend their job is."

"Huh?" Her face wrinkled up in annoyance. "What the hell does that mean?"

I straightened my posture in preparation for delivery. "It means if I sat here and pretended to have all the answers as to why your little girl had her innocence stolen and how I could fix everything, then I'd be a complete liar."

Her facial expression implied she was genuinely contemplating my answer. "So there's nothing you can do?" she pleaded.

"That depends on what you want help with, Amber. If you want me to 'fix' the problem, I can't, and if I sat here and told you otherwise, I'd be a liar," I offered sincerely.

The genuineness of my tone seemed to help her relax. Amber sat caressing the corners of her tissue, then she folded it in half over and over, firmly creasing each edge and then unfolding it, only to repeat the action again.

"I guess you're right," she said dolefully.

I looked at her in a way that requested she continue.

"There's nothing you can do to fix it. In fact, there's nothing *anyone* can do to fix it." Her teary eyes filled to the brim, droplets freefalling from her lashes to her blouse.

I nodded in sympathy. I made sure the tone of my next question was gentle. "So what did you want to talk about, Amber?"

She tilted her head, looked at me quizzically through her watery eyes, and smiled a faint smile. She stared vacantly for a time. I waited for her to speak, to see where she would lead me.

"Do you believe in God?" she eventually asked.

"Yes."

She looked at me with the kind of curiosity befitting a small child examining an insect.

"So you're a Christian?" she asked.

"Not in a conventional sense."

"Meaning?"

"Meaning, I don't believe God cares too much for organized religion. Why do you ask?"

Her curious look faded to torment. "I just don't get why God allows things like this to happen. It's so cruel."

"Yes, it's extremely cruel," I said. "The world is full of injustice."

She looked up from her tissue-folding. "So you believe God just lets bad things happen?"

"Nope, not at all."

She looked at me quizzically. "So why do you believe bad stuff happens?"

"I think you answered that very question earlier when you made the statement that life can be cruel."

She frowned slightly. I watched as she seemed to be carried away by her own thoughts, somewhere beyond the four walls of my office. Her gaze rested on me, but it was as if I wasn't there. Her eyes suddenly darted; she had returned from her "journey."

"So shit just happens," she said quietly.

"Yes." I nodded empathically. "Unfortunately in life, shit just happens."

Her face reflected her mind's tortured state; she was battling to accept such a simple rationale for the suffering of her daughter, not to mention humanity. She shook her head violently. "That philosophy is cruel in itself. It just makes light of my little girl's suffering."

I mimicked her head shake, except mine was soft and gentle. "We weren't discussing your daughter's suffering; we were discussing why bad things happen in life."

She was earnestly considering the dialogue; I waited for her to catch up. "Besides," I said softly, "who's suffering more—you or your little girl?"

She looked at me with her head tilted—her nonverbal gesture that she was pondering deeply. "Me," she whispered. She looked at me poignantly. "That's weird. I'd never really looked at it like that."

"Like what?"

"Who's suffering most; Carly seems relatively okay, except for a few issues. I'm more stressed than she is."

"With good reason," I said, leaning forward. "You're her mother. You want to protect her because you love her. She's a little girl with no idea yet of the gravity of what's happened to her."

Amber concurred with an enthusiastic nod.

"So," I continued, "if what you just said is true—that Carly is not as traumatized as you—wouldn't it make sense for you, as her Mom, to understand how best you can help your daughter so as to lessen her suffering even further?"

She nodded again. This time it was slower and more deliberate. It was a nod of acknowledgment upon hearing truth.

"And," I resumed, "in so doing, enable Carly to fully believe that she can come to her mom at any time in the future—a time perhaps when she might be struggling with her past—in full knowledge that you, her mom, won't become stressed in reliving the event, and thereby enabling an open line of communication that will decrease your daughter's suffering and, in turn, increase her potential to heal?"

Amber's expression was one of seriousness. "That's the majority of my concern," she said. "My concern is about the future, how damaged Carly will be."

"Of course," I offered frankly. "I think most people would instantly fall into that mode of thinking because they want to try to control the future. Instead, what would be more beneficial is you working through the here and now, doing what you can now to lay the foundation for a better healing platform in the future."

"God, that makes so much sense," she said less gloomily. The dark cloud enshrouding her dissolved for the time being. "So how do I do that?"

"Aren't you doing it now? Being here?"

Amber paused. "But we still can't fix it," she said wearily.

She gifted me an opportunity. I pounced. "What did you just do, just then?"

Amber looked confused. "Um, I don't know. I said we couldn't fix it?"

"And how did it feel when you said that?"

She appeared to be backtracking—rewinding her thoughts to recollect her emotions. "I felt an overwhelming sense of powerlessness."

"Why?" I asked, ignoring Amber's tears.

She looked annoyed. "Because it's a normal reaction for a mother whose daughter has been messed with and wants to fix it," she stated defensively. She could be feisty at times.

"Yes," I agreed, "it is a perfectly normal response for a mother in that situation who wants to fix it," I repeated.

"And?" she said derisively.

"There's no 'and.' You are perfectly correct in what you said."

The session ended. She left upset, pissed off, and puzzled. I was sure to call through to the receptionist to ensure Amber rescheduled. I had observed she was a thinker. I banked on the notion she would give due consideration to my repeating her statement. I gambled on Amber developing awareness of the point I was attempting to help her see.

Amber made herself comfortable. "I worked out what you meant at the end of that last appointment."

"About?" I played dumb.

"What you said right at the end when you repeated what I said. The bit about it being a normal response to the situation for a mother who wants to fix it."

I smiled. "Yes?"

"I was right in feeling helpless," she stated. "I felt like that because of the way I went back to thinking about how nobody can fix the problem."

She sat back, folded her arms, and looked at me as if to say "so there."

"Very good." I grinned. "And the most important thing to obtain from that insight is?" I hoped she might have taken it to the next level.

"Well," she began. The swiftness of her need to talk indicated she had given our discussion deep thought. "It seems to me that how you cope and how you feel is really dependent on how you think."

"Go on?"

"If I allow myself to think about the need to fix the situation, then I lapse straight back into negative feelings. That's because in saying stuff like that I am creating a sort of false reality."

"Can you explain that for me?"

"I mean, it's quite pointless to keep telling myself it's not fair and that it needs to be fixed. That's what I mean by a false reality. It's a sort of fictitious way to process things because it makes you feel so cheated. So robbed."

"I see. So what is true reality?"

"True reality is that life *is* unfair. That's just the way it is. There shouldn't be animals like him, but there are. It shouldn't have happened to my little girl, but it did. Someone should be able to fix it, but no one can. That's the truth; that's true reality."

I admired her capacity to be honest in the face of such adversity.

"I even thought of an analogy for it," she said matter-of-factly.

"Yes?" I enquired.

"It's like I'm caught in a rabbit trap. The trap is what happened, you know? As in what happened to Carly."

I nodded to clarify I understood.

"If I lapse into false reality and simply think how unfair it is that I was the one who got caught in that stupid trap, then all my energy is wasted on the injustice of it all. If I get to grips with reality—the fact my damn ankle is caught in that iron contraption—I can begin working out a way to escape, using my energy productively. And once free, I get to heal quicker."

I liked it. "That's awesome!"

She grinned. Something she hadn't done a lot lately.

"You know, Amber?" I said. "It's actually unnatural to think the way you are."

"Why?"

"Most people aren't strong enough to do it with the consistency you do. It's unnatural what you're doing, but a damn sight more productive."

Amber smiled. "It's very hard work. It's really difficult at times."

"How often have you found yourself entertaining that false reality—those negative thoughts—since I saw you last?"

"Often," she declared despondently. "But most times I catch myself and remember what you said." Her body language changed, from exhausted to committed.

"What did I say?"

"That if I focus on what I can do in the here and now for Carly, then it will build a solid foundation for her healing in the future, if she needs it."

"Did you hear what you just said, Amber?"

"Which part?"

"The bit about 'if' Carly needs healing in the future." I hoped she would get the point.

Her head tilted. "Yeah." She smiled a little. "I didn't say *when* Carly needs healing. I said *if* she needs healing."

"Correct. And that's reality. You cannot possibly know if Carly will need to heal because it's in the future; even if it's tomorrow, it's in the future. You are simply doing what you can today, and, in effect, that's all you can do."

She sat staring at me. "This all comes down to one thing, really."

"Which is?"

"Acceptance."

Perfect!

Things were going too well. It was time for an exam of sorts.

"Has Carly demonstrated any adverse behaviors as a result of the abuse?" I asked, my motive masked.

"Yes," replied Amber dejectedly. "I've found her touching herself in the bath a few times."

"It happens." My tone was not pitiless but blunt.

Amber looked up somewhat astounded by my reply. She observed me. Suddenly she recognized my agenda. "Yes," she said, "it's an understandable reaction, given what she's been through."

"And how do you intend to fix it?"

She shook her head. "I don't intend to fix it. I intend to talk to her about it and help her understand her behavior because that's all I can do."

I smiled. "Very good. It sounds like you've accepted that she has a problem."

Amber's eyes became a tad teary, but she soldiered on. "Yes, so if I see her doing it, I will utilize the moment to address the problem because that's all I can do in the here and now."

I relaxed into my chair, tilted my head, and stared at the ceiling. After a while I looked Amber in the eyes. "You're a strong woman and a good person," I said respectfully.

She frowned. "What makes you say that?"

"What you are doing is selfless. It demonstrates your absolute love for your daughter. You have every reason to collapse emotionally, every right, but you refuse to do it for the sake of Carly's well-being."

She blushed and beamed simultaneously. "Thanks."

Amber melted into her own chair and drifted off in thought. "To tell you the truth," she eventually said, "I don't even think about my own needs when I'm with her—probably because I have none until I get here. Then I'm able to release what I feel. I just focus all my attention on Carly at home. Things come up regularly, but I can sift through them in my own head pretty quickly. I know I can save them until I get here. The funny thing is, all those mini-breakdowns generally go back to me thinking too far ahead or too much about the past. All the things I can't control. When that happens, I just go back to what I know."

"And what is it you know?"

"Acceptance."

Amber persisted with therapy for a sustained period. She had difficulties from time to time but maintained her acceptance of the philosophy that "shit happens." While this mind-set may seem harsh, it is the means by which recovery is possible: acceptance.

What you resist persists. Don't get me wrong—plenty of the time spent talking with Amber revolved around major emotional issues. Some days she would unload her anger on me; other days she simply cried. She became an expert in using therapy for its intended purpose: growth.

Over time, little Carly developed a few of the typical signature marks of having suffered sexual abuse, but with Amber's guiding hand and selflessness, the child too was able to address and overcome these difficulties. Of course, Carly may encounter more difficult times down the track. However, her mother gave her the best possible foundation to heal.

AMBER—PART TWO (ONE YEAR LATER)

"I just don't know what to do. I'm at a complete loss."

I assumed Carly had demonstrated some sexualized behaviors that may have resulted in problems.

Amber's eyes were a cross of rage and fear. "That bastard is pleading not guilty!" she cried.

"So it's going to trial?"

"Yes!"

I knew why she was struggling. I didn't need to ask.

"I know shit happens—I know that—but what do I do? I'm pleading with you to help me with this, John. I don't know what to do."

This wasn't a time for silence; it was obvious she was caught in the dilemma.

"It would seem to me you have two options—"

"Yes," she cut me off. "Either I let them put Carly on the stand—cross-examine her and make her relive the whole thing—or I drop the charges, and that pig walks free. It's a totally fucked-up system!"

The despair saturated her soul. Her helplessness suffocated me, but I knew, for her sake, I couldn't be consumed by its force.

"What do you want to do?" I asked calmly.

"I want that animal to get his just desserts!" she shrieked. "I want him to pay!"

She was too caught up in what she wanted for the perpetrator. "No," I offered softly. "What do you want for Carly?"

Amber sighed. "I don't want her to relive the shit. I don't want her going through the whole thing again."

She waited for a response. I paused. I didn't want to jump in too quickly.

"Amber, I didn't ask you what you didn't want for Carly, I asked you what you wanted for her."

She collapsed into her chair and exhaled deeply. "I want her to be okay."

"And is she?"

The question seemed to surprise her. As if she hadn't really considered the obvious.

"Well, yeah, as weird as that sounds, she is okay. She doesn't know what's happening yet. I guess it's me who's having the breakdown."

I smiled. "Have you accepted the situation?"

"I think so," she lamented. "I'm here in tears about it, aren't I?"

I nodded and tiptoed into my next statement. "You were here about a year ago too, but you hadn't accepted the situation then."

She looked annoyed. "So what's your point?"

"In order to make a decision on what's best, you need to first accept that you have to make a decision."

"I know I have to make a decision. That's why I'm here," she stated with spirit.

"No, Amber, you know a decision needs to be made, but you don't want to make it."

A few seconds passed, and her eyes welled with tears. In due course they rolled gently down her cheeks. She was an honest girl, and I knew reasoning with logic would jolt her back to where she needed to be.

"Yes, that's true," she eventually agreed. "I don't want to make a decision because either way I lose."

"Not necessarily. Let's look at the options and the pros and cons."

She reluctantly gave a nod.

"Okay, option one is you drop the charges. The pros are that Carly doesn't have to give evidence and therefore doesn't have to relive the experience. Correct?"

"Correct," she said, sniffing.

"The cons are this guy walks free with no consequences, thereby, potentially putting other kids at risk, and Carly gets no justice. Correct?"

"Correct."

"Option two is you take him to trial. The pros are he may be found guilty by a jury—"

Amber waved her hand at me. "What do you mean 'may be found guilty'?" She fretted.

"There're no guarantees, Amber. Juries are made up of people, and people screw up sometimes. So the potential for a 'not guilty' verdict exists depending on how well the prosecution delivers the case."

"That's bullshit! He did it! He should be punished!" she yelled as she put her face in her hands. Eventually her fingers made their way to her scalp, where they rested between the strands of her hair.

"I understand," I said after she eventually looked up. "Remember, we are simply looking at the options and the pros and cons."

She gave a slight nod that seemed heavy. I imagined her head must have been pounding.

"So the pros are that he may be found guilty by a jury, suffer some form of punishment—"

"What do you mean 'some form of punishment'?" she demanded as her eyes once again ignited with anger.

I wanted to be honest. "It's highly likely he will go to prison if found guilty; depending on the presiding judge that day, his sentence may vary."

Amber's knuckles were white. "So not only do I have to trust a bunch of people on a jury to make the right decision, I also have to trust some judge will do the right thing by my little girl in putting that piece of shit behind bars for a long time?"

"Yes."

"It's not worth it," she declared in exasperation.

I didn't react. It wasn't my place to move her toward what I thought was right. "Are you sure that's what you want for Carly?"

"Yep. Positive. I'm not putting my little girl in that predicament based on 'possibilities.'"

Her statement, I felt, was more passive-aggressive than what she genuinely desired. It was simply born out of total frustration and the rebel in her that wanted to give the world a big, fat "fuck you." However, I hadn't played my trump card. I still had an ace up my sleeve.

"The decision is up to you, Amber."

"The decision's made," she stated tersely.

"Okay. However, I would like to add something before you entirely commit to dropping the charges."

She looked at me with a mixture of hope and insurgence. "What?" she asked anxiously.

"He'll be banking on you not wanting to put Carly through a trial."

"What do you mean? Who will be banking on me?"

"The offender. Even though he knows he's done this to your little girl, he's willing to use your love and need to protect her as a means to emotionally blackmail you into dropping the charges."

She looked a cross between curious and extremely pissed off. "So it's a bluff?"

"More than likely."

Amber sat up straight. She looked intense, like a general mapping out a full-scale military attack on an unsuspecting enemy.

"How do you know it's a bluff? How can you be sure?" she probed.

"I don't know and I can't be sure. I'm basing it on his selfishness. I expect when it comes to the crunch, and his lawyer thinks the evidence is too strong, he will be advised to plead guilty on the day. That way he will get a lesser sentence than if it went to trial and he put Carly through the trauma of testifying. All his actions are about protecting his own ass."

She smiled sheepishly. I think she may have felt bad for taking her frustration out on me. "Now I'm back to not knowing what to do," she said in a manner indicative she once again wanted help.

"Good," I declared strongly.

"Huh?"

"Not knowing what to do is much better than not wanting to make a decision."

"What would—?" She stopped midsentence and smirked. "I was going to ask what you would do, John."

I smiled and looked at her in a way that implied she should know better.

"Let me ask you this," I said. "If you were Carly, and in twenty years you asked your mom about the time you were sexually abused and whatever happened to the guy who did it, what would you hope your mom said?"

Amber's eyes went from a general gaze to intense focus. The notion seemed to slowly infiltrate her mind until it hit an area suitable to twisting her sense of self into her daughter's position. She then uncoiled from that standpoint to provide an answer.

"I'd like her to say she gave the decision much thought. That it was a very tough decision, but she had to do what was right." Her stature was now bold and her voice full of courage. "I'd like her to say she made that bastard pay, and then she picked up the pieces."

"What pieces?" I posited.

She look quizzical. "The broken pieces," she replied. "The pieces leftover from the trauma of the whole situation."

"Who's suffering trauma?"

"I am."

I paused to allow her to take that confession in.

"You're suffering trauma because . . . ?"

"I'm worried. I'm really terrified I will make the wrong decision. That my potential wrong choice will harm my little girl."

"Naturally," I comforted as I leaned closer, "but why are you struggling to make a choice?"

"I just said, it's a hard decision, and I don't want to make the wrong choice."

"Because?"

"I might harm Carly."

"And who would struggle more in dealing with that? You or Carly?"

She stopped. "Me," she answered with a tinge of shame.

I ignored her need to have me wipe away her misplaced feeling of guilt. "So earlier, when I posed that hypothetical situation, the one in which you were the child abused and asked what you hoped your mother did, you replied that you would hope she would do the right thing."

"Yeah?"

I lowered my voice. "What's the right thing according to *you*, Amber? What's your principle on it? What's your sense of right?"

She didn't think. The answer surged out as if it had been waiting for the first opportunity to escape. "Call his bluff!"

"Why?" I pressed, seizing the moment with a question. One designed to cement her decision in her own values.

"Because my daughter deserves justice," she stated with absolute conviction. "My daughter deserves what is right. I don't want that fucking pig doing what he did to another little girl, putting another family through this shit!"

"Do you have faith in your ability to help Carly if it goes to trial?"

She nodded convincingly.

"So what does Carly need from you?"

"To do the right thing and screw the consequences. Not to worry about my fears. Not to worry about her potential suffering. Accepting that whatever happens, whatever comes at me, I can handle it. I'm strong. I'm definitely strong enough to put her first. I'm strong enough to help her overcome anything and everything. We're strong. We're stronger than that pig!"

She was inspiring.

"How might you do that?"

"By accepting what I can control and what I can't. To do the right thing with the right intentions and not worry about fixing stuff out of fear it might need fixing." She paused. "Oh, and remembering 'shit happens.'"

Amber came to see me not long after. She stood by her convictions and did not drop the charges. On the morning she was getting Carly ready for court, she received a phone call from the police prosecutor. The offender had changed his plea to guilty. He was sentenced to a lengthy prison term. I never heard from Amber again.

Much respect, "Amber," wherever you are.

CONCLUSION

Did Amber make the right decision?

I don't know. Who am I to say?

What is obvious is Amber, upon accepting a decision needing to be made, acted. As a result of being brave enough to commit to a decision in pureness of heart, she was able to make meaning of the circumstance. By that I mean, for the rest of her life, Amber will have no regrets about her decision to "call his bluff." Amber made the right decision for Amber (and Carly). What decisions you make, through acceptance of *your* situation, is entirely up to you. There is no right or wrong. Especially—and I cannot emphasize this enough—when the decision is made in pureness of heart. Intent is everything!

Amber's lesson to us all is this: in difficult times, accept reality; don't fight it. Acknowledge the facts, then act. When you accept your situation, in time, something amazing happens: you begin to create meaning.

Chapter Fifteen: Meaning

"Often finding meaning is not about doing things differently;
it is about seeing familiar things in new ways."
~ *Rachel Naomi Remen*

Grace

Grace came to see me for many years until she passed away. Therapy was more an opportunity for her "to chat to someone with half a brain." She was a very independent woman and extremely proud. She did not suffer fools gladly and was somewhat of a hermit. Every session started the same; Grace would insist I make her a cup of tea. Once she was settled, we would sit sipping and conversing on whatever topic Grace felt of importance—usually something highly political. On one such day we sat sipping and watching the raindrops slide down my window. I always felt peaceful in her presence.

"I love the rain," she whispered more to herself than to me. "The rain always reminds me of that night," she said tenderly.

I sipped my tea as I looked at her, waiting for an explanation. The way she peered back, I knew Grace was recalling something of major significance.

She smiled at me sweetly. "The rain was my saving grace as he raped me."

I knew my expression was one of shock. I nearly spat my tea all over the window.

"My uncle," she clarified as she gently picked up her cup and went back to staring out the window.

I was left wondering what the hell just happened.

In session, I never have an issue addressing anything. Yet, turning to this elderly lady who commanded respect and broaching the subject she had just divulged scared the shit out of me. I mustered all the courage I could and faced her.

"How?" I managed to eke out.

"Pardon?"

I swallowed my tea to cover my nervous gulp.

"The rain," I explained tentatively. "How did it comfort you?"

Grace turned back toward the window. "The sound on the tin roof; it was comforting," she said.

I didn't know what to say. A silence ensued. I can't say it was an uncomfortable silence—more a space of anticipation.

"I knew it wouldn't rain forever, just like I knew he couldn't rape me forever."

I stared straight ahead. "How old were you?"

She ignored me and traced a droplet down the window with her skinny index finger.

"It made me aware that all things eventually come to an end. The rain will stop, the sun will shine. And so it goes."

Again we sat in silence. Then Grace looked at me. "Thirteen," she belatedly replied, in reference to my earlier question.

"It always ceases to fall at some point." Grace directed my attention to the change in weather. The rain had eased.

I thought about what she was saying. All her visits for years were a buildup to this. I felt peaceful in her presence once more. I relaxed and gave myself permission to explore the conversation Grace wanted to have.

"So you accepted what was happening in the moment?"

She smiled. She knew I'd embraced her wish. "I've never thought of it that way, John. But yes. Yes, I did accept the situation as it was happening."

Her head turned to face me. "Is that normal?"

I shrugged and sipped my tea. "It is what it is."

She gave a look as if to say "I guess so" as she daintily pressed the bone china cup to her old creased lips.

"I used to feel very guilty," she stated as she turned to face me once more. "Guilty because I didn't struggle. But I honestly didn't see the point at the time, John. Uncle Norm easily overpowered me to get me on the bed in the first instance."

"You felt guilty for that?"

"For a little while." Her response was calm in spite of my accusatory tone.

I'd never seen someone so tranquil in describing and discussing their sexual abuse history. The tinkering of her cup hitting the saucer brought me back to the moment.

"What made you stop feeling guilty about not struggling?"

"I knew I had nothing to feel guilty about. Not a thing." She smiled. "I was a lot wiser than your average teenage girl, John. I worked out that I am only responsible for the harm I do to others, not what others do to me."

I wondered at the profoundness of the old lady's statement. I vowed to remember it for the purpose of helping other victims struggling to rid themselves of misplaced guilt. I watched as she closed her eyes and enjoyed her tea. I wondered at the old lady's ability to love the simplicity of a hot beverage and raindrops.

"It exists for a reason, you know?" Her voice was soft and comforting.

"What does?"

"Guilt."

"Yeah," I agreed as I turned back to the window. The rain began to fall a little harder. "It keeps people from doing shit things to one another."

She looked up abruptly. "That's one way to look at it." She remained unruffled, but I got the impression she was disappointed in me. Disappointed my point of view was so cynical.

"How do you see it then, Grace?"

She smiled. "It's a reminder."

"Of?"

She looked at me serenely, the wrinkles of her aging face a road map of experience and wisdom. "It's a reminder for people to do better, John."

My thoughts immediately jumped to some of the psychopaths I'd interviewed over the years. I opened my mouth to debate the point, but then something occurred to me. It didn't matter. Those psychopathic types felt no guilt anyway. They don't get the reminder. They can't do better. She was right.

I listened as the rain became heavier and the dull roar of a million droplets hitting tin roofs somehow only added to the ambience of the calm in my office.

"Have you ever read *Brave New World?*" Grace asked from left field.

I eyed her oddly. "The Aldous Huxley novel?"

The old lady nodded.

"Yes, I've read it, Grace. Why do you ask?"

She gazed through the window out into the gray day, her eyes seemingly transfixed at something beyond the glass.

"It contains an interesting quote," she said. "Huxley writes: 'On no account brood over your wrongdoing. Rolling in the muck is not the best way of getting clean.'"

At surface level it seemed brilliant, universally true.

"And you agree?" I asked.

"No," she replied sternly.

"Why?"

"Because it is only pertinent to misdemeanors on a small scale. When it is applied to matters that can affect people's lives for the duration of their existence—such as raping a child—I think the muck needs to be acknowledged."

"Rolled in?"

She stopped sipping her tea and shook her head. "No."

"Then what?"

She paused. "Scrubbed clean, polished, maintained." Her voice was strong and purposeful.

"By?"

"In my case, the perpetrator—my uncle."

I considered her philosophy. I couldn't entirely make sense of why or how a perpetrator could "clean a victim." My nonsensical considerations led to my next question. One I'm glad I asked.

"How would a perpetrator cleanse a victim?"

Grace turned and faced me. She frowned slightly with a look designed to ask: "Are you not getting this?"

"They can't," she insisted. "I'm talking about the need for the perpetrator to clean *their own muck.*"

She stopped speaking for a period. She wanted me to absorb that statement.

"The stain they leave on humanity is their responsibility to remove," she continued with certitude. "Besides," she said, turning to me intently, "victims don't need cleansing."

"Many feel they do."

She smoothed out her long skirt. "There's a good reason for that."

"So what is it?"

"Because they think they're to blame in some way."

I didn't respond. I thought she was stating the obvious. Then she faced me once more, and I felt her insistence to pay attention. Her eyes pierced me.

"They have yet to come to the most obvious acceptance of all."

"Which is?" I requested curiously.

"They didn't do anything wrong. Once they accept *that,* they're finally free."

I embraced her words completely. I felt they held the surety and pureness of truth. The idea of acceptance being relative to not only the event (the abuse) but the victim fully accepting the fact they did nothing wrong was paramount to healing.

Grace interrupted my thoughts. "The hardest thing for a victim to comprehend is the 'why.'"

"The 'why me'?"

"Yes," Grace said as she gazed at the drizzle. "There is no 'why me,'" she said with conviction.

I looked at her in a way to request she explain.

"To ask that question—'why me?'—means you have to find a reason as to why your abuser did what he did." She faced me intently. "How do you find a logic to such perversion?" She went back to staring out the window. "It cannot be done," she muttered.

I sat in contemplation, silently agreeing with her theory.

"In the end, most victims do the only thing that makes sense," she said. "They turn on themselves." Grace finished the remnants of her tea. "It is easier to make sense of it if you turn the whole thing into something you did wrong, John."

I nodded in agreement.

"That's why I'm so grateful the rain hit the tin roof that night. Its soothing sound has forever helped me avoid the 'why me.'"

"So you've *never* asked 'why me'?" I noted her cup was empty. I motioned to see if she would like another.

"Once," she replied. "Once I asked the universe to explain itself as to 'why me.'" She declined my offer with a gentle wave of her hand. "But not in a way you might think."

My quizzical gaze prompted her to extrapolate.

"It was one night when I was in my twenties. I was alone camping in the middle of a beautiful rainforest. I started thinking about my past. During that episode, I felt such a strong commune with nature. I have never felt that close to the heartbeat of the earth. I felt the pulse of life. All life. And in that moment I recognized something."

"What was it?"

"I recognized that if my uncle had never done what he did, I would never have experienced that moment right there and then in the forest."

I must have looked confused.

"If it—the rape—hadn't happened, I would have assumed what might be described as a normal existence. I wouldn't have sought isolation from people in that beautiful forest. Sometimes things happen in life, and we perceive them as terrible—and often they are. But that's only because we don't know the paths they will take us on. We hardly ever look at the bigger picture because we are so caught up in our immediate suffering."

I considered her theory while listening to the delightful sound of the rain and gazing down at our empty cups.

"So suffering has a point?" I asked.

"Suffering is a choice."

"But isn't it rightfully human in nature to see sexual abuse as worthy of sufferance?"

"Of course." She smiled. "Take grief, for instance. Grief is healthy. It's healthy for humans to grieve." Grace looked at me squarely. "*For an appropriate amount of time*," she emphasized.

I knew by her tone that her last sentence held the key to the conceptual framework of her entire philosophy of dealing with her past.

"Who decides the time frame, Grace?"

"The individual. It's their personal journey."

"And if it takes too long?"

"John," she said, laughing, "there is no 'too long.'"

"But you just said—"

She interrupted. "It's about balance. It's all about balance. Balance to acquire inner peace. Too long and you overbalance. Too little and you overbalance. Life is a balancing act. We constantly walk the tightrope of life."

Again we paused while sharing in the visual blessing of the tumbling rain.

"For what?" I asked.

"Pardon?"

"What's the point of walking the tightrope?"

"To learn balance, silly." She chuckled politely.

"Balance?" I queried.

"Yes."

"So you have to learn to balance life's tightrope?"

"Yes."

"How do you learn?"

Grace slowly eased her frail, aging body from her chair and reached for her walker. "That's a question that can only be answered by every respective soul on the planet. It's all relative, John. The balance they seek is found in their own history."

I helped her to the door. "How did you discover your balance, Grace?"

She slowly shuffled through the doorway. Upon crossing the threshold, she turned back and smiled at me meaningfully. "My balance?" she asked.

I nodded.

"Whenever the rain hits the roof at night."

CONCLUSION

What must be understood in the context of this chapter is that the assigning of meaning is unique. Grace's meaning is by no means universal. It is the meaning she assigned to her childhood sexual abuse that made sense to her. The manner in which she assigned that meaning enabled her to live a fulfilling life in spite of her trauma. The progression from simple acceptance to application of a deep, profound personal meaning empowers the victim to become a survivor. It is a key ingredient that makes inner peace possible. It is a healing agent. And eventually, it leads down the barely trodden path to a fork in the road: the crossways of forgiveness.

CHAPTER SIXTEEN: FORGIVENESS

"Of one thing I am certain:
the body is not the measure of healing;
peace is the measure."
~ Phyllis McGinley

"So, I JUST WANT TO finish by saying that I'm very sorry for what I did. I know I've hurt you immensely, and you have no reason to forgive me, but I hope you do. Sincerely, Jeff."

I felt the eyes of the group move from Jeff to me. I didn't budge, simply because I never like the feeling of a bunch of grown men needing to look at me as if I were a schoolteacher and hoping to obtain permission to speak or—worse—wait for me to condone what we've all heard before they overtly approve.

Finally Scott offered feedback. "That was really good, mate," he encouraged.

"Good?" The question was derisive. The tone implied there was a nasty critique forthcoming. The voice belonged to James, an inmate with a rape conviction against a woman he met at a nightclub.

"I thought it was pretty good," said Ian, feeling the need to rescue Jeff from possibly being made to feel bad, and in the process highlighting his obvious issue with conflict.

James shook his head. "I'm not talking about what he wrote."

"Then what the fuck are you on about?" scolded Jeff, upset someone was not approving of his effort.

"I just don't see the point of the exercise; it's fucking stupid."

"What don't you understand, James?" I asked.

"I don't get the point of writing a pretend letter to a victim. What's that supposed to achieve? I mean, I understand we can't send it, but it just seems stupid."

I agreed. I understood the reasoning behind the inclusion of the exercise in the victim empathy module; however, it reeked of academia. The great chasm where theory and practicality never match up.

"It's supposed to make you think about your victim's feelings and what they might be going through," said Jeff knowingly.

"Yeah, I get that. I'm not a dumb fuck," chastised James. I always got the impression he didn't think much of Jeff. Like me, he seemed to see straight through the façade. He seemed to know Jeff was full of shit.

"So you still haven't told us why it's pointless," Jeff protested.

"Because it isn't gonna change a fucking thing."

Jeff shook his head disapprovingly. He held a look in his eye suggestive that James was a very lost soul who needed guidance. "Well, it would seem to me, the problem is you just don't care about your victim."

"No, you're so far off you have no clue. You're an idiot."

There was a silence, then James cleared his throat. I could sense he was deciding whether or not to commit to following through with what he had been thinking. He exhaled heavily, and I immediately knew he had decided "fuck it."

"I'll tell you something," he started. "I've sat here and listened to this shit over and over again, and it's always the same stuff." He pointed aggressively at Jeff. "For example, you signed that letter 'sincerely,' right?"

"Yeah, so what?"

"Well, I don't see a fucking thing sincere about it. It's just a bullshit exercise we get done because we have to. You don't write that for your victim; you write it for him," James said, pointing at me.

I didn't respond. James seemed to think he had to clarify the assertion.

"I'm just being honest," he pleaded with me.

"You're allowed an opinion, James. I have no issue with what you said," I told him.

"It's just that I've listened to those things being read and I feel nothing. Why would anyone need to write how their victim feels?"

"I already told you," Jeff yelped. "To help you understand the damage; it helps you to never do it again." He was annoying me. His protestations were nothing more than trying to win my approval and earn "Brownie points."

"That's complete bullshit." James was emphatic.

"Well, that might be how it is for you, James, but for me and everyone else who has presented our victim letter, we got something out of it," insisted Jeff.

James ignored Jeff's pretense. He knew the design of the impression management plan—he'd seen it in group often enough—and continued with his train of thought. "I'll tell you how I know it's bullshit."

"Go on," said Jeff. He kicked back in a pose designed to say "This should be good."

"I've listened to five of you read your letters now, and not one of you showed any emotion. Not once! But you know what?" James asked.

"What?"

"You all did when you talked about your upbringing and your trials and tribulations in life. Then you were willing to shed tears. Ya know why?" James lowered his voice. "Because when you did that, you felt the emotion," he said as he tapped his heart. "You were being real."

I liked what he was getting at. "So what are you saying, James?" I asked. It wasn't so much a question to understand where he was coming from as it was to lead him to where I wanted him to go.

"Don't get us to write the shit down," he stated boldly as he looked at me. "Make us speak from the heart."

I smiled.

"So how about you demonstrate?" Jeff chortled. His suggestion wasn't an act of encouragement; it was a trap to put James on the spot and potentially make him look small. Naturally James baulked. Then I saw the "fuck it" kick in.

James spent the following ten minutes focused entirely on his victim. It didn't all make sense. But it didn't need to. He was right. It was the emotive aspect that appealed as opposed to reading some letter designed to impress me. He cried throughout the entire discourse. He wasn't the only one. Almost everyone in the room (Jeff excluded) with the capacity to feel with others shed a tear, inclusive of myself.

At the completion, no one really said a word. We just sat. I suppose the rawness of the emotion was so overpowering, no words were required. I knew James would never reoffend; you can't feign raw emotion.

I sat pondering what I'd just witnessed and thought how I wished as a therapist in a government setting I didn't have to follow bureaucratic protocol. This was real therapy. Raw emotion, spoken from the heart, nothing rehearsed. It was cleansing. Soulful cleansing. Then something else occurred to me. James had not once mentioned forgiveness.

I waited as he sat with his head bowed. There were teardrops splattered on the floor between his legs. Brad, sitting next to him, had an arm around his shoulder. Eventually James looked up.

I respectfully gave him a nod. He acknowledged it with a forced half smile.

"James, I noticed you didn't mention anything about forgiveness."

He looked at me curiously. "I don't believe that's something I should mention."

"Why?" Jeff demanded. He was jealous that James had produced the goods.

"Why? I'll tell you why, Jeff. Why did you mention it at the end of your letter?"

"Because I really want her to forgive me."

"Exactly!"

"What the fuck are you on about? I don't get you."

James sat up straighter. He looked commanding. "You want her to forgive you, Jeff. That's just you imposing your wants on her again. I don't believe I have that right."

Jeff looked bitter. He went quiet and brooded.

"I think all people should forgive," said Warren, an ex–church pastor with crimes against his own daughter. "It's the right thing to do."

"Says who?" responded James with a touch of condescension.

"The Bible. Jesus taught forgiveness."

"So you think the person you sexually abused should forgive you because the Bible says so?"

"Yes, otherwise they aren't doing the right thing," the pastor said, sitting with his hands resting in his lap. I guess it was his "nonthreatening" pose.

"That's bullshit. You're the one who put them in that predicament."

The pastor looked nervous but seemed evangelical. It was as if he had been waiting for this precise moment to proselytize to the group and save our souls.

"Yes, I did," he stammered nervously, "but I also deserve to be forgiven."

"So what happens if they don't forgive you?" James insisted.

"They have to answer to God."

"But you don't?"

The pastor's countenance was sorrowful. "I've repented."

"So you're clean, but your victim is stained if they don't forgive you?"

"That's right." The pastor grinned nervously. "I don't make the rules, James."

James shook his head in disgust. "What a load of crap."

That was my cue. "Warren." I got his attention. "Aren't we all, according to the Bible, sinners?"

"Yes."

"So to get to heaven, we have to repent of our sins?"

"Yes."

"So even the Christian God requires us to be sorry for our indiscretions?"

"Yes."

"So, what if we aren't sorry?"

"You don't enter the gates of heaven."

I waited a while before proposing my next consideration. The pastor sat grinning, thinking he was on the path to delivering home a bunch of prodigal sons. "So even the Christian God reserves the right to forgive only those who are truly sorry for their sins?"

The question stumped him. He didn't respond. I continued.

"So, that being true, why wouldn't your victim reserve the right to forgive you?"

"Because I've repented," he shot. "I've said I was sorry." He was becoming a little frustrated. "It's between me and the Lord now."

"That's bullshit." James once again utilized his favorite phrase.

"How's that BS?" asked Warren incredulously.

"It's bullshit because everything you just said is all about you."

"How?"

"Everything you just said is about you wanting to get to heaven, what's in your best interests. So you think you just cut out all the suffering you've caused by saying sorry to your God? What about your victim's apology?"

It was a good point. I waited to see how the pastor would respond.

"By saying sorry to God, I'm saying sorry to my victim."

James rubbed his eyes with his index finger and thumb signaling his level of frustration. "How is that being sorry? You don't have to do anything."

The pastor's countenance changed again—he gave the look that said he "knew" he was enlightening us heathens. "That's the blessing of grace. The Lord died for our sins."

"Yeah, well I'm pretty sure he didn't plan on having us running around sexually offending against innocent people just so as we could say we're sorry to Him."

The pastor shrugged.

"Yeah, he's right." Ian reentered the discussion. "There has to be some sort of suffering for us. Not just prison. Emotional suffering. To be truly sorry, you have to be like how James was when he talked about his victim."

"Yeah, that's kind of weird," said Neville, a former bank manager convicted of sexually assaulting one of his own employees. "Ironic really, because I don't see you like that at all, Warren, and you're the one who's supposed to be the Christian."

"If I were God, watching all this unfold, I'd be allowing James into heaven before you, Warren," declared Ian.

"Why?" asked the pastor, insulted.

"Because he's truly sorry toward the victim. He's not just saying he's sorry so as he can forget what he did and pretend he's all good in the eyes of God."

"How do you know I'm not truly sorry, Ian? You're not God."

"Because there's no emotion," stated James emphatically as he reengaged in the conversation. "You, like him"—he pointed at Jeff—"demand forgiveness. And because you demand forgiveness, you don't empathize with your victim. No one has to forgive you unless they want to."

"The Lord does."

"Your victim isn't God, Warren. They're a flawed human being with emotions," said the bank manager.

"On the cross Jesus said, 'Forgive them, Father, for they know not what they do.' What do you think he meant by that?" The way the pastor delivered the question implied he didn't think James would be able to answer him. He was wrong.

"To forgive the people who crucified him because they were ignorant. See, that's the problem—you weren't ignorant. You knew what you were doing was wrong."

The pastor looked lost, so he reverted back to a response he felt was tried and proven but in reality was merely a reflection of his lack of willingness to think outside of his training. "I've repented."

"Yeah, and because you repented, you think you have a clean slate," James said in disgust.

"Correct."

"Which means you don't give any thought to what you did because you believe you're completely washed clean. Total bullshit! You're no cleaner than anyone else here!"

James sat stewing in his own frustration. The group went quiet.

"Ya know," started Fred—an old park drunk with sexual molestation convictions against the kids of his drinking associates—in his gruff, raspy voice, "the original ancient Greek meaning of the word repentance—*metanoia*—didn't mean saying sorry to God. It meant changing your ways."

Everyone looked up and paid attention. The old man didn't speak often.

"I have changed my ways!" insisted Warren.

"Maybe," said Fred softly, "but your lack of empathy for your victim speaks volumes."

"What is that supposed to mean, Fred?" asked the pastor in his fake-genuine tone.

"Put it this way: if I were James's victim, I'd be more inclined to forgive him as opposed to if I was your victim, Warren."

"I don't expect my victim to forgive me," James interjected. "As I said, I don't have the right."

The room fell quiet again. For once it wasn't due to an uncomfortable silence; everyone seemed deep in thought until Ian spoke up.

"How do we make up for what we've done, John?" he asked.

It was a question I had experienced in many groups prior. I answered it honestly. "I don't know."

They looked shocked that I had no idea on the matter, as if I should somehow have been bestowed with and the keeper of this knowledge. "Luckily"—the pastor thought he had the answer—"we aren't going to make up for what we've done by being sorry forever. You see, that's exactly why you need God's forgiveness. So you can move on."

"Do we deserve to move on?" asked the old park drunk. I wondered what the extent of his intellect might be if he hadn't soaked his brain in alcohol.

"Do we deserve forgiveness?" he whispered.

James nodded. "Good question."

Again there was silence.

"I think I can answer my own conundrum," said the old park drunk as he shifted forward in his chair using his walking stick to support his weight in preparation for what I presumed would be sage advice. "I don't think we have the right to impose on anyone whether they choose to forgive us or not. The important point—being as clichéd as it is—is we must learn to forgive ourselves, and I will tell you why. Because if we can do that, then we are truly sorry; we give up imposing our needs on others. We no longer expect or hope for their forgiveness. We just learn to forgive ourselves. But it can only truly and sincerely and genuinely be achieved with a pure heart. Like James showed us."

Again, the room was still.

"I'd like to apologize to my victim," the bank manager said, upsetting the quiet.

"You think you have that right?" asked Fred softly. "What makes you think they'd want it?"

Silence.

"Yeah, I guess you're right, Fred," replied James after some time. "It would mean very little if some guy apologized to me for molesting my kid. I'd just want to punch the fuck out of him. Like, there's nothing they could say that would make a difference."

"What do you think you could say, John? Do you think there's anything we could say?" asked Ian.

"I agree with Fred and James," I replied. I was going to leave it at that but thought better of it. They were ripe for picking. "I don't think it's something that should be imposed on a victim. You took enough from them. However, if by some means it panned out that the opportunity arose to talk to your victim, personally I think I wouldn't make it about me. I'd make it entirely about them."

"Meaning?" inquired Jeff, who had gone mysteriously quiet. For once he appeared to be sincere in learning.

"He means he'd tell the truth," Fred answered on my behalf. "He'd tell them what he did happened for no other reason than he was a selfish prick."

Spot-on!

Again a period of contemplation followed.

"Do you think victims suffer more if they don't forgive us, John?" The question surprised me, not least because it was deep but because it was asked by Jeff.

"It would depend on the meaning they create from it," I replied, still reeling from the source of the inquiry. The group looked at me in a way that told me I knew I needed to elaborate.

"Some victims might use the anger generated from not forgiving each of you to do great things. Alternately, that same anger and lack of forgiveness might cause others to suffer for their entire lives."

"So it depends on the individual and how they make sense of what we did to them," Jeff instructed the group.

All seemed to be in agreement.

"Yes, yes," old Fred acknowledged, "so, hoping they forgive us is okay. It all comes down to our motive for seeking their forgiveness."

"In what way?" asked Jeff.

The old park drunk shifted in his chair again, a sign to pay attention. "If we hope they forgive us so we feel better about ourselves, that's not a pure motive because it's still about us. It's our responsibility to get to a point where we're okay again, not theirs. Whereas, if we hope for forgiveness for their sake, to help them heal, then the motive is pure."

I've remembered that statement for the duration of my career. Offenders need to forgive themselves through earnestly understanding their wrongs to help themselves heal from their abusive ways. Why am I making comment on offenders forgiving themselves when this book is about victims? Because victims need feel no guilt for not forgiving if it helps them heal. Forgiveness is your choice. No one has the right to deprive you of that. However, a survivor—a true survivor—understands that the choice to forgive or not is a *great* responsibility. Because either way, the survivor comprehends the resulting decision must be used to benefit their own healing.

ELAINE

Elaine was a nice lady. She had overcome a tough upbringing. In fact, she was one of those people who went through life with misfortune after misfortune but could still smile. However, her latest misfortune was the straw that broke the camel's back. Her son had been sodomized at a night club after having his drink spiked. The perpetrator left seminal fluid at the crime scene and was captured due to a previous offense, for which he was convicted. The police were of the view the perpetrator had many similar unreported crimes.

"I'll never forgive that son of a bitch. Ever. Not in a million years."

I knew she wanted me to buy into her rage. I didn't see the benefit, so desisted.

"It's your right," I said calmly.

"I know, right? It is my goddamned right!"

Again I didn't purchase what she was selling. My composure kept her talking.

"It's weird, ya know. Society has this *thing* about forgiveness. This idea that if you don't forgive someone, then somehow there's something wrong with you."

I shrugged. "Do you think there's anything wrong with you?"

"Are you kidding? I'm a friggin' mess!"

I actually laughed out loud. She seemed to like that I could connect with her humor.

"But seriously, in answer to your question, I don't think there's anything wrong with me in choosing not to forgive that bastard. I feel completely justified and comfortable in that decision."

I began my "pen mechanics." "What's the feeling it instils in you, Elaine?"

She looked confused. "When?"

"When you think about what happened to your son. How do you feel?"

Her jaw clenched. "Angry, bitter, vengeful, spiteful, hateful. I want revenge."

"What would you like to do to him? If you could spend an hour with this guy, what would you do?'

"Everything in me says I'd like to knee-cap him with a baseball bat and inflict physical pain on him in torturous ways so he suffered immensely until he begged for mercy."

"Is that ever going to happen?"

"No," she said with a trace of disappointment.

"Why not?"

"Because I'd get into trouble." She looked at me a bit bewildered. It seemed she thought the question was dumb. "It's unrealistic. But the more I consider your question, the more I think I'd like him to know how much pain and suffering he's caused. How much my son has changed, how it's destroyed him."

"So what would you say?"

I sat back in expectation of Elaine rattling off a diatribe of insults and profanities. She took her time before answering. Then, what came forth absolutely astounded me.

"That would depend," she finally said.

"On?"

"Whether I thought he gave a shit."

"And if he didn't?"

"Then I wouldn't bother wasting my time."

I know I must have looked perplexed. "The emotions would be wasted," she explained. "I mean, someone who doesn't give a shit about doing something like that isn't going to be unsettled about how it impacted others."

She was entirely accurate. It was a key element I always look for in offenders: "Does this guy care? Can he change?"

"Think about that horrible crime. It's terrible what he did to my boy, just awful. To perform such a low cowardly act in the first place, you'd have to be a selfish son of a bitch. But to not care about the aftermath—well, to me, that's a whole other ballgame. Expressing your emotions to someone who doesn't give a shit—being vulnerable to someone like that—would only make me feel worse, even more disempowered."

She was a smart lady. "Why?"

"Because they already took so much. Stolen so much. I wouldn't want to give over more of myself that they could use or—worse—maybe even enjoy."

Elaine was shaking, literally. She clung to a handkerchief but didn't use it. I think it was her way of being valiant. Her way of not allowing that "son of a bitch" to steal any more from her. She requested a drink of water. I obliged.

"Have you ever met people in prison like that?" she asked upon receipt of the beverage.

"Like what?" I answered as I sat back down.

"Evil bastards. Pricks that enjoy hurting people physically and emotionally?"

"Yes."

"So they actually exist?" she asked as her glass of water trembled in her hands.

"I believe so."

She took another sip. "Can you fix them?"

"Personally, Elaine, I don't believe those types can be rehabilitated. Even if they can, it would take a very stupid person to allow them a chance to reintegrate into society."

"Why?"

"Because their second chance comes at the potential risk to innocent people. I prefer to work from the framework of protecting the innocent as opposed to giving some guy an opportunity who likes to inflict harm on the basis that he *might* be rehabilitated."

"Are most sex offenders like that?"

"No, Elaine, absolutely not."

She looked shocked. "Really?"

"Really."

She placed her glass on my desk. "How many of those evil-type bastards have you met?"

"Many."

"But you said most aren't like that."

"They aren't. Ninety percent of sex offenders would not fit into your 'evil bastard' category."

She picked up her empty glass and ran her finger around the edge; she looked pensive. "So you're saying that most sexual sickos can be rehabilitated?"

"Yes."

"Do you think the guy that raped my son can be rehabilitated?" I felt the question had a spring of hope attached. I perceived Elaine wanted me to tell her that her son's rapist was an "evil bastard" and should be locked away forever. It wouldn't have mattered; I would have told her the truth regardless.

"No, I don't believe he can be rehabilitated."

She looked pleased. "Why?"

"Because his offense is premeditated and his behavior extreme. He is incredibly deviant and has a history of doing it before. Past behavior whereby an offender has already come into contact with authority for the exact same offense says a hell of a lot about his future."

"Hmmm. Evil bastard."

She placed her glass back on my desk. I noted she was no longer shaking. Her belief this offender was in some way beyond help, for some reason, eased her anxiety. Perhaps it was because she expected he would never see the light of day again and therefore be no threat to her family—or anyone else's, for that matter.

"You see, John, that's why I wouldn't want to express my feelings to him of how he has harmed my son—my family—and all the destruction he has caused. To me, it would be wasted breath; I'd be too scared it would be more fuel for his fantasies."

"I can see your point."

She was deeply contemplating something. Suddenly she snapped out of it and laughed. "But I'd still love a few minutes alone with him and that baseball bat."

I didn't join in the humor on this occasion. Not because I had any moral issue with her and that baseball bat. It was simply obvious to me that her mind-set and accompanying emotions about it were not helping her.

"How does that help your son?" I asked.

She looked affronted. "It doesn't. It would help me feel I got some justice though."

"Isn't that what prison is for?"

Elaine seemed confused as to why I had suddenly begun challenging her. She looked nervous that she had said something "wrong." That I didn't approve in some way.

"I suppose," she forced out, "but his sentence will never be long enough." She paused and then articulated the status quo wish for sex offenders: "I just hope he gets to share a cell with someone who rapes and bashes him every day."

"That likely won't happen." I stated the truth. My agenda was designed to keep Elaine engaging in verbalizing her intense hatred for this individual.

"Why not?" she asked. "I thought sexual sickos were hated in jail."

"That's all media hype. He will be in a protection unit with people just like him. He won't do it particularly tough."

"That's so disappointing." She was earnestly dejected. I sat watching as she seemed to fall into despair at the prospect of her son's perpetrator not getting violently torn apart sexually, physically, and emotionally. Eventually I addressed the matter.

"Tell me—you said earlier this need for vengeance—this hate you have, this anger, this need to punish to the point of inflicting physical injury upon this guy—you said it doesn't make you feel good?"

She shook her head pitifully.

"Elaine." I made her look at me. "So what's the point of it?"

She looked at me with hate in her eyes; it wasn't directed at me. It seemed misplaced in such a lovely person. It was doing her harm.

"Eye for an eye," she said bitterly.

"I didn't ask for a rationale to your proposed behavior. I asked, what's the point of all this negativity?"

"Isn't it natural?" There again was the bitter edge to her tone.

"I didn't say it was wrong or unnatural. If it were me, I guess I'd be exactly like you."

My comment seemed to bring her back, to remind her that I was on her side. The iron was hot, and I had to strike pronto.

"So, Elaine, the crux of the matter is this: What are you actually getting out of it?"

"Nothing, I suppose." The standard client response to such a quiz. The one they expect I want to hear. The one that somehow means they have to give it up for no other reason than they get "nothing out of it." Subsequently, my next statement rattled her cage.

"That can't be true."

"Why?" she asked defensively.

"It can't be true because you hang on to it so tightly. You cling to it like a safety blanket, like it's all you have. You must get something out of it. I'm not saying what you get out of it is productive, or likely even healthy. I'm just curious as to what the payoff is."

"Why does there have to be a payoff?"

"Pretty much with everything people do, there's something in it for them in some way or another—not always a good thing either."

She looked down at me. "Seems a bit cynical."

"I know." I smiled.

"Give me an example of someone who might do something for a payoff but the behavior isn't healthy," she said.

"A woman in a domestic violence situation who keeps returning to her partner because she gets loved some of the time."

"Ah, I see what you mean now." She retreated into her own thoughts. She went silent for too long; I asked the question again.

"So what's your payoff?"

Elaine didn't hesitate. She had already worked it out, but rather than openly offer it up for discussion, she preferred to be asked. Probably because such an offering is a great deal more frightening than being asked for such private information. People do not like to offer up the parts of themselves they prefer to hide not just from others but from themselves.

"I get to express my total hatred for that piece of shit," she said.

"So you get to vent?" I asked gently.

"Is that unhealthy?" she defended.

"Do you like the feeling?"

The question settled her simply because it made her think. "I'm not really sure, to be honest. I've never really thought about it."

"So let's assume you like it," I angled in.

Elaine sat in a state of contemplation. Minutes passed and I let her be.

"Holy shit!" she suddenly exclaimed.

"Yes?" I asked in the hope that the "eureka moment" had occurred.

Elaine looked stunned. "Oh my God, John!"

"Yes?"

"I just worked out if I like it, then I'm kind of like those people I was asking you about earlier. Those evil bastards!"

I paused for a moment. Not because I thought she was evil but because I wanted her to rest with that thought before I took it away.

"I wouldn't say you are like them, but I definitely see where you're coming from."

She looked relieved that I didn't think she was an "evil bastard."

"So let's say you don't like the feeling," I probed.

"Then I'd want to get rid of it; it's not healthy. It's awful."

"So whether you like it or not, you don't want it?" I intended to make *her* decide if she wanted to keep the "security blanket."

"I don't want it, but," she stammered, "I feel if I just all of a sudden forgive him, it means his crimes aren't really that big of a deal."

"That he's gotten off too easy, or that you are being disloyal to your son?"

"Yeah, both!"

I leaned in for emphasis. "So tell me, Elaine, if you hang on to it, does he suffer any more or less because of how you process his offenses?"

"No. He will still do the same amount of time in jail."

I leaned back. "So explain to me what the payoff is again?"

"That I get to express my hatred for him."

"And that benefits you how?"

"It doesn't. It just keeps me bitter."

BINGO!

"So how do you want to be toward him, Elaine?"

It was a difficult question. Searching for an answer meant going against some serious prior programming.

"Apathetic," she said after some time. "I want to be apathetic."

I waited for more. I knew she would want to clarify.

"I don't want to be apathetic about what he did or what he might do in the future. I want to be apathetic toward *him*. He's unworthy of me. He's nothing, of no significance, not enough to worry about. I don't want to care about him because he's a person unworthy, undeserving, and a complete waste of my time."

I assumed "pen mechanics."

"So in saying that, Elaine, would you ever forgive him?"

She contemplated the prospect. I could tell she didn't like the idea. When Elaine finally spoke up, I knew she had come to a point where her feelings toward the "evil bastard" and forgiveness made sense to *her*. It felt healthy to *her*. "I don't need to forgive him," she declared. "That's his shit to deal with; he isn't dropping that at my feet, my family's feet. He did that once. *Never* again."

PAUL

"I've often wondered about the concept of forgiveness. It's an interesting conundrum when you break it down," Paul stated. He was a church elder. A victim of childhood sexual abuse at the hands of his stepbrother.

"How so?" I asked.

"Do you forgive irrespective of whether the person is sorry or not?"

"What do your teachings say?"

"Jesus said to forgive seven times seventy—meaning, always forgive. But I've thought about that. For example, let's say you forgive your abuser; they may learn nothing and possibly recommit the same act."

He pushed his glasses back up his nose.

"Or," he went on, "you might not forgive your abuser and feel bitterness and hatred all your life. I mean, the choices are pretty limited, aren't they?"

"So which is right?"

"Is there a right choice?" His question was one of the reasons I liked Paul; regardless of his religious doctrines, he earnestly sought truth. He would not allow unreasonable religious dogma to convolute his quest. In fact, by his own account, he wasn't supposed to see me; it was against church policy.

"I don't know," I replied honestly.

"Neither do I," Paul confessed.

I looked at him earnestly. "What *feels* right to you?"

He took a moment to reflect. "Forgiving."

"Why?"

"To forgive takes strength. In life, the things requiring strength are of worth. They develop you on every level. So on that basis alone, I would say forgiveness, to me, is right. What do you think?"

I took some time to think about *my* truth.

"I think forgiveness isn't a simple decision. It is often erroneously presented that way, but it isn't a simple choice that one just makes and moves on."

"How do you see it then?" sought Paul.

"It's a process. I have seen countless people who were hurt in all manner of ways over my career, and the one thing I've noticed is their capacity to forgive is never the result of simply changing their mind. It's a step-by-step process. Little by little. Until they get to a point where they aren't even conscious of the fact they have forgiven. It just rests within their being, within their soul."

"That's interesting," said Paul sincerely.

"Which part?"

"The part about the unconsciousness of the forgiveness in them. It's a beautiful thought. How many achieve it?"

I could tell he hoped I'd say the majority. Unfortunately that wasn't accurate. "Not many," I replied truthfully.

"Why?" he asked, surprised.

"Because when you have been hurt for no logical reason, when you have had your trust breached, your faith in humanity destroyed, you tend to want to protect yourself. When that happens, you build walls. Often those walls are built with blocks of anger cemented by a mortar of bitterness."

Paul didn't stir. He sat pensively absorbing my words. "So do you think forgiveness is important to help people like me heal?"

"You want my personal belief?"

He nodded.

"Absolutely," I stated emphatically.

"Why?" I could tell his question was honest. He asked to understand me, not to manipulate me into accepting forgiveness as a universal truth based on his religious beliefs. I respected him for that.

"Because it gives you power," I said with conviction. "It affords opportunity to reclaim your past, to reclaim what was taken. It stops your emotions from being dictated to you and instead empowers you. It helps you stop being a slave to your past, and therefore your abuser."

"Hmm. But can't you do that in anger?"

The question seemed misplaced, given that he was a man of standing in his church. "Yes, it can be done in anger. However, to achieve it in anger takes a highly enlightened and self-aware individual."

"Why?" requested Paul.

"Because anger clouds judgment; forgiveness doesn't."

Again Paul rested in profound silence. He looked up at me and simultaneously repositioned his glasses. "So you would give a person a second chance who sexually abused you?" he asked.

"Isn't the answer to that entirely situational?"

"In what regard?"

"I may forgive, Paul, but I wouldn't forget."

He pounced on me. "Then that's not true forgiveness, John."

I shook my head. "No, Paul, true forgiveness does not mean you erase the memories. If you erased them, there would be no need for the virtue of forgiveness."

That statement seemed to hit him between the eyes. "Yes, that's very true; a person who has healed definitely hasn't forgotten."

I smiled knowingly. "So what have they got, Paul?"

He gave the question much consideration. It seemed like an eternity before he answered. He didn't once stop processing the question in that entire time of silence. "I suppose," he began, "a person who forgives has a new take on the memory. They generate a new perspective."

Again I smiled at him. "Yes, it offers *everything* a victim needs to become a survivor. *Everything!*"

He stared at me. He desired this piece of information as if it was his holy grail. "Which is?" he asked.

"Hope."

Conclusion

IT'S AN EPIC JOURNEY, THIS thing we call life. In many ways a beautiful tragedy. But for all the joy we are gifted, one thing remains absolute: we will not escape suffering. Be it physical, mental, or emotional, as an existing conscious entity on this planet, you, like everyone else, will suffer. It's just the degrees that vary.

That said, some say there's no worse act than a sexual assault on a child. And as such—whether at the time or in memory—we expect the victim should suffer immensely. After all, they have been wounded in a manner that strikes at the very core of their being—sometimes to the point of brokenness. A wounding that defies comprehension because often its inflictions are not observable. Fear that rises from "nothing moments" to torment the sufferer and serve as a continued reminder that in some way they aren't good enough. They are unclean. Stained. Dirty.

Yes, this is suffering.

However, the human spirit is resilient. We have the capacity to soar "in spite of." Yet even though childhood sexual abuse victims possess the hardy attributes that are paramount in achieving recovery, most don't. For a myriad of reasons the majority remain frozen in their suffering—incapacitated through sheer terror. Too scared to step out from what they have come to (erroneously) believe is their "safe place." It takes enormous courage to give up the "protective" confines of a prison cell that has been "home" for an eon. In my experience, those who (choose to) break out are those who embrace something the universe begs us all to understand and implement. That something is faith.

When you try to control all facets of life, especially those you have no control over, you begin to battle reality. Pretty much everyone who ever sets foot in my office has waged some war on reality. They have lost trust in allowing the universe to do its job, so they try to micromanage existence. What I've noticed, however, is the universe has a pretty strong aversion to those lacking in faith. It will keep thrusting the issue in their face and kicking them in the ass until they give over, accept the problem as it is, and address it. Those who refuse to heed the call either suffer their whole life, or typically end up in an office like mine—fighting tooth and nail to hold firm to their "comfort zone" despite the fact it is now doing them harm.

To heal, you must believe you can heal. You must let go. You must have faith. Faith that the darkness is not a permanent fixture. Faith is the force that powers your journey toward the light of healing—the same light you were born into. It is an eternal ember that illuminates the way back "home." A light that can only be snuffed by a person's diminished faith. You can get angry, bitter, resentful, whatever—just never lose hope. As the wise Bengali philosopher Rabindranath Tagore once said: "Faith is the bird that feels the light and sings when the dawn is still dark."

Hope, always.

In saying this, one must recognize hope is only the means by which the journey can begin. Without it, we resign ourselves to stagnation. With it, we can reclaim our rightful place in life. And as we climb those stairs to healing, hope will be required every single step of the way.

There will be hard, painful times in the process. Many piercings to the heart. In some instances a reliving of the trauma. There will be times you want to concede defeat and hoist the white flag. You can't. You must endure. Your faith in a desired outcome must be resolute because it's better to die clawing at your future freedom than to "live" your days as a slave to your past. And in essence, that is the goal of becoming healed: freedom.

Freedom is evidence of recovery. It can only be obtained through courage. The courage to confront and transcend fear by taking that first step out of your cell. Then another, then another.

The road to recovery isn't overwhelming if you approach it one step at a time. And then one day, you'll look back down that path you've trod and see piles of shit shoveled to each side. A parted clearing all the way to the horizon where, in the distance, stands the remnants of the crumbling prison that once caged your soul, and the only feeling that will transpire will be one of peace. At that moment you will know, with every ounce of your being, that you are finally free, that you survived.

Made in the USA
Lexington, KY
14 April 2019